Happy Camping Around

Europe

Thomas Lewin

Grosvenor House
Publishing Limited

This book is published by
Grosvenor House Publishing Ltd
Link House
140 The Broadway, Tolworth, Surrey, KT6 7HT.
www.grosvenorhousepublishing.co.uk

A CIP record for this book
is available from the British Library

ISBN 978-1-80381-321-9

MEDIEVAL TOWNS AND CATHAR CASTLES OF FRANCE
FROM THE COMFORT OF A MOTORHOME

When I was a child, we lived in a free democracy. We could speak our mind, tell the truth as we saw it. Oh yes, I know you today, of the woke generation, feel you live in a free society, a free democracy. My generation knows different.

Today, if and when you want to say something, you have to stop and consider your response. Can I say that? No, oh, find a different way of saying it. You think that's freedom? No, you're brainwashed. Worse, its stress-inducing. We might live longer physically, but we will end up more and more with stress-related illnesses. This came home to me even more forcefully when my daughter came in one day from her job as an accountant. She had been given an informal notice to be careful what she said in future. During a lunch break with colleagues, the conversation turned to the immigrants entering our country. She made the mistake of saying, "the problem is there are far too many in this country, and they should be sent back." It was clearly something she had overheard in our home and with other people.

Without further ado, one of her colleagues jumped in and pointed out her boyfriend was a person of colour, and she resented the comments. As well as feeling embarrassed in front of her new colleagues, she was reported to her superior. Upon hearing her explanation, he accepted that there was nothing racist or untoward in her statement but cautioned her to be more careful in future and not utter the statement again. Freedom of speech? You're having a laugh.

Today she is in the top ten percent of wage earners in a fully responsible position. But she has changed out of all proportion to the straight-talking girl she was.

People today mourn the loss of the "character." I lived in the days of those characters, most of whom have disappeared like the dinosaur. Every road or street, mainly in working-class areas, had one or more characters. Our markets had characters who gave those same markets the colour and vibrancy abounded. My dad was a character, being a market trader, "come and get your nice plump tomatoes." Slowly those characters in the markets have almost disappeared. Driven out by the new woke brigade. The Jewish lady in Birmingham market selling her wares had the most ear-splitting annoying voice you could wish to hear. Loud and piercing. She would shout out her sales pitch, "come on, darlings, you won't get better than this." But at the same time, she was fascinating. Today she has gone along with many others of those characters. Driven out by the 'wokes.'

Those characters in our streets and roads have also been driven out. Firstly by the growing politically correct brigade. A term that was never known when I was a child. To me, it was more of a snobbish-driven progression. As working-class people were moved out of their homes, where they had lived for generations, they had the confidence of knowing their neighbours next door, on the next road, a mile away. Then they were moved to new estates, in different areas where they knew no one, and no one knew them. As soon as they opened their mouths, they were chastised and shut up straight away.

Slowly, surely dying away in the process. It was a slow progression. None of us properly noticed until it was too late.

First, it was the racism bandwagon. Fine, racism is not nice. Using the n****r word is obviously grossly offensive, except when they use it on each other. But where does racism start and finish? For years, we have called the French 'Froggies' due to their penchant for frogs legs. We used to call the Americans 'Yanks.' This went right back to the 17th century but was commonly used during the first and second world wars. Partly banter, partly a snipe, I suspect. They called us Brits or Limeys, for the same reason. No offence was taken. Unless it was said in an offensive way, and that's the gist of it. Maybe that is part of the problem in itself. If people were not so delicate, the words might die out naturally.

But a far more unpalatable series of expressions or alternatives have come into usage today. It's the unspoken. It's the nod or the wink. I know fellow hoteliers who would take a booking, only to find when the couple turned up, they were black or Asian. A suitable excuse would be made, "sorry, double-booked," deposit handed back, no mention of racism. The Welsh have a similar mindset. Whilst viewing a smallholding in Wales, I was struck by the two beautiful daughters. Only one had a part-time job. They had been in Wales since they were ten years of age. In junior school, they were made to learn Welsh, yet the locals made it clear they would never get a job in Wales.

More offences are rushing into English law faster than we can blink. Homophobia, a dislike of gays. Something that used to be a crime many years ago now it's not only accepted as normal, it spanned out into other variations. Now we have terms such as allosexual, androsexual, asexual, bisexual, fluid. For lord's sake, fluid. No wonder we are all becoming mixed up as a society. Today, we are becoming less and less aware of who and what we are. Children are growing up far less happy or as well balanced as my generation were.

I do not consider myself racist in any way. Much of my comments are well-meant banter. Today, sadly, the lines are becoming more and more blurred. So for anyone reading my books, please try and remember that I came from a more enlightened and freer democracy. Where we could express our likes and dislikes without fear of upsetting someone or being threatened with court action if we used the wrong phrase or expression. Today, I suspect many of us don't know what's right or what's wrong to say.

DEDICATION

To my wife, Betty Jean Lewin. My wife, my life, who left me on 22nd August 2014. I miss you and think about you every day. You were the most wonderful, decent, caring woman in the world. We had so much more to share.

To my fellow motorhomers, campers and those who aspire to own a motorhome. You don't have to have the most expensive model around to enjoy the quality of life whilst touring Europe. A bed to sleep in after a day on the beach or sightseeing, a cooker to make a simple dish and a toilet and sink are plenty enough. Anything more is a bonus. Have a great time, and share your memories for others to enjoy.

Happy camping

FROM THE SLUMS OF SUMMER LANE TO MEANDERING AROUND EUROPE IN A MOTORHOME.

It certainly is interesting what life throws at us. Was it Tom Hanks who once said in a film, 'life is like a box of chocolates?' You just don't know what's going to come out of the box. People are being slaughtered, tortured, mutilated and murdered on a daily basis throughout the world. Six million people, including Jews, were tortured and murdered by the Germans in WWII, through no fault of their own. Stalin is accused of killing millions of Russians, yet he's venerated as a hero to the Russian people. The mind boggles on both counts.

People are suffering in different parts of the world while the people ruling over them live off the Hogg. Billions in hidden bank accounts throughout the world. Saddam Husain, Gadhafi. Where is God in all this? Yet in Africa, India and Pakistan, every time you look at the kids on the telly, they have big happy smiles and gleaming big white teeth, yet they are wearing rags on their bodies. They don't know what a comb or a pair of underpants are. For the most part, they don't even know what a toilet roll is. The owners of the cotton fields in the deep south of America in the 1800s thought they were being kind to their black slaves by feeding them, giving them a roof over their heads for the work they were doing picking cotton. The odd whipping didn't hurt them—why you had to do that now and again because they got belligerent and out of hand. They had to be kept in their place like naughty kids.

Then you have the kids, the people, dying of various illnesses and diseases every hour, every day, throughout the world. What answer is there for the six-year-old, just starting to learn about life or how to ride a bike, being diagnosed with cancer. The young bride, deliriously in love on the threshold of a new life with her husband, being told that she only has a few months, maybe a couple of years, to live. Where is God then? Over 1,000 people died when the Titanic sank, yet what did the survivors say? The first words that came out of their mouths? 'Thank God. Thank the Lord, he saved me.' But where was he when the other 1,000 plus drowned? God didn't care too much for that lot. Maybe they weren't Christians. You hear the same time after time when someone is killed, and one survives. 6,000 died in battle, but three survived, 'thank you, lord. Yes, God was looking down on you that day. Yes, just not on the other 5,997.

I was born in the so-called slums of Summer Lane. Grew up in the slums, or so-called slums of Nechells. I didn't know what a pair of underpants or a toothbrush was until I was fifteen. Toilet paper was unheard of. Toilet paper? Don't be stupid. You wiped your backside on the daily mail. Everyone did. If you were posh, you cut them into squares and hung them on a nail in the Kazi. If you were like us, you just used to pick the mail up as you needed it and ripped a sheet off. If you forgot, you would just hope there was enough there for you. In Morocco and other places, they use their fingers. In Afghanistan, they use pebbles; that's a bit more upmarket. For our bedding, it was a sheet with an army coat on top. In winter, ice formed on the inside of the windows. I still remember the priest and the whole family being around my bed as I was dying with double pneumonia. I wasn't expected to survive, but I did. I went diving in the canals around Birmingham, clogged up with filth and green in colour. How I survived, I don't know. But I did, and I feel all the better for it.

When I left school, I didn't know what to expect. I know the teachers didn't care a hoot. We were just factory fodder, and that was it. All I knew was that I wanted to be something. I wanted more than just to live in a scutty little slum house in one of the many slums around Birmingham. I didn't want to be a millionaire. The boxer Johnny Prescott was my hero. Reaching that position would satisfy me.

As it happens, I didn't reach the dizzy heights in boxing. Still, I had enough in me to work hard and achieve a modicum of success. I provided for my family, together with my wife Bet, we had nice houses in nice areas. We gave our kids the springboard in life to go for and achieve more. The rest was up to them. For us, our dream, having achieved what we did, was to retire early. Get out and enjoy our life, maybe buy a villa. Which we did in Tenerife. We ended up deciding to buy a motorhome and see and travel around Europe. When we got into the hotel business, my plan was to buy a yacht. With that in mind, I did a two-year inshore navigation course. Then our son and I got our class-three divers certificates. We were almost up and flying. Within a few months of buying our first hotel, I got the opportunity to buy a very nice 32ft ketch. Unfortunately, sailing was never going to be part of our dream. The Bristol Channel has one of the highest tides in the world, over 30ft, couple that with force ten gales, and that was it. Our hotel was right on the seafront, the sea our back garden. When Bet saw those waves, that was it. No one wanted to get on the water, especially with me. Sadly, my wife had a completely unexpected stroke. Then a heart attack. After a few years of seeing Europe, my dearest Bet passed away. Now I travel alone. On my own, continuing with my dream. Our dream.

COVID AND THE JABS

Well, by design and a force of nature, bad news has to come with the good. Maybe it's Gods will. Over 60% of the country has had the Covid jab, and after yet another six months or so. Is it? I've gone brain dead. I suspect I ain't alone. Like anyone in or with a motorhome, even a caravan, we are self-isolating by our very situation. We have toured all over Europe well, a fair whack of it, even down to the Sahara. Mostly wild camping, occasionally, going on sites. I've never been closer than six feet to the next door van, never mind another human being.

So ok, I know we all have to follow the same flag, sing from the same hymn sheet. Maybe. Really? According to the government, if I travel around in my motorhome, I risk spreading the virus. Yes, of course, so if I take a ride into the country, I'm going to give someone the bug right. Well, in truth, all it's really doing is giving those Welsh and the Scots the opportunity to keep us out. Both of the miserable bleeders don't want us in their country. This goes back to William Wallace and Robert the Bruce. In Wales, Lord Llewellyn of Harlech, well, someone like that, it doesn't matter. The fact is they hate us, and this lockdown is a hidden blessing to them. This is their opportunity to keep us out. I swear if they could have a time limit on how long they had to be self-contained, they would take it as a God-given opportunity to kick us out for good and claim independence.

But then we all know where that would leave them, don't we? Both would starve to death. As lockdown was easing a bit, I had a little tour over to Llandudno and Rhyl. Around Anglesey, and to Barmouth, and boy were they pleased to see me. Put their grubby little hands out to take some money. Oh yes. No bugger off English then. They even turned a blind eye to my parking overnight in certain places along the beach.

Last week, my grandkids had a few days break over the bank holiday. Ringing up sites, they were dismayed to find the site owners were doubling or trebling the charges. Barmouth wanted over 90 quid for three nights. 90 quid to pitch a tent up on a patch of wet grass? So, I suggested a break in the motorhome. Off we set on Thursday night, reaching Rhyl by 9pm. It was still light. After a short walk around, we got to bed. We had three full days in front of us until Sunday night. After a comfortable night's sleep, in a car park right on the seafront, the kids set off for a little preamble around the town and seafront. By lunchtime, they had had enough. They were not too impressed with Rhyl. I thought the seafront was very nice, but, sadly, much of the place was still closed up, so was the fair, so that did it.

After much faffing about—they didn't want to upset me—they agreed that they preferred Barmouth. We got to Barmouth by 3pm in the afternoon. But that was it, sorted. Out they shot, filled up their little bellies, and were swimming in the sea at 9pm. Beautiful, and well worth it. We had headed to our favourite little spot on the far side of the car park by the train lines, making sure I was backed up into the one bay and not impeding anyone.

I had spent two nights there a couple of weeks earlier with no problems. Yes, of course, there was a sign saying no overnight camping, but who was to say we were camping? Anyway, I had had a chat with a traffic warden some years before who had told me they turned a blind eye to campers as long as we paid for a ticket. I always did. This is a two-way street. Being totally self-sufficient, I resent going on a site and paying through the nose. For their part, they are getting the extra money that I had saved. Sadly, the Council doesn't think like that. The fact that Barmouth is empty for ten months of the year is irrelevant. We had arrived on the bank holiday weekend, though the car park was empty when we arrived. On the Saturday, it started filling up. By Sunday, the sun was beaming down, and the tourists were steaming in. Most, just for the day. The council saw us as an obstacle. We woke up to find a little ticket on my windscreen.

Not for camping in the car park overnight, no, simply for parking in the wrong designated spot. Looking around the car park, I just couldn't see any other designated spots. Sadly, I think Barmouth Council just saw this as a way of getting some extra money. To make up for the Covid lockdown. The night before, a guy came over to say hello and asked if I felt it was alright for the overnight parking. I told him I had never had any problems, and his little face lit up. He was parked in the disabled bay overlooking the seafront. Later on, we met up in the local pub and had a chat and a drink. The next morning, my daughter told me he had called over and wasn't very happy at all—we had both gotten a ticket—he didn't come back but buggered off. I don't think I was in his good books.

Getting home after three very pleasant and enjoyable days with the grandkids, I decided to front the fine head-on by writing to Barmouth council. I had given the kids £250 spending money plus another few quid for the two great-grandkids (well, that's what granddads do). I asked the council to explain to me where the correct designated spots were. I also told them I was refusing to pay the fine anyway and that maybe others might also. If not, they may not return again. Hence maybe why Barmouth was so empty for most of the year.

Barmouth has car parks stretching the whole length of the seafront (has anyone seen the number of car parks Barmouth has? They must stretch at least a mile along the front). Yet, they are empty for eight parts of the year, maybe longer. Even in the busiest periods, the very far car park is empty. How stupid is that? So, I wrote to the council, pointing this out. As a builder-developer, the cost of putting in a disposal tank/point for the cassettes, plus a water tap, two simple yet cheap jobs to do, would enable them to cut off sections of the car parks for motorhomes. Maybe all the car parks at certain times of the year. Very simple, very effective, yet without being greedy, each motorhome would generate circa £10 per night for the council. A polite note added on to please spend in the town would generate further income. Doesn't take a lot of brains, does it? Even if just ten pounds are spent in the local supermarket, its money going into the economy. This applies to many seaside resorts around the country, yet these councillors are so blind to this they don't see it.

Calling into Bewdley, Worcestershire one weekend, I couldn't get into the car park. Height barriers. I pulled the traffic warden, who eventually told me the barriers had only gone up last year. I had parked there previously. Carefully he told me it was because of the gipsies. A few years previous, a group had camped up in the car park. It cost the council a good few grand to get rid of them, plus another two grand to clear up the mess. Dhu?? Well, excuse me a minute for being so dumb, but how come this is still being allowed in our country? How come a bunch of itinerants can demand being treated as a special case? A protected race. Allow their kids to go without a decent education, dump rubbish, defecate wherever it suits them, and get away with it? The warden said the council were working with other councils throughout the country to find a solution. In the meantime, everyone suffers under the same umbrella. The gipsies are laughing their little nuts off contemptuously in the knowledge that they can't be touched unless they are caught bang to rights nicking something. I have a nice six-berth motorhome, shower and toilet on board. But because of the trouble caused by a small group of itinerants, we can't be seen to show favouritism. Oh no, it's that union mentality. All out, everyone out.

I can fully understand the caution. Some campers do take the piddle, some pull in the side of the road putting their awnings and chairs out, others leave rubbish scattered on the floor, this shames us all. What shames me, in particular, is when I hear of someone defecating anywhere they feel like, but this isn't just motor homers. It's happening to kids who go to festivals, people who go out for the day in the car and need to relieve themselves, empty their bowels. What's the answer? Well, it might be a help to build more facilities, that's what. More toilets. But oh no, that means spending money, taxpayers money. Our money, and the council don't want to do that do they? They have better things to do with our money. Put in their own bins more likely, and I don't mean bins, bins.

How come I don't see this problem in Europe? There are 70 million people in England, great for the government. It means more money. More money means being able to strut about on the world stage, giving it the largesse, distributing millions to the poor and needy. Whilst we have to defecate in a field, or the homeless have to sleep on the streets, great ay? Ok, ok. I know it goes on in Europe as well, but we don't seem to be learning.

In contrast, I find driving, touring, holidaying in Europe so utterly different. To me, now, I look on England as suitable and great for little short breaks of two or three days. To do that I've had to learn over the years to find little hide aways where, if not wholly welcome, I can park up for a day or two and enjoy a short break. Of course, I daren't mention or recommend it to anyone on social media for fear of so many heading to it and destroying it for me. Oh no, one has to learn to be quite selfish. Scotland is different for sure. When I get around to doing that, I intend to spend at least a month or so touring the great country if I get the time. England? Well, you may as well stick a big ten-foot sign up saying motorhomes are not welcome, so no, Europe it is for me. In France, you can't go five miles before seeing the signs for an Aire. These are free parking, camping sites. Many have toilet or washing facilities. All have rubbish bins, most seem to be respected, some even have electricity.

Many are run by small or medium businesses like wine merchants, olive oil producers, cheesemakers, etc. It costs them very little to provide facilities like water and waste disposal, and hopefully, the idea is you will buy a case of wine or some other goods, much of which you might have brought anyway. It's a win, win, all around. Some Aires are set in beautiful locations or positions like Chateau Gontier in the Mayenne region. Right on the side of the beautiful river Mayenne and town. Obviously, you will spend a few days there, and obviously, you will spend a few euros. There are medieval villages and towns with parking facilities for the price of a parking ticket. One such place was an olive grove in a small medieval town where the Abbey of Sainte Marie, Lagrasse stood. Delightful. Another was a purpose set aside Aire in a small alpine ski resort called Martinet on the Spanish side of the Alps—absolutely great—free camping and toilet water and dumping facilities. Electricity etc. a five-day limit.

There are many, many more dotted throughout France. That's all quite apart from the service stations and what a contrast again to England. No big signs saying three-hour maximum stop. Just enough time to spend the money you are about to spend, then bugger off. These places are massive. There is the service station itself, for fuel, then the café, restaurant, eating area, then the lorry parks, whilst just for lorries I often sneak into one of the bays as I consider it safe and secure. If you can put up with the noise, you have the picnic areas, parking for cars and parking for campers. No sweat, no worries, no jobs-worth walking around with eagle eyes waiting to pounce with a ticket. Oh no, complete freedom. I never knew or discovered this until my wife and me, Bet, bought our motorhome in 2006, then, slowly, the world started opening up.

We had stood for that mantra for years, you can't beat England. England is the best country in the world. You have everything in England, beautiful countryside, quaint little seaside towns. Why go to France? The French are pig-ignorant and hate us. The French cops hide in every corner, ready to pounce when they see an English number plate. The Spanish are peasants who can't wait to crack us over the heads when they see us. Mind, that's partly true when it comes to the brit drinking yobs. Me being one of them at some stage, all stuff and nonsense.

We would set off for Wales, our favourite destination for many years, even though the Welsh hate us. It would be a nice sunny day, and with the measly few quid we had in our pockets, we would set off, and what happens? As soon as we hit the Welsh border, the skies would open up, and it would pee down with rain. We found the same when we had the hotel business. Guests would save up all year to spend a week or a fortnight in our hotel, in August or July, the height of the season mind, only to get a couple of days or more with it peeing down with rain. I felt heartily sorry for them, and the last thing we could do was tell them we were having a month in sunny Morocco or the Canaries. Oh no, we had to keep our gobs shut, the less said, the better, and they never asked.

So no, now I look forward to spending my time abroad, mainly alone. We bought our motorhome new in 2006. It was all we desired and needed. An Autotrail Cheyenne. It had a fixed bed at the back above the garage. The garage could house a scooter/moped plus chairs, etc. After a hard day travelling or lying on the beach, the fixed bed was made up and ready to dive into. Inside were two side by side sofas, ideal for when we came back from sightseeing, shopping or a day on the beach wanting to put our feet up for a nap without having to get into bed. On the one side next to the sofa was the decent sized fridge with a small freezer compartment, a full-size cooker, and an adequate wardrobe. On the opposite side, a full-size shower, toilet and small sink. Small but adequate. Plus, an outside shower was an absolute bonus for washing the sand off after a day on the beach. On the other side, a gas fitting for the BBQ that we never used.

After a few nice years touring just getting the hang of it, my wife, Bet's, health deteriorated, until eventually, she passed away. Only someone who has had that experience will know what it is like to lose your partner, soul mate and best friend. I took her for granted without realising how much I loved her or needed her. I took her skills and abilities for granted without realising how talented she was. Following further complications, we decided to spend the summer in France, where she could recuperate. Sadly, she suffered a heart attack on a lovely campsite outside Limoges. Whether she knew, I don't know to this day, but I certainly never knew. All I did know was that it was serious, and the next day, I drove to Calais like a man possessed with the devil beneath my heels.

The specialist treated her, and even then, as she recovered and recuperated, I never realised how serious it all was. A few years later, in August of 2014, she passed away after a short spell in hospital. On the Friday morning, we were looking forward to her coming home on Saturday. She got up, joked and laughed with the doctors and nurses, went to the toilet, got up and fainted. Low blood pressure see, she never came out of it, as she had a few times before. I like to think she waited for me to get to the hospital before slipping away in front of me. I will never know. I know that she had told me before that she could hear everything around her when she was unconscious. Did she know I was there? It is something that haunts me and will do until the day I die.

Whilst in hospital, she had brought up our planned tour of Italy the following year. Venice, Rome, Pompeii. She had heard the roads were bad in Italy. She used a mobility scooter, but I said, "ok, no worries. If we visit a certain spot like Pompeii, I will have a quick look around whilst you have a tootle outside. Then we'll get off somewhere else." Well, I never got to see Italy the following year. For a couple of years, I couldn't go anywhere, really. Wherever I did go, she was with me, in the motorhome. Even now, her presence is with me. Though it took me about three years to find the courage to visit Italy, and even then, I had to do it with friends for some comfort and support.

VENTURING FURTHER AFIELD

Now, here I am planning my next assault on Europe, this time in France. Initially, our plan was to spend our summers in England, short breaks here and there. Our winters abroad, mainly in Spain, the main destination for us English. We would get on the ferry at Dover, get over to Calais for 1am-ish, then drive straight through and down to Spain. To me, I thought France looked ugly and desolate. Everything seemed to be closed and shuttered up by 8pm. What is the problem with those French? To avoid it completely, we very often caught the ferry to Bilbao or Santander. Cutting out France altogether. Failing that, we tried Caen. Cutting out a big portion of France. Either way, it was a big mistake on my part, something we had only just started to realise.

On my own, I would start to set off from Calais, across France, into Switzerland, then Italy, into and through Slovenia, Croatia,

Serbia, Bosnia, into Montenegro, Albania, Greece. Sometimes I would hit and pass through some 12 or 14 countries without experiencing the benefits of each, so busy was I in my intent to get there. Maybe it was partly to do with Bet. Maybe I was just desperate to say I had visited these countries. Now I was taking my time, going at a slower pace, savouring the countries I was visiting. France being one of the main ones. How much time did I have? There was so much to see in France, from the medieval towns and villages, like Carcassonne, to the chateau's, vineyards, and Riviera. Having seen and experienced some of them, I wanted to see them again.

Now here I was planning my next little foray. This time I wanted to spend the summer in the south of France, down along the Riviera, on the beaches soaking up the sun, once nicely tanned like a little berry, getting out and about into the little villages, seeing a few chateaus. Although I miss my wife terribly, I feel it would be nice to share my experiences with someone, obviously, and preferably, female. My granddaughter, Sammy, would often get a cheap flight to wherever I might be in Europe and enjoy a nice relaxing break, as do my other kids.

It's great to have my grandkids or kids fly over, and we have a lovely time. But it's those moments when you're in a beautiful spot. Like the little cove on Corfu, right on the beach, shower and toilet right there, a couple of nice restaurants across the way. And there you are, eating beautiful fresh mussels, chunks of fresh bread overlooking the beautiful scene of your motorhome there by the surf, on your own with no one to share it with.

I met a couple of nice ladies who I thought might be ideal companions to share my life with, but none worked out yet. Val was a very nice girl. Quite knowledgeable about a lot of things, including France. The problem was Val liked a drink. Wine being her favourite, but if I brought two bottles, she would drink them, then her own that she had hidden away in her bag. Sadly, Val was an alcoholic. Whatever had gone on in her life, I don't know. She had four lovely respectable kids. She had been married 25 years when her husband did a runner with another woman. I don't know what Val found worse or the most hurtful, the fact that his new girlfriend had a house and money or that the affair had been going on for some time. I think that really p****d her off. At any rate, she sunk back and hit the bottle, emerging after four years to find herself another bloke. Preferably someone with money. There was the farmer, but after two years, that didn't work out. Then the barrister, that was a no, no.

For the first few weeks after I met her, she hid the drink problem well. "I hope you've bought the wine," she'd say as I picked her up from work. Course, this was just for chilling after a hard day. Perfectly understandable. And if she got drunk by 9pm, so what? It was perfectly normal. But after a bit, if we went away for a few days, it would start creeping into the days. If we went for afternoon lunch, she would be ordering double wines and slurping it back like a good un. Walking to the toilets as stiff as a board whilst trying to hold herself upright. Sober, she was nice company. P****d, she was hopeless. The problem was she was p****d eight hours out of ten.

Worse, she was quite calculated and mercenary. "What do you do with your money Tommy?" she'd ask.

"Why?"

"Well, I know you have money, but you never spend it." It was quite funny really, she was 55 and hadn't got a clue about the value of money. I didn't mind her being skint. I'd come from the slums of Birmingham, Summer Lane, but it was the calculated way she was asking. But then I was finding this with a few women once they reached forty or fifty and got divorced. They had blithely gone through life, bringing up their kids, maybe waiting and relying on their husbands to bring in the wage packet, having a nice night out. A nice meal, buying nice clothes. Putting a bit aside each week for the annual or more holiday. Then all of a sudden, the proverbial s**t hit the fan. Maybe the kids had grown up. The husband had had enough. The marriage broke up.

Most people don't fully realise that if you buy your own house, the biggest part of the mortgage term is made up of interest. Only in the latter few years do you actually start paying off your mortgage. Worse, a lot of people start borrowing on the equity in their property. 'Oh, darling, the house has increased by twenty grand. Let's borrow ten, put a new bathroom in and have a luxury holiday. A cruise, maybe?' The older I get, the more I'm astonished at how many people, couples do this. In fact, I'm staggered. It is only then that they find how little they have got. Even allowing for property increases. This is all fine and dandy, but what happens then is the bloke normally hunches his shoulders in. Accepts his fate, maybe gets himself a flat or a council house, but the woman? Oh no, she sets out with a vengeance to find someone with money, to give her the life she feels she's entitled to. I tell you, finding someone is hard work.

Carolyn was different. Carolyn was a smart, savvy girl who had her head screwed on. She had various businesses, including jewellery shops, antique shops etc. She knew how to make money and was the type who could see the potential in something, even an old folks home she went into business with. Carolyn grew up on the same council estate where we had lived, Kitts Green. We had travelled the same road, experienced the same hardship. She knew the score. She was a friend of a friend on Facebook, so she could see my sense of humour. I first met her outside the hospital in Redditch, where she was undergoing chemotherapy for a few cancer spots in her stomach, or so I thought. She was absolutely stunning in a designer dress and coat with expensive jewellery to match. At a nearby pub lunch, we got on like a house on fire. I had never heard of her, but she told me she had loved me since she first knew me when I lived in Kitts Green. I was married. Now, sadly she was married. That in itself wasn't a major issue. She could always get out of her marriage. No, the problem was, Carolyn didn't just have a few spots around her stomach. She'd had the whole of her stomach taken out ten years earlier as she was ravaged by cancer, now she had a colostomy bag on her stomach.

We went along for some fifteen months before I found out about the colostomy bag. I didn't mind. We were on a little break in Barmouth when it had to come out. The truth and the bag. Much as she tried to deny it, we both knew there was no way out. The cancer was not going to disappear. It was another few months before the reality hit her, and the pain became too much. Though I offered to look after her, she chose to die in her own bed, in her own home with her husband looking after her, Que Serra Serra. I got to the hospital minutes after she had died. Even though she was made up with her full face on, she was hardly recognisable.

I had plenty of time to plan my journey. We were in lockdown. Boris was dithering between complete lockdown, part lockdown or freedom. One minute, the virus was flying around the country; people were dropping then dying like flies, then it cleared up with no fatalities. Then it would flare up again. We had the Nepalese strain. Then the Indian strain. Like mugs, we've all got to stand for this crap whilst the Indians are still allowed to fly in by the zillions without checking. And those that are here, in the usual hotspots of Bolton, Bradford and Alum Rock, are refusing to have the jabs because they think us whiteys are out to eliminate them. What do the government do? Why, they reel in as many Asians and people of colour as they can to beg people to get the jab. Actors, comedians, newsreaders. "Look, it's fine. I've had it, and I'm still alive." In the meantime, millions more are still flying in because we can't be seen as racist. Funny, they cannot seem to see that they, themselves, are creating the divide.

What p****s me off just as much, if not even more, is we are all lumped together in the same boat. So my neighbour can get the bus or the train to work surrounded by other potential human virus carriers, but I can't go away into the country somewhere with not a soul about, except maybe a sheep in the next field. Once, even before the first lockdown centuries ago, I decided to have a drive over to Brecon. Calling into town, I pulled into the local car park. I was the only one to point out that I was alone and self-isolating. I posted a picture on a Facebook camping page. Jeez, the outpouring of self-righteous vitriol that spewed out was unbelievable. And this was before any lockdown. The stupidity and short-sightedness that seems to be growing in our country is getting beyond a joke.

So here I am. Waiting for Boris to give us the all-clear when we get the latest virus, and things are teetering. France is a no go. Spain wants us in. It wants our money, that's why. I'm giving some serious thought to getting the ferry to Spain. Once in Europe, I knew there were no borders. What will the French say if I try sneaking in through the back door?

GETTING READY

With no need to rush, I started getting my motorhome ready for the off. Like the layout, everyone has their own view of what suits them. One painful story the sales rep told me was of the guy who bought a motorhome with bunk beds, only to find after less than a week it just wasn't suitable at all. It cost him a right few grand. For that reason alone, Bet and I spent over a year looking at different motorhomes. Nothing to do with cleverness, oh no, far from it. We were just that bogged down in different models, layouts, different manufacturers. We couldn't see the wood for the trees. Now, having got the one we both wanted, and I'm still content with, I double-check and keep everything stocked up.

My wardrobe is always full, socks, underpants, slacks, shoes, shirts, T-shirts. I always carry three bath towels in the shower. Scissors for cutting my toenails. Trimmer for trimming my hair. Oil, perfumes, aftershave, plenty of razors, skin balm, soap. Plenty of toilet paper, air fresheners, washing up liquids, bleach, disinfectant, etc. One can never have too much. Plates, cups and cutlery are a fixture. A few video's, games for those boring nights. Then the little bits like WD40, a set of screwdrivers, a small multi toolbox, and super glue. Stupid as it sounds, super glue is a great asset to have around. A sewing kit, well, you never know, a small USB air conditioner that I bought off my mate Mark Dale. Loads of continental plugs for all around Europe, a converter to turn 12 volts to 240 volts, great for running the telly or computer. Then the solar panels, I've got a 100 watt on my roof to keep my two 85AH leisure batteries charged up. Plus, belatedly, a small solar panel in my windscreen to keep my main battery topped up. It's no fun being in Bulgaria for a month having to worry about your battery all the time, giving it a run every few days to keep it topped up. I'm a slow learner. It's taken me years to find all these little things out, and I'm still learning. With hindsight, I realise I should have had at least a 200 watt solar panel and then connected to my mains battery also.

I always keep my food larder topped up more than at home, with packets of salt, pepper, and a few sauces. At least half a dozen Fray Bentos tins, tinned vegetable's, beans, packet and tinned soups, powdered milk, much better than fresh milk, and sweeteners rather than sugar. Most times, I split between eating out and cooking the odd simple meal. A Fray Bentos pie in the oven for twenty minutes plus a small tin of vegetable's make a decent meal for just over a quid. Sorted. I eat the pie straight out of the tin, which sits on a plate alongside the vegetables. This leaves only a small saucepan and a knife and fork to clean off. I know some people like to have and cook a full-blown breakfast or dinner. Fine, we used to try it, but frankly, we found it easier, more convenient, to eat out. It's everyone to their own choice. Some people might like to go away for a week and live and eat well, cooking a full-blown Sunday lunch and eating out with all the finery, and that's great. On a country and western site just outside Preston, I got pally with a plumber with the same model motorhome as me. He spent his time and money entertaining girlfriends in his luxury camper. Even down to little crystal chandeliers. Absolutely great. He completely cracked me up.

Having doubled checked everything, I was now ready for the off. It was just a matter of when and where. This is where the motorhome or camper comes into its own. The real aficionado's don't like the word camper or camper van.

Oh no, it's the motorhome. Higher up the rankings, see, not a mere camper. This is your home on wheels, not a camper on wheels. One does not go camping, oh no, one just moves home, and in truth, that is the actual truth. When you first look at a motorhome, it's just an object. Inside its set out with just inanimate objects, furniture, fridge, cooker, seats that double up as beds. Much like a caravan, probably more so than a caravan, I mean, a caravan has separate rooms. Statics are proper houses with a nicely set out lounge, a feature fire, nice bedrooms with posh built-in wardrobes, great if you like that and like being stuck in one place. But then it's not your caravan, is it? Oh no, you think it is. But when it gets a bit old, a little bit worn, the site owner can and will tell you to take it off and dump it. If you don't, he will.

I've heard horror stories of people whose partners have died, unable to get to their van, they eventually turn up only to find their scant belongings in black bags, the caravan gone, dumped, smashed to smithereens. Too bad. See, a letter had been posted through their door whilst they were at home grieving the death of their partner. And, typically, there is nothing the law can do about it, and for that, you are or have been paying the princely sum of some four grand a year plus. Great ay? But your motorhome? Oh no, that's different. For the first few excursions, it will all feel strange, where to put this, where to put that, what does that Sargent thingy do in the cupboard. Why is that light flashing? Bit by bit, you start to learn about your little home, your little house on wheels. You learn to read and understand the instrument panel. How much water your tank holds, mine holds 80 litres. How to be careful with your water usage, especially if you are mainly wild camping. How to read your battery usage, both leisure and mains. One silly little tip I learned once was to buy non-stick frying pans and saucepans. Once you've fried your eggs or cooked your beans, instead of wasting water on washing, just wipe them down with a paper towel, utterly simple, utterly stupid, but it works, and it saves water. I've met people who hold something like a dozen batteries, with a roof full of solar panels to keep them stocked up. For that, they run televisions, radios, computers, etc. No, sorry, not for me I'm afraid. A tad too over the top, but ay, that's the great part about it, you see. It's your individual choice. Because the thing is, it's all yours. Lock, stock and barrel. It's your home.

For the first few outings, I was terrified. I hit walls with my wing mirrors. I backed into objects hitting and smashing my light lens. I've lost a couple of my side windows with the kids not closing them properly and tightly (my fault for not double-checking). After a couple of £400 replacements, you soon start to make sure you double-check, I can tell you. But after a bit, after all that, your camper, your motorhome, becomes your home. It becomes like your favourite jumper, coat, or pair of slippers. If you've been away from it for a few weeks, it may feel a bit strange getting back into it. But after a few hours, starting that engine up, listening to its little purr, it all comes back to you. You start to learn its little foibles, its little habits. A little edging strip came off the front of my step into the bathroom. I tried sticking it down once with some 'tough as nails,' it soon came away again. Ahh. Into my little cupboard I went, brought out the superglue, scraped off the 'tough as nails,' super glued it, job done, until the next time.

I have throws over my two sofas, which keeps them clean and from accidental spills. After ten years, they are still as good as new. I love my little motorhome. "Our little motorhome," for in truth, I still consider it to be mine and Bets. When we get into our double bed, it is "our bed," it has our smell. Shortly after buying it, we decided to take it down to visit our daughter in Oxford. She and her husband Justin were holding a pig roast. Middle-class people do that, you know. Well, we pulled up outside their house, Louise, our other daughter sitting in the back, waiting for someone to clock us. It didn't take long.

Now Justin is a barrister, and like a lot of these legal experts, he is so far up his backside he has a permanent tan. When he talks to you, he doesn't look at you. He holds his head back and looks down his nose. He's a lawyer, you see, superior to everyone else, but his mother, who is also superior, pointed out how much Justin loved it. Eventually, our daughter, Rachael, and Justin deigned to come out and view our new acquisition. Both were holding their excitement in. Rachael asked if they might borrow it, "of course, when we bring it back, we will have it valeted. It will be cleaner than before we had it," she had said.

"But it's new?" I replied. Oh, ok. With five kids, we always valued the idea and benefits of sharing. Like the Greeks and the Asian community. How wonderful to think of a couple of the siblings joining up for a weekend or a week and sharing our not inexpensive motorhome, enjoying the experience of visiting a site where their mom and dad had spent a few days, reminiscing about the experience. But no, Rachael and Justin were privately educated. University groupies. They wanted to take their friends, loads of them. "But where will they sleep?" I asked.

"Well, anywhere, a couple can sleep in your bed, two on the sofa beds, and me and Justin in the overhead cab, anywhere, what does it matter." They were that engrossed in the thought, in the planning of it, they didn't see the horror in our faces.

"But Rach, that's our bed, our own personal space."

"Oh, dad, for Christ's sake. When you go to a hotel, you never care or think that a thousand people have slept in that bed, do you?" Of course, she was quite right, but this was our bed, little domain, personal space, and home, and she never saw that. It was bad enough that they thought it was that simple and straight forward they could just get in it and tootle off like it was a car. Typical university kids, see, all brains and no common sense. Sadly, that was it. Justin and Rachael never borrowed our motorhome.

I popped down to see Rachael on the boxing day after my wife passed away a few years later. By now, she had divorced Justin and had gained the house. She had gotten two massive dogs that she was into breeding, long-haired, smelly things. Taking us down to Henley-on-Thames for a walk, it had started to rain lightly. Once we got back, the dogs walked around the house, soaking wet and stinking the place out. "Oh, dad, do you think we could borrow the motorhome sometime?"

"Err, what about the dog's Rach?"

"Oh, they will be fine, and of course, when we get back, we will have it valeted?"

I wouldn't have minded if she had at least said they would sleep in the garage, but oh no, Rachael wouldn't lie. Again, the thought made my nose curl up, dog hairs all over the place? I would be picking them out for months. Sadly, Rachael had forgotten the first time she asked. Again, she never got to use or share the motorhome. I ask you? A forty-odd grand motorhome. It really is a joke. My kids have a word for me first espoused by Nicky, 'conditional dad,' because everything comes with conditions. But of course, it does. That's how family life works.

The virus was and is still spreading around the world. No world leader knows best how to handle it. Dickhead Donald

Trump even suggested that maybe swallowing disinfectant might stop it—this is the American president. Think about it. What does that say about the American people who voted him in? The one little consolation is it's only him seeming to raise the thought that it might not be such an accident that this virus has escaped from China after all. Maybe the other world leaders are too diplomatic. After WW1 and II, it was said there would never be another world war of such magnitude and loss of life, not to mention the enormous cost. No, it would just be skirmishes around the world, small guerrilla outbursts like in Iraq, Afghanistan. Up to now, they have proved right, but after Blair, the American president's puppet and warmonger, led us into a totally unnecessary war in Iraq. I don't, like many people, have much confidence in our world leaders.

What would be the simplest, cheapest and most effective way to destroy a country? Well, financially, of course. And what better way than to release a little bug? A little virus? I bet Hitler wished he could have thought of that. Hang about, he did. So here we are, all housebound. Pubs and shops are closing down galore, zillions of pounds being lost worldwide on a daily basis, and famous names going bankrupt and under. All the while, the politicians are trying to act calm whilst pooping their pants, desperately trying to find a solution. Now we've got the Asian virus, the little Napoleon Macron, president of France, has put Britain on its red list. In return, our prime minister, Boris, the buffoon, has put France on its red list. The French hate us anyway, always have done from the hundred-year war, Napoleonic wars to the second world war. The mantra has always been don't go to France. The French hate us. The French police hide on every street corner, ready to pounce on any English car they see and smack us with a fine. Besides, they eat frogs legs. How bad can that be? But hang about, that's not what I found from my experience, well, apart from the frog's legs, of course.

In exasperation and desperation, Portugal had opened its doors and welcomed the English. Soon, Spain followed suit, "come in, visit us, we need your money." But I wanted to visit France. I was getting to love France. The more I saw, the more I wanted to see. Ok, it was hotter in Spain for longer, you could sunbathe and swim in Benidorm on Christmas day. France was also more expensive, but I could compromise. Spend the Summer in France, tootle down to Spain in the Autumn. But how do I get to France? Hang about, once in Europe, all the borders are open. Why not book my ferry to Spain then simply sneak in by the back door into France?

By now I had had my two injections and my little certificate to go with them. The one-way ferry to Spain was £345. The one-way ferry from dover to Calais was £85; with one tank of diesel at circa £85, I was saving some £300. Now in anyone's language, especially mine, that seemed like good value, and I was on my own. There was no more to be said, but what about French customs? It had been made clear that they didn't want us in France. I decided to take the bull by the horns, went online and booked my ferry for the second week in April of 2022. No objections, no queries, no refusals, I couldn't believe it, what's going on? Why did no one tell me I wasn't allowed into France? Arriving in France two hours later, I disembarked with stomach knotted. There could be only one explanation: Europe was all open borders; I was heading for Spain... how could they stop me?

Duly arriving at Calais, I was quite apprehensive because I'd had a bad cough and sore throat for a few days. I wondered if one of the grandkids had given it to me in Barmouth on our little jaunt. Had I got the virus? The Covid? Onboard I was warned that I would have to fill out a destination form with a phone number etc. Getting into my camper at Calais, it was warm. Worse, I was sweating like the proverbial. Over comes one of the staff with his little gadget and holds it to my bonce, this is it. But he walked away. Yikes, my lady friend who had tested me a couple of days earlier was right. I didn't have Covid.

Getting off the ferry, I was met by passport control. No worries, as I was waved through. Then through customs where I was pulled over by a pretty but stern woman who asked where I was heading. Benidorm. "How much money do you have?" she asked. To which I replied, "£700."

"Only £700?"

Jeez, did they have to be so obvious? How much English money do you have? Whether she was satisfied with that, I don't know. £700 doesn't sound like a lot of spending money. Maybe it might have dawned on her that I was possibly carrying credit and cash cards. Getting out of the port, I clicked Cannes into my sat nav and tootled off, heading straight across to France. Taking a wrong turn, I ended up on a motorway, but I didn't mind too much, normally I avoid motorways as they take the fun out of seeing the sights, but this time I was quite grateful. The driving was a doddle, the motorways mostly empty or with very little traffic. One great thing about lockdown and Covid is it empties the roads. Pulling into one of the Aires halfway through my journey, I pulled into the garage, filled up, then went into the restaurant for a light meal. I then settled into my little bed for a peaceful nights kip. Thank you, Covid.

MARSEILLAN LA PLAGE

On one of the camping sites I was on, someone had mentioned a place called Marseillan Plage, where there was plenty of motorhome parking along the seafront. This was just about forty miles further on from Narbonne, a place I knew well and liked. I put this as my next destination. With no signs of where I was, I was a bit nervous when I was pulled over by a guy in uniform at the tolls. "Where are you from?" he asked.

"Spain."

"Yes, I know Spain, but where in Spain?"

I was puzzled, "Santander. I have been there a few days." I don't think he was too bothered. He was friendly enough but just going through the motions, then it occurred to me, is this France? "Yes, you are in France." And that was it. I'm here, in France, sweet as a nut, no worries, no palaver.

What the hell is all the fuss about? After a few hours, I was in Marseillan Plage.

Driving steadily along the main thoroughfare, I kept my beady eyes out for a berth. I suspect many motorhome owners do this. We get quite expert at it, glancing up and down as we drive along. Where can I park up? Where can I get some water? All little questions and queries that have to be answered as we go along?

Along a side road adjacent to the beach, I clocked a couple of motorhomes, French, of course, parked up alongside a big car park. I pulled in behind a couple of them, settled down, opened my roof lights and put the kettle on. Plenty of time later to explore the town. Marseillan Plage is very pretty. Smart, well to do. Plenty of shops and restaurants serving good quality food, especially seafood, which was in abundance. Unlike Narbonne, it was also quite a bit cheaper, more reasonable, a glass of beer three euros. The money

I am saving on campsite fees, I spend in the town, even more so, so it's a win-win, all around. There is a campsite in Marseillan, and after a few days I went in to have a look at it. I was curious. Having seen the motorhomes driving down, I wasn't impressed. The site looked untidy, pitches overgrown. No swimming pool. And the charges varied between 30 and 50 euros a night, in high season. That's £210 to £350 a week. Oh, ok, that's fine, I suppose, if there's a group of you coming away for a week. But I still consider it, well, stiff, just to park up your camper, use a bit of electricity. Fine if you can get away with it. And they are, especially after lockdown.

I find motorhome users split into different groups. One neighbour of mine in Sutton, not short of a few bob, will not use sites on principle. Others will use them for the odd night to top up their water and batteries, empty their waste and cassettes, which makes sense to me. Especially if there are two of you. Then you have those who would not be seen dead wild camping. It's beneath them. Besides, they want to put their awning out, put out their tables and chairs, relax. Cook nice food, eat at the table at leisure. This also I can understand. It's everyone to their own, were all different.

A couple of years ago I stopped at a car park in Italy by the seafront. Sitting on my sofa with the door open, I saw a little dog walk past, the only thing was, it wasn't a dog at all, it was a baby wild boar. Soon its mother appeared, then the whole family. You don't get that on a campsite. A few days later, having a friend visit, I booked into a campsite a mile further away from the sea. Ok, it was nice. But the only benefit I felt we got was the swimming pool and the laundry room to wash my sheets and quilt covers. For that, I was paying 150 quid. Here in Marseillan, the beach was fifty yards away, and the Mediterranean Sea was nice and warm. It was a bit of a no-contest, I'm afraid. Even more so on my own, yes, with my kids for any longer than three days, I'd go on a site.

I had now been at Marseillan for over a week, I don't think anyone would mind or even notice if I stopped longer, but I feel it's maybe time for a change. Last Monday I went to bed only to get a loud bang and shouting on the back of my motorhome. My initial thought was it might be a traffic cop or warden, so I ignored it. Then I heard a bit of noise outside and felt it's best to have a little nose. It's a good job I did. It was the market traders setting up. They took over the whole parking area on a Tuesday, which stretched from the seafront down to the main boulevard. I got out quick sharpish. It was only later I saw the tow-away sign for Tuesdays only between 6am and 2pm. I must pay more attention.

I decided to visit the small town of Meze, a few miles away and on the edge of a lagoon. As the waitress told me in the Bodega Bar, it is a beautiful place to visit. She was right, but there was just nowhere to park. I pulled up right on the beach by the small slipway, had a swim and did a bit of sunbathing before going back to my camper and seeing a ticket on my windscreen. Hearing a couple of ladies with Irish accents sitting nearby, I asked them if they could speak or read French. They could and told me I would be fined if I didn't move. I did, but where too? Not the side of the road here. Driving to the port was a no-no as well. After driving around four times, I decided to give the town a miss, shame, but they obviously didn't want motorhomes. I decided to give Sete a try a few miles further along.

Sete was a very big town, a fishing port and harbour, on the Mediterranean and just a few miles further up than Marseillan. Driving around a bit, I decided to give that a miss as well. I'm just not into big thriving places. It was getting on a bit, so I decided to head back to Marseillan. Before setting out from England, I invested in a couple of books covering all the Aires in France, Spain and Portugal. Together they cost over forty pounds from vicarious media, who also supply ACCSI books, a great cheap campsite guide for Europe. But it was to be money well spent. Heading back to Marseillan, I saw an Aires to the side of the road. Pulling in, I was given a ticket from the machine that raised the barrier. It was a short walk to the beach and cost ten pounds for the night. For two people, it was good value for money for someone who wanted a beach and seclusion. It was packed with French. Nice, but on my own, it didn't suit me.

The next day I made my way back to Marseillan. The car park was now all cleared of the market traders. I decided to park up near the boulevard. After the first night, I realised my mistake. It was kept busy from cars coming and going and boy racers on their little motorbikes. The next day I moved up to my little quiet spot at the far end by the beach. Now, tomorrow, I'm off, along to Narbonne and Gruissan, further back along the coast, forty miles away. Between them, they had three Aires right by the beach and harbour. Another little adventure.

There are only three things I feel that can give you the freedom of a motorhome:

1. The tent, oh I don't mean those great big, three-roomed monstrosities that take you four hours to put up and five hours to put back down and put away, losing the most important bits as you do. No, I'm talking about the small, two-man, or two-person backpack tent thrown over the shoulder. A nest of Billy cans and the sleeping bag, together with a box of matches and your away. A train to Devon or Scotland, a plane to anywhere in the world. Off the plane, train or bus and away you go. Complete freedom. Great when you're fourteen, exciting when you're twenty and with the girlfriend you love, but forty? Fifty? Nah.

2. I read an article once about a couple who, being young, sold their home in London, came out with six grand in cash profit. They sold everything up, caught a plane to America, once there they called into a local car sales pitch,

bought a cheap estate car, went to the local Wal-Mart, bought a few spare clothes, a small gas cooker and a couple of sleeping bags and off they went. They spent twelve months touring the whole of America, doing the odd job for food as they went. What a great idea, how original. But my first thought was, so ok, with the property prices, how they are in London can they ever get back on the housing ladder? So that's a no straight off.

We had a friend in Devon, Anne. Anne had been diagnosed with cancer. Having worked in a circus, she was now a qualified teacher. Instead of working full time, she worked as a part-time supply teacher to suit herself. Wanting to see China, she got herself a two-year contract teaching English. Great. She got to know and see much of the Chinese culture and lifestyle. The real nitty-gritty parts. Dogs, being sold at market as a delicacy, babies put on show in demijohns in small villages as a warning to all not to have more children. Only one.

Wanting to see and tour America, she got a flight to New York. Travelling east to west, south to north, she would visit a town, spend the day or two touring, then get on one of the famous Greyhound expresses, travelling overnight to another city. Once there, she would make use of the modern facilities, have a wash, shower or whatever, tour and visit the town or city before heading off yet again overnight to another destination. Again, I thought this was brilliant, but Anne was clocking on 50 plus with little money, and she knew life was short.

3. Well, to be rich, of course, and when I say rich, I don't mean 70 grand a year rich with a half-million-pound house, you might think your rich, you ain't. No, I'm talking really, really rich, when you can afford the yacht to take you and the staff around the med. Bored with the

yacht? Then to get on a plane, private or first class, fly to Botswana, or the Bahamas, Iceland or Australia, hiring the best guides in the area to show you the sights, now that's the way to really travel, but then Richard Branson's got all that and what does he do? He lies in a hammock all day on his little island.

Failing all that? Then it only leaves one option. The motorhome, oh, ha-ha, I forget, there is the caravan, hump that onto the back of the car and tow that down to the Sahara if you want. No, it's the motorhome, your own home, everything at your fingertips and the ability to drive anywhere in the world, and I mean the world. In Igoumenitsa, Greece, one year, I was parked up by the harbour seafront along with a few others when a Chinese couple pulled over in a colourful motorhome. Shortly afterwards, a German couple in front of me came over and started chatting. The Chinese couple had travelled from China itself, they plan to tour Europe. Awesome, I thought. The German soon brought his Hurly Gurley out and started playing the songs on it, a brilliant night had by all.

In my Aires book, there is one Aire in Narbonne right on the seafront, two in Gruissan, one on the seafront another by the harbour overlooking the boats. I decided to try Narbonne first. Narbonne is a beautiful little place with a massive long beautiful beach. The only problem is they don't want it spoilt by motorhomes. Every other post had a sign on it, in French, but the camper bit was international. I drove up and down a couple of times before heading out of town for the Aire. Found it alright, but no one was available to open the barriers. Not to worry, I wasn't desperate yet. There was Gruissan to check out. There were plenty of Aires all along my route, and don't ask me which way I came. I hadn't got a clue.

My sat nav is now a few years old. It's a Tom-Tom, XXL Europe. I gather there are better ones on the market that tell you heights of bridges, traffic disruptions etc., all singing and dancing. My problem is I find it difficult to adapt. I've got three computer's, my kids gave me two, but I'm used to my old, slow one. My Tom-Tom does its job. It gets me from A to B. If I get off the ferry at Santander and input Benidorm, it will take me there. It might Lose me an extra 50 miles or so, but it will get me there, as it did to Marseillan Plage from Santander. No problems, no worries. Many times, while travelling in Spain, I find my little car on the screen is driving alone in the desert, and the correct road is a few miles to my right or left, in red. This worried me for quite some time until I realised, since joining the euro, the Spanish were borrowing money hand over fist to build new roads. Someone had whispered in their ear that it would be a fantastic idea to borrow billions off the European banks and have a massive infrastructure build. Our money, taxpayers money, used to bribe its citizens into voting for it. They were building roads that fast the sat nav companies couldn't keep up with them. Worse, the developers got in on the act, borrowing billions off the banks to build new towns, villages, and communities all over the place.

Once we were all in the euro, the logic was simple: where would everyone want to go? Why Spain, of course. From cold Germany, Finland, England, we will all be flying down those newly built roads and buying up those newly built towns and houses. The only problem was it never happened. Developers were going out of business left, right, and centre. Banks were stuck with zillions of properties they couldn't sell. Now, here they are, opening the doors to let us in. They need our money.

From Marseillan to Narbonne, I just put in the coordinates from the Aires book, some 45 miles distance. Twenty miles or so were fairly straightforward, nice roads, all avoiding toll roads. Then? Well, I went off track. The roads were reduced to tracks, then winding lanes amongst what looked like sugar cane. To be fair, I passed some lovely scenery, picturesque rivers with boats moored up. There were plenty of places to camp up and enjoy the local scenery. Seeing other motor homers pulling in, it was obvious some had the same idea. But I was only a few miles from Narbonne. Well, I thought I was only a few miles from Narbonne. Had I put in the wrong coordinates?

Eventually, I got to Narbonne. Disappointed, I headed off another few miles to my next destination, Gruissan. I had visited Gruissan a couple of years earlier. Gruissan is a beautiful port town with a very nice yacht club, very fancy yachts, and a nice selection of restaurants from reasonable to expensive. I had parked in the yacht club car park only to be told fine, but not overnight. I drove around until I found a very nice car park, shops and restaurants nearby, right by the beach. If things didn't work out with the Aires, I had a backup plan. On my way to the Aire, I saw and looked at two other free Aires on the side of the harbour, great. But it was 85 degrees. I needed to be by the water for a swim. It is coming up to the high season. It's going to get hotter. I soon found the Aires, and it looked ideal, right on the seafront, lovely beach. And it was packed. At ten euros a night, those French ain't slow.

Pulling in front of the barrier, the girl came out, indicated a pitch, asked if I was on my own. When I said I would get some shopping first, she did an about-turn and said she had no more room. She was packed. She handed me a map of the town and directed me to another Aire. This sounded fishy to me, even more so when a Frenchy pulled in behind me, and she let him in. No, no, no, that was a bit of favouritism alright. Ok, fine. I drove off, familiarised myself with the area, then found the trusty little car park right by the beach I had used a couple of years earlier. About five other campers were dotted around there before me. It didn't take me long to get my bearings, find a little pitch, back in and settle down. Sorted. Now, all I needed was to get my tan topped up and get on that beach.

I've heard all the horror stories of what some campers get up to. 10,000 people can go to a festival, defecate on the grass and leave rubbish and tents all over the shop. But if five campervans leave some rubbish behind, all hell is let loose. To be fair, there is no need or cause for it. We are self-contained individuals, so there is no problem in taking our rubbish away with us. As regards toiletries, well, that is another matter indeed. I have heard stories of people with campers defecating in open view. Well, in all honesty, I find it staggering to believe. How can anyone do or be like that? Some people say it is the small camper vans with limited facilities and no toilets, in either case, I don't think that's any kind of an excuse. Many years ago, when we first visited Morocco. I was impressed and staggered at the sheer number of motorhomes on the beach in Agadir. It was rammed. The following year it was empty. When I asked Mohammed from the hotel what had happened, he said the King drove past one day and was appalled by seeing so many filling the beach. Worse, it seemed the French were emptying their cassettes into the sea at night. Whether this was true or not, I could never figure it out. Surely the French would not be so stupid as to empty raw sewage into the sea? On the beach? It seemed too blatant to accept or believe. Quite a few people told me that there are Arabs who go around in trucks emptying your cassettes for a fee, and why not? Everyone's happy, the Arabs earn a few dirhams, you get your tank emptied. I know they also come around with fresh water and food as well as fresh fish right off the boat. It can't be bad.

But who could possibly be so stupid and inconsiderate as to empty waste into the sea? The mind boggles, but then over the years, I started to hear different stories. One camper boasted that he kept emptying the fluids out of his cassette to leave more room for solids. Ok, fluids, urine does take up a lot of space but crikey, a cassette full of solids? For myself, I found the best solution was a separate container for fluids and only rarely used the toilet itself. When my wife was here, or my kids were with me, we rarely spent more than three days wild camping. That's about as long as I can put up with the kids anyway. (Love you, kids). With my wife, it was different. She had priority over everything. It was her toilet, her shower, her sink, even on sites.

FRANCE AND THE RIVIERA

El Campello in Spain had a beautiful car park right on the beachfront where motorhomes pitched up. One year I noticed very few, then across the main road next to a garage and the rambler, I saw a line of motorhomes. Walking along, I noticed all were Spanish, except for one brand new, very expensive motorhome, towing a KA car on the back to boot. The couple were sitting outside their van overlooking the rambler, swatting the flies away as they sat, both in smart clothes. The woman dolled up like she was ready for a ball, full makeup on. And this was 10am in the morning.

When I asked why they were not on the seafront, the male told me the gendarme had moved them back a few weeks earlier due to flooding from the rambler. They had just never bothered moving back to the seafront, only popping out now and again to do a bit of shopping.

"But what about your cassettes?" I knew the garage supplied water, but it didn't have toilets. With a casualness that surprised me, the guy pointed to the rambler and said, "well, I suppose most of them will empty into the rambler." Then pointing to some blue-tinted bits of tissue directly in front of him, he said, it looks like someone has dumped there. There were two feet in front of them. No wonder they were squatting flies away. They were in a sixty grand plus motorhome, and they weren't bothered about effluent dumped right in front of them.

Some small CL sites, even in England, can be found for just a few pounds a night. Anyone should be able to afford even that once or twice in the week. For water, it's a different thing again. Our motorhome has an 80-litre tank. We never drink from it. It is purely used for washing or flushing the toilet. We carry a separate five-gallon container with fresh water for coffee or drinking, another one-gallon container that we keep topped up from the big one. Both containers will last us at least a couple of weeks, on my own a month. If and when I run out, I search out a new supply tap. Marinas always have a water supply, as do cemeteries, also many garages. Failing that, and if need be, I will go on a site or an Aire.

I have a solar panel for my main battery, a 100-watt solar panel on my roof for my two leisure batteries. It is plenty adequate for living aboard needs, at home I have the telly on all day, news during the day, a couple of good films at night. Here in my motorhome, I don't miss either. I've got a telly hung up on the wall, video's to watch in my cupboard. Maybe one day or night I will watch one or two. For now, I'm quite content to enjoy what's around me, doing puzzles, and reading free magazines that I save up out of the Sunday papers. Sitting in the nude on my sofa after a day on the beach is quite satisfying, roof light and side windows fully open. The weather here in Gruissan is 85 degrees at the moment, so it's deck chairs out, lotion on. The rest of the day on the beach.

My main and underlying reason for visiting the Riviera was threefold. Cannes, St Tropez, Narbonne and Gruissan all had fabulous beaches. Monaco did not impress me at all. Why anyone would want to go to such a cramped up little place is beyond me. Surely it can't all be about tax dodging, for lord's sake, impressing your peers? What is to gain by that? I once read that Aristotle Onassis, the oil billionaire, was always competing to outdo his cousin with a bigger boat. I could see the advantage with Cannes, St Tropez. I might even get a peek at Bridget Bardot. Although the last time I saw a picture of her in the papers, she looked like a wrinkled up little prune. Great body, shame about the face.

No, all along the Riviera was/is beautiful, nice long sandy beaches, the crystal clear blue of the Mediterranean. OK, it was a bit more expensive. A lot more expensive than in Spain. Maybe the French have got to try and find a way to pay the debts they are in, but in a motorhome, you can compromise. A bowl of Moules Mariniere in Spain is about nine euros. Here in Gruissan, with frites, it's fifteen euros. In Marseillan Plage, thirteen euros, a nice entrecote steak with frites (that's French fries to you ignoramuses. I'm worldly-wise), is about 17-19 euros, which compared to a nice restaurant in England isn't too bad I don't think. So, to me, I compromise. Some days I would eat something simple in my van, like a couple of cooked chicken legs, maybe a Fray Bentos pie with a tin of vegetables. Each makes a nice meal, twenty minutes in the oven and that's it, very filling. In the morning, a cup of coffee will set me up for a bit. In truth, I eat to live. I just don't live to eat. Food, nice as it can sometimes be, is just a necessity. If I'm in the mood, I will have a snack at some local restaurant. Yesterday I had a very nice jambon and melon at the local restaurant here. I felt obliged as I use their Wi-Fi. But at twelve and a half euros for three slices of melon and a few slices of ham with a coffee, I won't rush to try that again. There was hardly enough to fill a tooth.

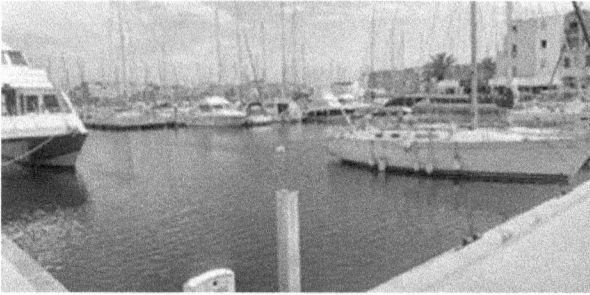

But the real reason I chose this part of the Riviera is it has so much to offer. First, you have the beautiful sandy beaches, the pretty, smart little towns and resorts, and its convenience and accessibility to so many places. Languedoc, the medieval village of Carcassonne, just a few miles inland, has many medieval villages in the surrounding areas. I just never knew France had so many medieval villages. Lagrasse, with its famous Sainte-Marie Abbey. Villerouge-Termenes, with its Chateau. There are just so many of them. All within a short drive of the Riviera. My plan was to visit as many as possible, maybe spend a couple of days in each one, have a meal, savour the atmosphere. Then there is the Loire Valley with its abundance of beautiful magnificent chateau's.

The first and last time I called into La Cite of Minerva, a small medieval village northwest of Carcassonne, I had a nice chat with the proprietor of a little bistro who wasn't a happy little bunny at all. He had only owned and set up in business a few months earlier. Now, the next day, he had been ordered, along with the rest of France, to close down completely because of Covid. The poor bugger was gutted. But then, he would not be alone. I think many businesses, big and small, will be affected by this coronavirus. I think, for many, it will be enough to make them go out and get a 9 to 5 job.

What constantly surprises and impresses me is the openness and friendliness of the French people themselves. I used to think they were pig-ignorant, frog-leg eaters. They look on us as 'la boeuf' eaters. But is this part of the age-old rivalry between us? Many people are starting to visit and see the real France, but how many are put off by the horror stories passed down? Don't trust the French. They hate us. French cops hide in the side streets to nick us left, right and centre.

My friends Keith and Janet own and live on a beautiful farm in the Loire valley, just outside Chateau Gontiere. It is absolutely amazing, so peaceful, so calming. Driving to it down a short country lane, it's like entering another world. Keith and his wife had bought the fifty-acre farm some fifteen years earlier. They loved the French way of life. Their plan was to make a living from the farm and supplement their pensions. Keith was an engineer, his wife a teacher. Unfortunately, they were not to know that you can't make a living with fifty acres. Even the French couldn't make a living with fifty acres unless of course, you could get into turkeys, chickens, or caravan storage. Sadly, Keith's wife died. Within a very short period, Janet's husband and my friend, Ken, died. Janet and Keith both decided to pool their resources and live together. It was a win-win for both of them. An even better win for Janet, who lost everything on Ken's passing.

In Chateau Gontiere, the River Mayenne runs through the town. Lovely little bistros are dotted about, all reasonably priced. A camping Aire sits on the banks of the river. Each time we went out to Gontiere, we were met with friendliness. Once I was helping Keith spread some gravel chippings he had just delivered, fifteen tons. The driver got out, approached Keith and immediately put his hand out in friendship. After discussing his requirements, the driver did a great job of taking the trouble to spread the gravel along the whole of the drive, making it a lot easier for us to spread with a rake. After he had gone, I commented on the driver's friendliness and willingness to shake hands. Keith just threw it straight off as normal, "oh, they all do that." Well, I thought it was a lot different to back home. Don't get me wrong, I love England. I love visiting many towns, resorts, Barmouth, Llandudno, Weston-Super-Mare, the Derby Dales, and the Lake District. But it's the people, the locals. In Weston, they might as well put big signs up saying bugger off campers. In Devon and Cornwall, they call outsiders grockles and with a sneer. And they want our business? Here, in France and in Spain, I was met with nothing but friendliness. They are supposed to be our age-old enemies? In Normandy, I called to see where the invasions took place by the British and Americans, Omaha Beach, Gold, and all the other invasion points. There is a war museum there dedicated to the British and American forces. At Pegasus bridge, there are tributes all over the place in gratitude by the French. Around the towns in Normandy, there are tributes painted on the walls and buildings. You cannot hide the admiration and respect the French clearly have for us. Yet it embarrasses me to see or hear whenever there is some petty argument over one thing or another, we have to throw up how much they owe us from WW2. They know. I'm sure it must be the politician's, or the press, constantly stirring up trouble.

Sitting on my sunbed, soaking up the rays, looking at my fellow sunbathers, I can't help but notice even the skies have their own ambience, their own personalities. Looking up, the skies are friendly and blue. The clouds were lazy, laid back and easy-going, chilled, relaxed, very French. The Spanish, just across the border, were different again, random. Laidback with a sense of cheekiness about them, doing very little to hide the sun's rays from pouring down on us. Challenging us to see how long we can sit out in it. How vastly different to the British sky, clouds rolled up into dark, angry balls of blackness and anger. Always something hiding amongst them. One minute you might see an angry dog, or a wild horse, never anything nice like a flower, a cherub, a buttercup, and then there is God moving his furniture. It was always so angry, so malevolent, so brooding, our parents had to find an excuse for it. "It's alright, son. Don't be frightened. It's only God moving his furniture." I stood for that for years. I believed them.

The Russian clouds are even worse. Cold, brooding, silent, watchful, evil. I dread to think what the Germans must look like with their history. One day, maybe someone might do a survey on cloud formations around the world. It might explain much of the personalities within and under it.

It was hard enough for me to learn the English language. Growing up in the slums of Birmingham, we were considered factory fodder. I never even knew or heard of an A or O level when I was at school. I didn't know what they were until my own kids were coming up into their teens. Oh no, we were left to sink or swim. Many of us sunk into the factories or building sites dotted around us, grateful for a job, any job. A nice council house was the height of our ambition. But as I started to get around in the world, I thought it was only polite to try and learn even a bit of the language.

In Wales, 'yaki dah.' Mind, I soon put a stop to that after a night in the local boozer in Tregaron Wales. Drinking over one night, I said to the old boy looking at me, "yaki dah?" Well, he started going off on one in Welsh until the landlady put him right and told him I was English. His face turned to thunder. He did a complete about-turn. His back didn't look too pretty. I don't know who felt the biggest twit. The Welsh hate us anyway. So no, I never do the 'yaki dah.' But around the world, I try to learn a bit. In Morocco, I took the time to learn 'guadan,' 'shokran,' and 'inshalla.' Which, if I remember correctly, means tomorrow, thank you, and God willing. I had to learn something to put a stop to the Arabs who are a pain in the backside and won't leave you alone for want of trying to get the last dirham out of you. By saying, "no, thank you, but I will come back tomorrow," God willing, will shut them up. In Spain, the word 'gracias' comes in useful, which I always pronounce as grassy arse, much to my kid's amusement. But means thank you.

SPEAKING LA FRENCH

Here in France, it's 'bonjour,' 'merci beaucoup,' or something like that anyway. I'm getting quite adept at it. Even to the extent that some of the French think I'm French. Well, at least I'm having a bash. When I see some of the French talent walking around, I wish I could speak it a lot more. Mind, it would be nice if some of the French talents could speak a bit of English. There are some beauties around, alright. But how can you chat a French woman up when you're limited to "Bonjour, mademoiselle?" No, I'm stymied, I'm afraid. Even more so in some of the restaurants. I thought it was bad enough in Marseillan Plage, the French are proud of their language and won't bow down to learning some German. Quite rightly so, as do we brits, maybe I should get an app on my phone? That's it. Otherwise, how on earth can I understand the menu. Calling into my little local just a few paces from my van and along the seafront, I asked for the menu. They understand that bit; it's international. But the actual menu? Oh no, that's in French. Why don't they put it in German or English underneath? I've noticed some snobby French restaurants in England, run by English if you don't mind, do the same, two penny halfpenny snobs. Here in France, I can understand it. Maybe very few English come here, obviously.

There are five or so items on the menu. The first one, Moules Mariniere, is top of the list. That is the top seller alright, everyone goes for the Moules, even I love my Moules, but not every night. No, I wanted a steak. The French love the word 'entrecote.' If you want a steak, ask for entrecote. In Marseillan it was entrecote. Pink? Yes pink. Here in Gruissan, no entrecote. So, I asked for steak, the young waitress looked totally blank. "Que?" The guy on the table next door asked if I speak Deutch? As in German? No. Eventually, I think I got the second item on the menu, down to meat. It was meat, but she couldn't say what or any more. Frites? Ahh yes, frites, ok. I took a chance. I will have that.

When it came, it definitely looked like beef of some kind, maybe a steak. Talking to the German on the next table, he and his wife seemed to agree that it was from a cow of some kind. They knew the word rump ok, but not sirloin. At rib-eye, they looked equally blank. I didn't even want to contemplate the word horse after my meal. After the Germans had finished their Moules, they asked if I was from England? Yes. Brexit, everyone in Europe knows the word Brexit, mention Boris and that's it, the two words tie in together. Boris and Brexit. The German looked a bit quizzical, leaving me to think maybe he deserved a bit of an explanation, from one European to another kind of thing. I explained to him that personally, my feeling is that if we hadn't been treated so dismissively, we would all have probably voted to remain but when that idiot from Brussels was asked on camera if they would be giving any concessions away to our Prime Minister Cameron, on our immigration problem and he arrogantly replied, "no. None," we might give him a few crumbs, that is all. Well, I was furious. And maybe that infuriated many others in England also.

That arrogant twit may have thought he was addressing the individual journalist asking the question behind Cameron's back and as a warning to Cameron himself. He wasn't. He was addressing us. All of us English. I tried to explain this to the German. But you know, try as they might, those Germans can't hide their arrogance. Their self-feeling of superiority. With a smug little look on his face, eyes looking down his nose, he explained he had voted remain. Whoopee doo. I said, "well, Finland wants to get out. Even here in France, there are murmurings of discontent. And I gather many Germans were not happy with frau Merkel on the mass of immigrants coming into your country?" He didn't like that too much. I thought maybe I was getting too near the bone here. Drop it and get out.

Without a doubt, those Germans don't like losing too much. They show it in how they nick the sunbeds wherever they are in the world. They even build little moated walls around themselves on the beach. How bad does that get? Once, in Morocco, the pool entertainer, maybe not realising the significance, decided to organise a game of water football in the pool. Well, there were a bunch of young English lads there on some kind of outing, all in their early twenties. They were right up for it. As were the Germans, of mixed ages. Knowing their keenness for winning, as against just enjoying the game like anyone else, I decided to give us an edge. I explained to the English lads that I would pitch myself in with the Germans right up by the German goal. Well, I'd got a bit of a square head and guessed the Germans would never clock on. Well, they didn't.

The lads were passing to me, and I was banging the ball into the net one after the other. We were about eight nil up before they started to clock on. At one point, they all tried to jump on me in the pool to give me a ducking, but it was too late. We will beat them. Off they went all sulking. That night in the bar, one of the older Germans came over to me and gave me a bit of credit for winning the game. He knew it was my positioning that did it. Strangely he then gave me a salute and clicked his heels. Ahh, looking at him, I could see he was too young to have served in the war. But he must have been in the Hitler youth? I almost said it. Biting my tongue quick sharpish. Yes, after all these years. It was still instilled in him.

GRUISSAN AND
THE LANGUEDOC

Gruissan, the beautiful port and harbour, is based in the Languedoc area of France. Languedoc stretches from Montpellier to the Pyrenees and is famous for its wine-growing regions. Whilst using Gruissan as a base, my plan was quite simple. To chill, relax and explore as and when I felt like it. I had had a pleasant week around Marseillan Plage. Visiting and sampling different places. Here, in Gruissan, I was some forty miles from the medieval town of Carcassonne. Around Carcassonne, in all directions, spread amazing and interesting medieval towns and villages.

Between Gruissan and Carcassonne lay the Fontfroide Abbey. Initially, I just assumed it would be another abbey occupied by a few monks. Solemn and serious-looking men were carrying the worries of the world on their shoulders, like the Sainte-Marie Abbey in the medieval town of Lagrasse, just a short drive inland from Fontfroide. They do like their Abbeys in France. The monks left the Abbey sometime before 1901. It was founded in 1093 and became Cistercian in 1145. It continued to evolve until the 14th century, becoming one of the most powerful Abbeys in Europe (how can an Abbey be powerful?). Anyway, it did, and following the departure of the last monks, Gustave and his wife Madeleine Fayet bought the Abbey with plans to restore it.

Oh, to be a fly on the wall when they decided to buy that. Gustave and Madeleine were respected winegrowers. Was it just out of love and respect for the Abbey and a genuine desire to preserve it, or was it a more cynical business decision? What does it matter? The Abbey obviously came with a few acres of land, lots of acres. Gustave and Madeleine spent a lot of time and money renovating, repairing and making the Abbey their home. Today it has passed down through the generations, and now their children run the Abbey. Its success is clear, yet it retains the peacefulness that the Abbey had exuded over the centuries.

Driving through Languedoc, mile after mile of wine-growing fields, was enchanting. Rugged rocks and cliffs reared up and surrounded the vineyards as though protecting them. Driving through small towns and villages was like discovering hidden gems in itself. Narrow streets got the old ticker pumping with fear of what lay in store just around the corner. Many of these villages and towns were built back in the days of the horse and cart before cars were even thought of. Beautiful sandstone houses are clustered and built tightly together for support. There are no gardens to the front, just shuttered windows and doors leading onto the narrow streets. Driving along, you had to keep your wits about you and look out for overhanging balconies as well as the little streets that narrowed away to a dead-end, many a time forcing you to reverse back on yourself, the locals looking at you with that certain look, the bemused look. "Ahh, la English. The stupido." Yes, they all give it. I just give them a big smile and a "bonjour." That throws them then. They think I'm French.

Reaching the Abbey was an act of discovery in itself. It was well signposted. And I soon found myself passing acre after acre of vine bushes. Eventually, I came to a well-signposted notice, cars and campers. Ahh, yet again. So typical in France. Motor homers are catered for, even to stop the night. Who is watching? The car park was massive, clearly signposted with cars lined up in rows. The car park held some 60 or 70 cars, lined in rows of four or five, and it was only a quarter full. Dotted around in their own spaces were the motorhomes, tables and chairs out, enjoying the ambience. It was all very relaxed and peaceful. But where was the Abbey? After a pleasant drive to find the place, I decided to make a cup of coffee whilst I soaked up the surroundings. Trees lined both sides of the field that was the car park. In size, it must have been about four acres. At the far end, the ground started to rise up, and I could see the newly arrived visitor's, walking slowly up the incline. After my coffee, I locked the van up and started to make my way to the steps leading up to the incline. First, I was met with a notice giving the history of the place, how Gustave and Madeleine bought Fontfroide to restore it and protect it from abandonment. On another notice was the ticket price to visit it. 12 euros, hmmm. Following on through the wrought iron gates, the Abbey opened up across the bridge over the moat and started to reveal itself.

Through a covered entrance, the courtyard opened up in front of me, the Abbaye and building's leading off to the right, the restaurants, outside seating to the left, the place was busy, I would pop in for a snack and a coffee later, for now, I wanted to have a look around and explore the Abbey, at the very least it was awe-inspiring. Although the Abbaye was approached from a clear and level road, it was still on the beaten track. Even more so in the days that it was built. The Abbey itself nestled between groups of trees and mountains at the back nestled around it in a protective blanket. Very clever indeed, those monks may have been doing God's work back in the days, but they sure knew how to protect themselves from the evils around them.

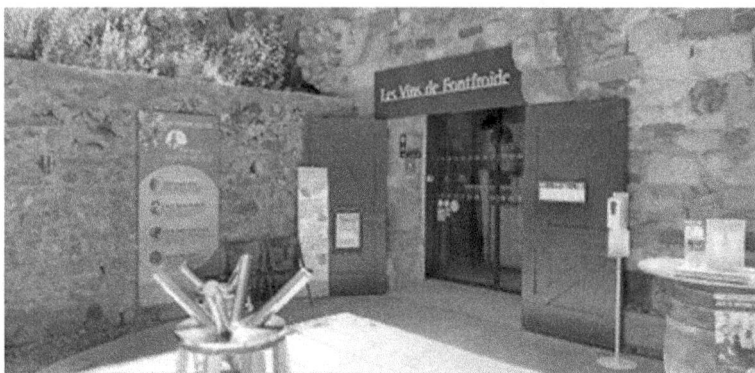

Getting my bearings, I decided to have a nosey around the wine shop. In the quietness of the building, the wines were set about in cases, individual bottles set out on shelves, tempting you to look, to buy. 9 euros for a bottle, 8 euros if you bought a case. I'm not a wine connoisseur. I know nothing of wines, red or white? Yes. Red with meat, white with fish. Until I read years later, one expert debunked that as a load of nonsense. Our favourite was a Liebfraumilch, a concoction of different German wines. Once, at a wine tasting at the national exhibition centre in Birmingham, Bet and I were invited to try a sample of wines by a couple of Germans in a small kiosk, and why not? It was only after sampling half a dozen wines that we found one we liked. Horrifyingly it was only sold by the case. We would have needed a second mortgage to buy a case. It was only then we realised the Germans had set us up in their favourite panzer movement. We were hemmed in like crabs. It took us all our willpower and effort to get out. We'll be back later. On the way home, we bought a bottle of Liebfraumilch. We couldn't taste any difference.

THE SNOBS

People are very snobby about wine, and I've found very few know what they are talking about anyway. Our friend Janet was the world's worst for snobbery. Opening a bottle, she would instruct Keith to leave it for a while, "let it breathe, Keith. Let it b-r-e-a-t-h-e." Once, she conned me into taking her to a fancy Michelin starred restaurant in Chateau Gontier. It was awful, pretentious, the wine reached over 1000 euros a bottle as I was paying Keith found one for just over thirty euros. Getting back to the farm, Keith poured us a glass of Merlot from the three-litre plastic wine container. "You know Tommy, you're right. I can't taste any difference from that wine in the restaurant."

Janet piped up, "oh Tommy, you do know a bit about wines then." See what I mean, utter snobbery. That thirty-odd euro bottle of wine was nothing more than a two-euro supermarket wine with its own label on it.

I took pictures of the wines and room for my records when I heard the little voice pipe up from behind the counter, "Monsieur? Monsieur? Ahh, Bonjour Monsieur, English, Ahh English. Will you be buying some wine Monsieur?" No messing. He was straight in for the kill. I guessed he was one of the descendants. "I certainly will indeed, but first, I shall have a look around." With that, I was out.

The Abbey and grounds were awe-inspiring. Beautiful and so peaceful, away from tourists' main body, you couldn't hear a sound except for the odd lift of wind or the birds singing in the distance. I wasn't a religious man, but some churches just forced you to sit back and contemplate your existence. Once, Bet mocked me in a beautiful church in Spain because I wanted to sit down and soak up the atmosphere. After she had passed away, if I was visiting a church, I would always light a candle in her name, sit on a bench and think of her. The Abbey in Carcassonne was almost intimidating in its presence. You can't help but question if there is a God. Is there another place, is there something after we have gone? Scientists debunk that straight off, no, when you die, when you kick the bucket, you've gone, kaput. But it still makes me wonder. It's something that keeps us all in check. Keeps us all in our place. Whoever came up with the idea of religion has to be given full honours for wisdom, foresight, and originality. OK, from the early Neanderthal man, we worshipped something. Be it a pig, or another animal, early man worshipped the heavens, the Vikings worshipped their God of thunder, but we shared him.

Early American Indians, before outside influences, worshipped their own gods of earth, wind and fire. But somewhere along the line, some clever human came up with the real McCoy, God. Then to further prove it, Jesus, son of. I bet those Romans could kick themselves for not thinking of it first. Pray to the lord or see hell and damnation. Wow. What a way to keep us in check. And there you have in the first and second world wars, two sides, each praying to their own God, the same God, to help them destroy the evil enemy across the other side of the trench.

Be good, pray to God and obey the rules, or you will go to hell, such a terrifying threat. Hitler never listened though did he, nor Stalin, a good few others neither. No, the threat of God was to keep us plebs in place. The catholic church got around that, though, by having the confessional. "Father, I have sinned."

"What did you do, dear child?"

"I did bad things with little Tommy in the woodshed, Father."

"It is all right, my child. Say three hail Mary's, and you will be forgiven." The Irish republicans used it all the time.

After a pleasant contemplative walk around the grounds, I called into the restaurant for a snack. Sitting down in the outside eating area, I noticed quite a few were eating salads. One couple was munching on a baguette. I decided to go for the baguette. Joining the queue, I changed my mind. It was a beautiful, worthwhile experience, but I felt I had soaked up enough. I walked slowly back to my motorhome. I got a booklet from the office. I could see that Fontfroide catered for everything and everyone, from quintessentially Mediterranean walking trails to treasure hunts, the library, and the museum. Festivals concerts, wine growing and selling. There were night visits. Invitations to businesses to dig down and support the Abbey, exclusive benefits to be gained, yes. But the Abbey was and is looking good. So well done to the family.

From there, I had planned to set out to Sigean further down along the coast about 14 miles away. It had a campsite for five euros a night that had a short walk to the sea. I felt it was worth a visit. All the Aires coordinates were given in north and south directions which thankfully were in my sat nav. The Aire was described as in Sigean, but it wasn't. So, trusting me just follows the sat nav. As I'm getting closer, I see the sign for Sigean going to the right. I'm being directed to the left, two miles further on. Oh well, my sat nav must be right. Into another quaint little village, narrow streets, meandering in different directions, then the little lane out of town, all the time my eyes are peeled, looking for interesting and potential places to pitch up and view the town. On the side is a group of men playing boules. It's the obvious main pastime of the French. They love it. Anywhere there is a bit of level ground, you will see them playing the boules. But now, I was heading out of town into the country. Where was this Aire? Another quarter of a mile, and I found it, stuck between the rugby club and the countryside. We were out in the sticks. I didn't like the look of this too much. It described a mile walk along the path to the beach, and with no views, which was fine. But where were the shops, the bars etc.? Pulling in front of the barrier, I noticed a cop pull up to me and open a set of gates to the main coach park, a coach driver waiting at the drive-in? I indicated to the cop who waved me away furiously, pointing to the pay machine opposite. Ahh, I get it. Over I go to notice the sign, 8 euros. That's gone up from five. I decided to have a bit more of a drive around first.

Further on was all country. I had seen one camper go into the Aire. As he drove on, I saw a small group in the far distance. If I had paid my 8 euros that, was it. I was in, trapped. I decided to go back and into Sigean itself. Passing the guys playing boules through the narrow streets of the town. With all the height barriers, blocked roads and no entry signs, I was getting frazzled trying to get out. I wasn't overly impressed. After another hour of disappointment, I decided to give Sigean a miss. I just wasn't feeling too confident about the place. The first rule is, if you don't like it, move on. I moved on. Gruissan was twenty miles away. It was a no brainer. After a nice drive, I noticed the Port La Nouvelle to the right. That might be interesting. Trying to find the seafront was a bit of a chore. Then the sandy beach opened up in front of me, dozens of motorhomes all set out dotted here and there. Fantastic. But then I realised I recognised it. Bet, and I had called into here a few years before. But there would be no internet here, I had to check my emails. Driving into Port La Nouvelle and along the river, I recognised it even more. The big casino. The big signs all along the front. No camping cars. Oh well, that was it then. I didn't fancy being stuck on the beach on my lonesome. No, it was back to Gruissan.

But I had no water. Heading to the harbour first, I asked a French yachtsman where I could get water, after a bit of figuring out the French for 'water.' Aqua. He got it, pointing to the electric points in front of him. Below them were the taps, sorted. I got my hose pipe out and filled it up in a matter of minutes. Within another few minutes, I was back at my favourite little parking space, the beach a few feet in front of me. The pub with Wi-Fi. Another few feet away.

It's very easy to slip into an easy-going, relaxed lifestyle when you're in the sun. It's even easier when you don't have to think or worry about money too much. I wake up about nine in the morning, the sun is shining through my roof light. Slowly, I will get up, kettle on, coffee made and on my table, door and window open to let in a slight breeze. I save up all the Sunday magazines throughout the months at home, so I've got plenty to read when I have a spare hour. I have a TV-DVD player, but I'm not too fussed about watching any films. At the moment I'm writing this book. My fourth. I didn't think I had it in me to write a second one, never mind a third and fourth, but I'm finding it therapeutic, but more interestingly, I like the idea of helping other people enjoy the experiences I am having. By reading this book, they may get to enjoy it as well. Motor homing is a completely different ball game. You buy a tent, by its very nature, and get back to nature. It's as cheap as chips to spend a week having a great holiday whilst spending very little money. Let's face it, you're not going to spend your time pitched up on Blackpool beach spending lots of money, are you? Mind, I suspect Blackpool council would love it if you did.

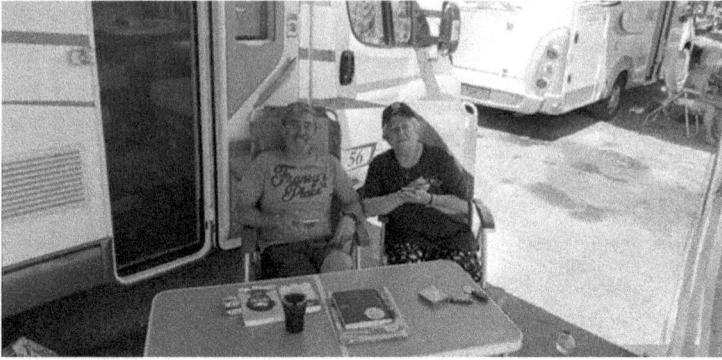

Then you have your holidays, hotel holidays. Packaged or not, yes, we've arrived now, very middle class, but now we have to live up to it. We have to spend accordingly. My mate Danny boasted that he would take two grand on a two week holiday with his wife and two kids, two grand? When the average wage was 200 quid a week? For Christ's sake, we were talking boozing here day and night to waste that kind of money. But motor homing? Where do you go? How much do you spend? How much do you have to spend? How much are you expected to spend? Well, the simple truth is, you can spend as little or as much as you want. You can spend ten grand on a tidy little camper. You're no worse than the guy who spent sixty grand on a camper. I met a very nice guy who had paid over 100k for his motorhome. It was a beauty, lift up hydraulics. Wind out extended lounge and bedroom. I was impressed. Until he told me what a nightmare it was finding somewhere to accommodate him, in England, where I met him. He had to spend the night in the council leisure car park because no one would accept him in the south of England. Looking at my Auto trail, he admitted he had looked at it and wished he had bought that model. I was feeling quite pleased with myself. But it doesn't matter.

In Chefchaouen in northern Morocco, a couple pulled up alongside us in a small one-tonne transit type van, A and B Couriers on the side. As we sat in the comfort of our motorhome, we watched as they first got out the table and chairs, then the small gas cooker. We could see the mattress to the side. It didn't matter. A few weeks later we met them again at the same campsite in Chefchaouen. When we enquired, they told us they had more or less taken the same route as us and seen many of the sights we had seen. They had set off the day before us from our campsite and headed south and down to the Sahara. From there, they turned west to the Atlantic. Before turning back north and heading home, back to the campsite. Ok, they didn't have the comfort that we had in our motorhome, but they saw the country just as we were, and after all, in most cases, you are hardly in your camper. You cut your cloth accordingly. We had seen young couples in Spain pull up alongside us in small, 5cwt vans and head for the bar. Back to the van at midnight, up with the lark in the morning, nightdress on, towel around their bonce, back fifteen minutes later all showered and sparkling clean. Then off out for another adventure somewhere. Great stuff.

Most Aires in France or Europe are meant for short stopovers, three or four days at the most, but who is there to watch over them? Over many years I had found some nice little hideaway spots to park up. In a certain quaint little village in Shropshire, free parking, clean public toilets nearby, a couple of nice village pubs and an ancient monument, to spend a pleasant few hours. I certainly don't like acting like a thief at night, hiding away in some back street, windows closed, curtains drawn. Just parking up to all intents and purposes. No, no, no, not for me, thank you. I heard one horror story of one guy who parked up on the main Benidorm road into town. Someone driving into town late at night, probably drunk, banged him right up the backside. I bet that shook him out of bed alright. His camper was a write-off. But there was no need for it. I parked in the hospital car park, free, minutes' walk from town, quite safe and secure with the added benefit of nearby hotels that kindly allowed me to use their facilities like toilets, swimming pools etc. In Europe, it's even easier to enjoy that freedom. Here in France, there are Aires galore. I think the French look at it as an expected right.

In Narbonne, the camping was very restricted around the seafront. Probably fair enough if millions of French campers had descended on the town and blocked all the car parks. So no, after a few turns around the town and not liking the Aires that were available, I decided to move on and give Gruissan a visit. In Gruissan, there are quite a few Aires, cheap at that, a couple free on the marina, a couple of cheap ones on the marina and seafront. I would have been happy to pay the ten euros a night for the one directly on the seafront. Shops and restaurants all around, unfortunately, it was choc-a-block full, so the girl said.

FINDING A PITCH AND A FRIEND TO BOOT

Then I found the one I was on. It's a matter of yards from the lovely sandy beach fronting onto a lagoon. Ideal. I find I'm spending very little on a daily basis to live and eat. I don't do breakfast. And my eating habits are very cheap and basic. In the nearby Aldi, I can buy a box of chicken wings or four legs of chicken for just over a couple of euros. With a small tin of vegetables, I have a meal for two people For two days. With pizza's aplenty, I reckon I could live on less than one hundred quid a week quite easily. At the harbour, there is fresh water on tap. If not, there are garages or cemeteries. So, for the cost of getting somewhere. Diesel etc., it's quite cheap to live.

I'm not cheap skating, though one lady friend accused me of being one. "Why on earth do you insist on parking up for free when I know you can well afford to go on sites?" Sadly, she just didn't get it. I do go on sites. I'm not averse to going on sites. Paying forty quid upwards a night to park up on a bit of scraggy grass is not my idea of heaven or a bargain for electricity? For showers? I have a shower, I have solar panels. I consider most campsites a rip off in England. Here in Europe, they are fairer in prices. But it's not even that. I'm often able to park in such a valuable spot, whether by the seafront or nearby amenities. On the beach or harbourside in Igoumenitsa. Greece. Many places around Spain.

After a few weeks, the initial outlay has almost been recouped with how little I have spent. Tonight, I shall go out and maybe have a nice entrecote steak. Maybe something different. But the choice is mine and the joy of knowing that I can do so, safe in the knowledge that I am not throwing away good money. If I had my children with me, yes, I would go on a site and take advantage of everything the site offered. On my own? It's just wasted. Some couples mix it about. I've met a few who will enjoy the benefits of wild camping for a few nights before heading for a site to empty their cassettes, fill up with water showers etc. It makes perfect sense.

My newfound friend is an English man with an apartment here in Gruissan, just a few minutes' walk from the seafront. Hearing his accent, I commented that it was nice to hear an English accent for a change, at that he pointed out that mine was the first English accent he had heard in some three months. This part of the Riviera is a hidden little gem then. Strictly speaking, this isn't part of the French Riviera. We are in the Languedoc region of France, but oh well. I thought he and his friend were both English, but he pointed out that his friend was Algerian. Then he pointed out that he was from Wednesbury and had never been married. Before I could react and step back, he quickly pointed out that he was not gay. Oh, that's ok then. I breathed a slow sigh of relief. In truth, the guy was in his 80s and was not in the best of health. He had decided to buy his apartment on a whim after hearing about it from a colleague he worked with. He was an engineer, and his colleague had a Dutch friend who wanted to sell his apartment here in Gruissan on a whim. He bought it. As you do.

He was quick to point out that if he'd known what he knew now, he definitely wouldn't have bought it. The apartments are made up of "the committee," a group of owners who set out and abide by the strict rules governing the apartments, which he quickly explained were shoddily built. Putting an aerial up for his telly, he found the satellite signal quite weak, so he decided to put up a much larger satellite dish. This didn't go down well with the committee, who sent him a warning letter with a heavy fine if he didn't remove the dish immediately. My eyebrows rose slightly. Then he told me that once, he invited a group of friends around to sit by the pool and enjoy a swim. He was quickly told this was forbidden and not allowed. Now my eyebrows really raised as I did my Roger Moore impression. Without a doubt, I thought this was quite disgraceful and told him so. He had paid some 85,000 euros for the apartment, and it seemed no better than a "casa"- a caravan or mobile home on a site. It also put the dampener on it for me. I'm not particularly keen on swimming in the sea and always try and find somewhere with a pool. In one fell swoop, my newfound pal had made it clear it was pointless even asking. When I asked how the "committee" would know if someone walked in and used the pool, he said, oh, they would know all right. That's it then. No pool swims for me.

I was starting to gather that my newfound friend was a tad unworldly wise for all his age. Personally, I would have had the apartment on the market straight off. With such restrictions, how can you enjoy its comfort? What if your children came to visit? Friends? No, maybe he's exaggerating a bit. With the Algerian man by his side, I asked what the talent situation was like here. I'm nothing but optimistic. There were no English women, so that only left the French ladies who couldn't speak English. It looked like I was in a no-win situation. But there is Danni? Danni is a French girl, slim, quite nice looking, and has a very popular party trick? Hmm, this was interesting, but Danni was in Nepal. I was deflated.

My new-found English friend from Wednesbury turned up today at our little bar in Gruissan after an absence of three days. I was a bit concerned. My feeling was he had either croaked it, and I didn't even know where he lived. I didn't even know his name. Or he was skint and having come down to see his friend who owed him money, only to find he hadn't turned up, went home suffering a bit of depression. Course, the third option was he'd had enough of my company and decided to avoid me like the plague. It wouldn't be the first time. But no, sitting there doing my emails etc., my friend Colin turns up. He's still looking suitably depressed. "Have you seen my Algerian friend?"

"No."

"Oh well, that's it then."

He owes Colin 90 euros. I said, "I think you had best say goodbye to that mate, learn from it but don't lend again." But it gets worse. It seems he's taken Colin's new 160 euro Samsung phone to get some downloads on it. Plus, his old phone to boot. Colin is looking depressed, and no wonder, I said, "well, I'm sorry to say, mate, you'd best forget him and your money." Colin doesn't know where he lives, except it's Narbonne. He's a gambler and a bad one at that.

I said, "look, unpalatable as it is, he's a gambler, he owes you 90 euros plus a 160 euro phone? He's into you for over 200 euros." Colin's face dropped another few inches. He knew I was right.

"But I haven't even got a phone. I couldn't even phone the hospital in an emergency." He replied. I debated giving him a phone. I have a few in my motorhome, but should I? Having brought up the hospital, I said, "if you don't mind me asking, what happens if you, you know? Kick the bucket." Clearly, Colin had given it a lot of thought. I said, "well, you're here on your own. You don't know anyone. Who would know if you just went?" Shrugging his shoulders, Colin admitted that someone would eventually notice. The smell, for one thing, someone would notice.

"But what about your apartment? I mean, you're not married. Would you leave it to your brother?"

"Oh no," he said, "I wouldn't leave anything to him on principle. I don't know really, I don't care."

I said, "you can't say that surely. You do realise the French government would just nick it?"

"Well," he said, I could leave it to a children's home." How sad. I took Colin a spare phone I had, insisting he has it until at least he gets his own back, maybe. Very reluctantly, he accepted. When lo and behold, his Algerian friend turns up with both of his phones, yippee, the guy was dead chuffed, and I got my phone back.

For a chat, my pal and I would meet up most days at the nearby bar, which was between his apartment and my motorhome. It coincided with me going to the bar and picking up the Wi-Fi to check my emails, having a gossip and a bit of banter on Facebook and WhatsApp with my kids. It passed a pleasant hour or two before going over to the beach and doing a bit of sun-worshipping. One morning we talked about relationships, how I missed my wife etc. My pal told me that he'd had plenty of women but never felt the need to get married. We are all different, and quite rightly so, whilst I was quite happy being on my own, I didn't like being alone most of the time. I explained to him that it's the little things.

Once I got the ferry to Corfu from Igoumenitsa from mainland Greece, you can drive around Corfu in two hours. Corfu itself, I found, was a bit of a dump, a favourite destination for the 18 to 30s. But the rest of the island was quite pretty and interesting. Coming upon a very pretty cove, I pulled in next to a small fishing boat lying on its side. A tap for water and a shower. Idyllic. I was quid's in. Water and a shower plus a beautiful spot, I was sorted for a couple of days. With three restaurants across the way, I went over. I asked if they would be open that evening, "yes, sir, do you have any idea of what you might be wanting to eat?"

"Well, definitely mussels for starters."

"Ahh, we have plenty in."

That was it. I was over there in the evening, got myself a table and ordered a bowl of mussels that came with nice fresh chunky bread.

As I sat there, eating my mussels, I looked over at my motorhome and went as sick as the proverbial as I thought of my wife, Bet. She would have loved this. The mussels started to go down like lead balloons. Corfu was a beautiful little island, and like most of Greece, Zante etc. was motorhome friendly. Passing through a village, the locals would shout out, "pull in over there." No problem. Yes, Bet would have loved it. Trying to explain this to my friend, I said it's the sharing. I miss those little nuggets I see on my travels, Pompeii, Italy, Carcassonne, the medieval city in France, the many medieval cities here in France. I see lots of little nuggets. "Well, surely you should find no shortage of women wanting to share that with you?" my pal had said. Surprisingly, no. Carolyn, I think, would have loved it, maybe. But she was the type who loved the glitz of the Savoy. Mind, she did say she didn't care so long as she was with me. Sadly, she died of cancer. Val was different. Val was reasonably intelligent but very petty. She knew France well as her husband had French relatives, but, sadly, Val was also an alcoholic. I said it didn't bother me that Val had no money. It didn't cost much more for two than it did for one travelling. I wasn't bothered about buying her a couple of bottles of wine a night, meals out. It was the fact that within a couple of hours, she was blotto. Plus, I found, a lot of women were damaged. If they weren't damaged after being married for so long, they set the bar high for any potential mate. Over 55, you had to have the body of an Adonis. Run ten laps every day and open the car doors all the time. Even royalty don't do that. No nasal hair, no ear hair, no baldness, no false teeth. They don't want much, do they? Plus, you have to like Fido the dog, or the three dogs or cats they keep. Then, and that's the big one, they won't have their weekends or Sundays interrupted as the grandkids visit. That puts the kibosh on everything.

It's the little things that give people away. Having explained all that, my friend gave a shake of his shoulders, shook himself quite vigorously, and said, "oh, I wouldn't stand for that, any of it. What? Spending money on a woman like that." That was strange. I was puzzled. He then pointed down to his groin. "Well, it's that," he said, "I'm impotent. I've got a tube fitted. I can't pee properly. I will never pay for a woman if I'm not getting anything out of it." Well, I was staggered. I couldn't believe any man could say something like that, well, not a man who had got some education. In one fell swoop, he had given himself away, for the sake of not being able to have sex, he wasn't prepared to spend or waste money on a woman just for company.

I had met a few men like that, though. There was the guy in the pub who would disappear every now and again. I was puzzled until I went out and saw him sitting in his car, a bag between his feet with cans of lager in it. Slurping from a can, he said, "I'm not paying those prices in there." What a cheapskate. Well, why go in in the first place if you couldn't afford to buy a pint? Then there was the woman who was going to marry my friend, Lindsey. She was doing a striptease one night in the pub, and a great body she had as well, I must admit.

"Are you looking forward to getting married?"

"Maybe," she said, "but no man will ever take me for a mug again." Spitting out venom, she said, "my first husband never gave me a penny. Kept me short of housekeeping all our married life. When I divorced the b*****d, I made sure the next one paid for everything. What was his was mine, and what was mine was my own. No one will ever take me for a mug again." Christ, I nearly choked on my lager. She was really bitter. Not surprisingly, she and Lindsey never got married. In truth, I wasn't surprised. They were both very selfish.

My friend liked his tipple, his lunchtime tipple. Surprisingly I found this many times around Europe. In Spain in particular. In Benidorm, even more. At first, I never gave much thought to it. You will see them all around Benidorm, around lunchtime, having a snack or a meal and the obligatory pint of lager, then another pint. Many times, you see the wives follow suit with a pint as well. At first, I never gave it much thought. Well, they are retired. They are entitled to enjoy their lives. Some were in mobile homes, some had brought an apartment, but they all liked the lunchtime pint or three. In Benidorm, you see them whizzing around on mobility scooters. You realise it's to get them to the bars quicker and easier. After drinking for most of the day, the scooters get them home drunk. From there, they spend the night watching Emmerdale or EastEnders. It was a lesson I was taking on board. My friend was a bit more upmarket. Being an engineer, he was into the shorts. Buying me a drink one day, he observed I was drinking orange. You don't drink? "Oh yes," I said. I drink alright, too much, in fact, but only at night. I can't drink during the day.

After a few drinks, he said, "I've got to go." Getting up slowly, he said, "my kidneys are very bad."

"That's the booze," I replied.

"Don't say that," he said and did the cross sign over his body. "I don't feel too well at all." With that, he slipped off slowly. He had been here over ten years, had never bothered to learn French. In a solely French-speaking community. He was certainly a bit strange. But a nice guy. I was pleasantly surprised to see him the next day, still ordering his shorts. Well, I am 84, you know, I mean! I could see he was accepting his fate. He was getting ready to die, accepting the inevitable. He only had one brother that he hadn't spoken to for years after a family argument. Whose he got if he kicks the bucket? Who checks on him every day? Every week? This leads me to my own mortality. If I kick the bucket, who is going to know? Who is there to check up on me? I've clocked these vans, these campers. The only way you know someone is in them is by their roof lights being wide open. One camper across the way has been solitary for the past week, with no sign of life. Is he living there or in a nearby apartment? He could be dead, and no one knows. We wouldn't even smell his body decomposing shut up as it was.

Once, a neighbour lived at the top of our yard, a real miserable old bugger. No one heard from or about him for a few days. Then my mom tried to look through the curtains, always drawn. Eventually, she called the cops. Carrying him down the entry, I noticed the men carrying the stretcher were bleeding from the nose and had plugs in. The old man had been dead a few days. His body had exploded. The stench must have been awful. Imagine me in my camper? A week in bed. In 85 degrees? The thought doesn't bear thinking about. And I bet the buggers would go through my wallet and credit cards like a rat up a drain pipe. My only consolation is my kid's details are on my phone. Eventually, they will know. I'm being burnt anyway.

My friend Edward had a pop at me the other night on Facebook. "You need to learn French, Tom. If you're spending so many months away, it's essential. If I was away, I would definitely learn it, Tom." Course it is Edward, and you know best. Why is it everyone and their uncle knows best? The year before last, I called in or spent time in about 14 countries, from France to Bulgaria, Greece, Italy, and then back to France. What a bonus to be able to speak every language, if not fluently, then enough to get by. Flemish, Bosnian, Serbian, Greek, Spanish, French, Italian? What a man of the world that would make me, ay? Yikes, when I left school, I didn't even know my tables fully. My alphabet was a joke. O-levels never existed. No, I will just have to struggle along and get by, ok Edward?

WILD CAMPING

With camping, it's a simple fact of life that you have to keep your eyes peeled. It's common sense. It's instinct. It's primeval. When you put that tent on your back and set out into the wilds, you go with eyes open, wide. Where is the best place to get water? Where is water in case something happens? Do we go for high ground or low ground? Flooding risk, high ground, bears and snakes? Don't make a lot of difference. Heavy snow coming in, build a nest, an igloo. In a motorhome, it's much of the same, on holiday, or even more so in the hotel business, you can see different people and guests' reactions. On their first day, the majority will go out on the mooch, the sniff. In all senses, casually, they will go out to explore and scope out the town. They will pop into a local café, the local pub, then another pub, feeling the atmosphere, the ambience, the price difference in each pub. It's something my friend, well, ex-friend Bernard, didn't realise, respect or appreciate.

He thought all the customers in his boozer were mugs. He had a fantastic boozer, The Salty Dog, with an outside dining area over the sea. Yet, he killed it with his greed and stupidity. He just never realised that the holidaymakers had done their homework within the first day or so. It's the same with all things; it's the same with camping.

When you buy your motorhome, you may see things one way. A lot of people join different clubs. Caravan clubs, motorhome clubs and the sites they have and advertise. Fine, that is great, if that's what you want, I have no argument with it, it's a purely personal choice. I would never say never to go on a site. My only real reservation is I'm self-contained. I'm fully self-contained. I can go four days in my camper. With nearby public facilities like toilets, water, I'm totally self-sufficient. Why on earth should I pay 40 quid upwards to sit on a bit of grass?

Campers, by and large, are split into three groups, those who feel happy to pay the rates. These are people who come away for two or maybe three weeks of the year. Those who don't like to pay the rates but feel they have no choice for lots of reasons. You usually find a lot of elderly people in this category. They just feel unsafe and insecure parking in the wild. Of course, there is the hygiene factor as well. In fairness, the ladies do like to go to the toilet proper, do the business and have a nice shower. The days of digging a hole, doing a squat are gone for many, me included. Then there is the third group. Even this subdivides into different groups again, but we like to wild camp in the main. As such, we drive with our eyes peeled, looking and observing different spots if not for now, maybe another time. Now think about it, would you go and pull up in a quiet street in Brixton or Handsworth, Birmingham, park up and expect to sleep in peace?

Once, after I had picked Keith and Janet up in France to have a tour of Italy, we spent about half of the time wild camping and the other half on sites. Driving through one area at the end of a long day, Keith kept barking out, "hey, that will do, another time. Ay, that will do." Pointing to a large parking area near several what looked like council blocks, I had to shout at him a few times. A couple of miles further on, we came to a very nice Aire on the side of the river where there were a few other vans dotted about. It wasn't that Keith was stupid, far from it. He just wasn't frightened. Being over six feet, he never considered it. As in all things, it's common sense.

When you set out to buy a house, you look at that area then the next. There are some beautiful Aires in France, Italy, Europe. But many are totally isolated. I have driven into some with my wife, pulled up at 12 pm at night, only to see other travellers pull in, use the facilities, then drive straight off, leaving the Aire desolate. No, thank you very much indeed. But then I've seen or come across other isolated pull-ins or parking spaces with magnificent views, that without a doubt, I have felt perfectly safe in. Sometimes you have to take some risk in life, maybe, if you're that worried, that frightened, then maybe you shouldn't be buying a motorhome at all? Some of the Aires are so pretty, so attractive, it's hard to believe that they were free, in 2020. Whilst driving through the regional park of the Catalan Pyrenees, I looked at and passed some amazing Aires, including one in Martinet.

The town was beautiful. It was quiet but busy, with people going about their business. It was one of the many alpine resorts hidden away in or around the Pyrenees. It had character and a feeling of romance about it. Driving through it, I realised it was somewhere I must stop and spend some time to take in the atmosphere, the ambience of the place. I was almost through it when I saw the car park. Returning on myself, I had to drive a fair bit back to be able to do a U-turn to get to the car park. Then I saw the other sign, Aires, with a camper van sign. Turning in, I drove across the bridge crossing the river to see a massive car park in front of me, some 5 or 6 vans parked up and facing me. Behind was farmland and the Alps. It was magical. I couldn't believe something like this was set aside and free. Parking up, I had a little meander around. To the entrance was a toilet block and shower, water and cassette emptying facilities. The sign on the wall offered electric hook up for a modest few euros. It had everything you could want for a few nights stay, and it was a few nights. Another sign said the stay was limited to five nights, but that was plenty enough anyway. And who would be monitoring you?

Checking my van and that everything was alright, I locked up and decided to have a little mooch around the town. Though it was a skiing resort, it was out of season and quiet, but the shops, pubs and restaurants were open and quietly trading. Getting some supplies, I then had a little walk around the town, through the back lanes and allies, along the many streams bringing water down from off the mountains. As with many councils throughout France, the council had had the forethought to realise the benefit of setting a bit of land aside for the many motor homers that would be passing through. Those motor homers would be stocking up with supplies, buying fresh goods, food and drink, eating in one of the restaurants. If we only spent £30-£50 each, that could be circa £400 into the local economy, maybe all year round. Why couldn't the British councils think of that ay? I'll tell you why, because they are short-sighted.

Barmouth west Wales is a pretty resort that went through a sad decline. My wife Bet and I saw this going right back to the mid-80s. Much of the decline is due to the surge in people wanting foreign holidays, cheap package deals with guaranteed sun. People were getting fed up with the rip-off British attitude, including hotel doors locked after breakfast. I should know, Bet and I had three hotels in Devon. Yet Barmouth has over a mile of seafront parking extending from one end of the town to another. Empty for most of the year. After buying our motorhome, Barmouth became our go-to place, amongst other little places, of course. Barmouth council were quite sensible about our camping up, the wardens told me. So long as you buy an overnight ticket, we turn a blind eye to campers. After all, six or eight pounds for the night is still something. But for some reason, whether it is abuse or what I don't know, they would change their mind according to who was patrolling and how busy it is. Consequently, you can go there one week and never get a ticket, go the next and it's coming up to the bank holiday, and they will throw one at you. I got one the other week. The car park was chock-a-bloc, with tourists driving in for the day then leaving early evening, the car park empty again. I refused to pay the fine and suggested they wake up to the fact that the car parks are empty most of the year. For the sake of a few pounds, why not put a tap and dumping facilities. Even at maybe the far end of the car park? Come on, it doesn't take a pile of brains, does it? Everyone would be more than happy to pay a fiver a night. I think a prominent notice asking people to respect the parking area and spend some money in the local community would be respected.

Driving through the Alps, yet another time on my way to Spain, I passed a campsite snuggled into the side of the mountains. It was coming to the end of the day, so I decided to pull in when I saw the sign saying 7 euros for the night, no electricity but with the internet. That suited me. It wasn't one of the nicest sites I had stopped on. The lady warden was as grumpy as she was ugly. The site was scruffy and uncared for. The mountain road passing us was quite noisy. But ok, 7 euros a night who can complain? But the next day, carrying on with my journey, I kept passing absolutely fantastic pull-ins with stunning views overlooking deep valleys and lakes. The parking areas were big and perfectly adequate to spend the night. To say I was a tad gutted was an understatement. It was not the 7 euros. I didn't begrudge that. 7 euros is neither here nor there. The views and parking areas that I was continually passing were far superior to the 7 euro a night campsite. I came across this quite regularly and will continue to do so as I continue my travels. For free, Wild Boar in the car park in Italy. Wild bears in the mountains in Italy. Utterly amazing and free. Mind, we made sure we kept the doors closed, just in case.

I read of a convoy of motor homers in one of the caravan magazines that travelled to and through Morocco. I decided to follow their route, stopping and visiting some of the places they had visited. At a campsite in Chefchaouen, I discovered they were right when they mentioned being grateful for the onboard facilities like shower and toilet. The campsite was dire. Visiting the city or the ghost town halfway down into Morocco was a revelation. To reach it, we had to travel nine miles along the dirt track and rickety bridges. The ghost town was a former mining town employing some 30,000 people, mainly Berbers. When it closed down in 1961, the town was left barren except for one Berber family, probably with nowhere else to go. Driving through the actual mining area of built-up dwellings stacked up one on top of the other into the side of the mountain, we could see little eyes peeking out from the dark window openings. Dirty washing hanging along every bit of space didn't help when I remarked to Bet that the hills have eyes. A reference to an American horror film.

Carrying on to the actual ghost town, we followed the winding river that snaked around the village. Sandstone mud huts were dotted around, a well in the centre. The villagers all came out to greet us. Much increased in size from the one Berber family. As Bet dished out toys we had brought, dolls and fluffy toys, the head man or leader invited me into his home to join him for mint tea. It was like something out of the scene of Bethlehem. No mirrors, no water, no toilets, no sink, just four walls. A rickety little shelf with a small battered Calor burner on top. Presumably, this would be for their mint tea or tagine meal. They made their meagre income from selling minerals that they dug out of the earth. God knows how they survived. There is no social security in Morocco. If you become ill, your family looks after you, if you have no family? You beg or die.

I wanted to camp up for the night down by the river. It was the pure wild west. Nothing around, no lights, no noise, just surrounded by mountains. And the river running through and around it. The clear stars lit the night sky. Bet was having none of it. "I'm not stopping here, they could creep over in the night, slit our throats, and no one would know we had ever been here." Of course, she was wrong, but I could understand, quite a few tourists visited this place. But that was it. My remarks about the hills having eyes were my undoing.

Driving back through Spain on our way back from Morocco, we ventured onto a long wide road that seemed to go on for miles. Probably built by the Romans. Following its length and to the right, we were hitting mile after mile of forest. It became too much for me. Davey Crocket and the Saturday matinee cowboy films were pulling me in. Seeing an opening, I said to Bet, "come on, we'll have a bit of this, set up the campfire, eat a bit of cooked chicken, a few bars of home on the range." Bet wasn't too keen at all. Lighting the campfire, I got out the bottle of vodka and started fulfilling my fantasy. Bet stopped inside the camper. Sitting up for a bit, I heard a car pull up in the distance. Shortly after, I heard scratching at the door. Looking out of the window, I saw the most beautiful little dog, pining to come in. There was no way I was going to stand for that. It would cost a fortune to get it through customs. The car that I heard had obviously dumped him. I'm a softy for sad dogs, but no, definitely no. By the time I got into bed, Bet was in bed. But she wasn't asleep, as soon as

I got in, she got out. She stayed on the sofa all night clutching a big kitchen knife, waiting for intruders. She listened for hours to the dog scratching before realising what it was. I never thought to tell her. The fact is she was quite right to be cautious. In truth, it was a bit of a risk to park up in such an isolated spot, hidden as we were from prying eyes. I didn't do that again, but hundreds do every week.

France is made up of departments, don't ask me why, and Gruissan is in the Aude Cathar country. Aude being the department for the area which stretched from Montpellier down to the Pyrenees and covered Carcassonne and further west. It also included France's famous Languedoc wine-growing region, famous for its table wines, Merlot, Cabernet Sauvignon, Sauvignon Blanc, Chardonnay, and others. It had every reason to be proud of itself. It held some of the most diverse and beautiful scenery in the whole of France, from majestic mountains to famous and medieval abbeys and towns to chateaus and castles. Fontfroide was just one of many. There is the medieval abbey and city of Lagrasse, Caunes-Minervois abbey. There are the castles, Usson Castle, Puivert Castle, just so many I don't know how I am going to get around to seeing them all.

The Cathars were a breakaway religious group formed in or around the twelfth century in France protesting the country's leading religion, Catholicism. But its roots go back much further than that, on the banks of the Indus several centuries BC. They believed that good and evil were equal, unlike the Christian belief. Their God created heaven, the devil created the earth, they believed in reincarnation and abstained from sexual pleasures. They were persecuted for centuries throughout France until, presumably, they became extinct. I haven't got around to asking if any still exist though the area is still known as the Cathar region. If any did, I should imagine they would be keeping their mouths shut. The way the Catholics were treating them was beyond horrendous. At first, they were simply ignored but as they grew in power, so did the anger and fear of the Catholics. No one was going to usurp them without a fight. Once they had got the Pope's blessing, innocent 111, that was it, the Cathars days were numbered, the battle started in earnest. There was no stopping them. Maybe the Pope was looking after his own wellbeing as well. These were harsh and brutal times. These were the times before Antoinette said of the starving peasants, "let them eat cake."

The catholic church was all-powerful. Thousands were hung, drawn, quartered and tortured for the pettiest of things, well, much like England really, I mean, look what our kings did to that poor bugger William Wallace. So no, I don't think the King had any great choice in the matter. Once he gave it his backing, that was it. The Cathars were doomed. They were killed in their thousands. Not just killed, killed and tortured. The city of Beziers, a Cathar stronghold, was burnt down, and twenty thousand were killed and burned. Burning being a favourite way of killing someone after the Abbot of Citeaux declared slaughter them all, God will recognise his own. No wonder then that the French were at war with the English. If they could do that to their own for simply forming a breakaway religion, what would they have done to us being protestant Christians? It doesn't bear thinking about, and we dare to call out the Arab's for burning eyes out or chopping an arm or leg for stealing?

It's no wonder that the area holds so much in the way of interest and beauty. But I think the French like to keep the best parts to and for themselves. Trying to find anything in English is nigh on impossible. The restaurants are a bit of a minefield. Calamari is clear enough to me and a definite no go. I read like a hawk to pick out frogs legs. I can't even think of them or snails, though to be fair, I like whelks, so who am I to complain? The difference in quality between the restaurants here and in England is clear to see. It has one of the highest densities of Michelin stars in France. Only the odd one is bland or of poor quality. Here, in France, the game is upped a bit. In Gruissan, every restaurant serves fresh fish, Moules (mussels) as standard. No wonder we have no fish or mussels. The French are nicking it all, and it looks like the British government are standing for it. Again.

Colin is the only English man I have met, and he reckons I am the only English voice he has heard in three months. That in itself shows what a well-kept secret it is. Gruissan is also famous for its kite surfing. The reason being its unique position on the Mediterranean coast and the Pyrenees mountains that cross west to east just along the border a few miles away, it channels a mistral wind right down into the town and along the coast. Fortunately, I quickly caught on to how deceptive it can be and make you feel. The temperature is into the 80s, and by mid-afternoon can get very hot. But with a heavy, blustery wind blowing, you just don't notice the heat. Gruissan is also famous for its houses on stilts. Today the town is linked to the sea by a channel, but it used to be isolated in the middle of a lagoon and served as a point of defence for Narbonne. But a new resort of Gruissan was built after a channel was opened linking Le Grazel Lagoon with the sea to protect the houses. The expected floods were no longer a threat.

Crossing the Aude Cathar country, from west to east runs the Canal Du Midi, entering at the Atlantic just above Bordeaux passing through Carcassonne and exiting into the Mediterranean at Sete, in all some 150 miles in length. You could spend weeks just exploring the length and beauty of that alone. When I last visited Carcassonne, the medieval city, I set out to visit a short stretch of the canal, where it passes through the new city of Carcassonne below. The difficulty was finding somewhere to park up. My plan, as always, is to enjoy the scenery and the area of where I am visiting, not wear myself out just getting there, fine when your twenty, not at my age which I don't like to mention. After a bit of tootling around in circles, I pulled onto what seemed a large car park with plenty of room to park my motorhome, in an out of the way section where I was of no hindrance or nuisance to anyone else. All this within a short walk of the Canal Du Midi, great. Switching off the engine and getting my bearings, I wasn't sitting there more than five minutes before two French cops walked over. Straight away they said, "you cannot park here." Looking baffled, I asked, "why not?" I wasn't obstructing anyone, and it was free parking. Mind, at 22ft and nine feet high, I suppose I am a bit obvious. Then I realised what it was, seeing the panic in their faces. They were concerned, thinking I was about to set up camp, a not unreasonable theory as many of us campers do and feel we can do, especially the French, they are used to it. Quickly, I tried to explain that I was not stopping for long, I just wanted to visit the beautiful and famous canal, they got the message, and after a quick chat with each other in French, they nodded and agreed, gesturing me to stop there with a wave of their arms.

Ok, maybe one day I will come unstuck and get walloped with a big fine for speeding or something, but up to yet, touchwood. I had been pleasantly surprised by how different things were from what I had been led to expect by the English press and even so many British people. Don't trust those French cops. They hate us English. They sit inside streets with speed cameras waiting to pounce with heavy one hundred pound cash fines. The thought alone terrified me. It's all stuff and nonsense. Well, up to yet, it is, maybe around Paris. In the big cities, the French police are a lot harder but generally, here in rural France, I find the police very different, very friendly, very courteous, as are the people themselves.

In the small towns and villages, I noticed that Keith and Janet would drive very cautiously, being very aware of the speed limits, but these were very quiet places anyway. The very slowness and pace of life lead you to slow down. It all seems very much unlike England, where the motorist is seen as the cash cow, and you get a heavy fine and penalty points on your licence merely for going 6 miles an hour over the limit. It's not so much the fine in itself. It's the resultant increase in your insurance premiums. We are a milking cow to the government whilst they strut about on the world stage being the 'big-I-ams.'

Locking my motorhome up, I set off across to the canal, which consisted of a basin with a good-sized marina in the town. As an ex yachtsman and scuba diver, I was quite surprised by how many French people were into sailing and motor boating. All around France were yachts galore. Here on the Canal Du Midi, it was no different. Just here were more motorboats. With the difference in weather here to England, who could blame them? Once, many years ago, Bet, and I had booked a hotel in Majorca. Whilst there, we were walking along the harbour at Palma. Seeing the British ensign on a boat moored up, I stopped to look. The boat looked old and knocked about. In fact, it looked more like a canal barge and was about 40ft long. On the foredeck were dozens of plastic water containers linked together through the handles by a length of rope. A wiry looking old boy in a tatty pair of shorts and T-shirt hopped about on the deck. "Ahoy there," I said, "you're English?" He stopped whatever he was doing and came to chat with me. I was curious as we had the yacht at the time, and I considered bringing it over to Spain and using it as a base to fly to. The guy was from Liverpool, and when he retired, his wife asked him what he was going to do. Without a second thought, he said, "well, you know, I've always wanted to buy a boat and travel around the Mediterranean." I was just getting over that surprise when I asked what his wife's response was? "Well, she said if that's what you want to do, then I will do it with you." Now that really shook me. He did no more than put his little terraced house up for sale, told his kids to help themselves to whatever they wanted, dumped the rest just keeping a few personal prized possessions. He then bought the boat he was standing on. Seeing my face, he said, "oh, don't be deceived by its looks. The engine is rock solid and has carried us all around the med as far as Morocco." Never having been on a boat in his life, he then brought a British atlas road map. Setting off from Liverpool docks, he navigated the British waterways using the map as a reference until he got to Dover. From there, they spent the winter whilst learning about navigating. He then crossed the channel, sailed down to the Canal Du Midi, and travelled to the Mediterranean. Course he followed up with, "we were retired, so we never rushed."

I was amazed and full of admiration. For both him and his wife, he then told me there was no snobbery at all, pointing to a million-pound yacht along the way he told me he was often invited aboard for parties, the owner often giving him little jobs to do, inviting him to help himself to the leftover paints, hence the different colours on his boat. "Oh, I hardly even touch my pension," he said, "it's so cheap to live." Saying goodbye, I turned to Bet, "Christ, when is enough, enough? We have a yacht, a nice hotel. Yet this guy is rich in comparison to us?"

The canal was beautiful, peaceful and majestic at the same time. I wanted to walk alongside it and out into the countryside to get a real feel for the canal and the area, maybe even find somewhere to camp up and spend the night. There is nothing quite like the peace and serenity of a flowing river or canal to contemplate and relax. But after a couple of hours, I was growing a bit anxious about my motorhome and the local police. I didn't want to get back to find a nice fine stuck on my windscreen or, worse, my van clamped. I had seen enough for me to want to see more. Next time I planned to maybe visit some more out of the way stretches of the river, do a bit of walking. Maybe passing through some lovely French villages. Now, this was the next time. I planned to spend some months here in France, visiting more medieval towns and villages, abbey's and chateaus, and Carcassonne itself. An amazing place. I want to learn more about the medievalist Violet Le-Duc, who began reconstructing the site in 1844, rebuilding the cathedral and ramparts that were built circa 1258. Carcassonne itself was named after Mademoiselle Carcass, who, famously under siege, ordered the last sheep to be stuffed with the last of the grain then thrown from the highest point of the castle ramparts. The enemy below, who had the castle under siege, concluded that if they had so much food that they could afford to give a sheep the best grain, there was no point in continuing the attack. The townspeople were so overjoyed they rang the Sona Bells of Carcass loud and clear, hence the name of Carcassonne. Then maybe after seeing some more places of interest drive down to Spain, the world is my oyster. Well, at least Europe is.

After over three weeks in France, almost two in Gruissan, I was still trying to get used to balancing and using my money. In Spain, it was quite simple, being a lot cheaper for starters. In Benidorm in particular, I went out, over the corner bar and had breakfast for 3.50 euros. In the evening, I went out and had liver and onions, or fish and chips for just over five euros. It was easy to balance my money. Actually, it was not good for me, the food being that good meant instead of getting rid of the pounds I was piling them on, I was spending barely 100 euros a week. Here in France, it was more expensive. I didn't mind that. I knew it anyway. But I just couldn't see where or how it was going. I had brought 750 euros in cash with me. My plan, as always, is to pay for diesel etc., by credit card for security. The cash being just for daily spending, drawing on more from my cash cards as needed or required. Up to yet, I had left some £250, in cash having spent £450 over the four weeks, not a lot, really. And well within the parameters that I had more or less set myself. Ok, my kids say, "spend it, dad," but what on? I can only eat so much. And I didn't anticipate eating out every night. Life is a balancing act, really. I've known some wealthy people Lose everything, and only be trained in one thing, finding it impossible to get back on the ladder. How many celebrities do we see reach the dizzy heights of success only to see them fall and disappear? I couldn't imagine anything worse than making millions, building up to a mansion, a nice big yacht on the med, only to Lose the lot and end up in a council house.

I saw that happen to a well-known jeweller in Birmingham. Maybe his wife was sucking him dry, but at any rate, he flipped, ramped the credit upon the couple of shops he owned, raided them and nicked all the jewellery, then did a runner leaving his wife and two kids who were at private school behind. The only problem was he didn't handle it right and got caught out bang to rights. His wife and kids, humiliated, had to be pulled out of a private school and lumped in a council house, shudder, the mere thought of it. So no, I live nicely. I have what I want when I want. I see what I want. I can and do have a cruise or something different if and when I choose.

Finding a small shop up the road and a very nice looking delicatessen next door, I decided to try their lasagne one night, then a portion of Moules, followed by a very attractive rum baba. Fifteen euros. Nice as the lasagne was, the cold Moules were not very appetising. I may as well of had a meal in a restaurant. Friday being the market day, I decided to buy a half chicken off the rotisserie man, 4.50 euros, which actually made a very nice meal. The prices seem to fluctuate for no reason. In most restaurants, a burger is 13-15 euros. 15 euros for a burger? It must be gold plated. Yet a tidy burger bar did a nice burger for 4 euros, a bit more like it. Yes, the prices certainly took some getting used to. I'm off out now to Le Teatro for an entrecote steak. Maybe 20 euros.

I just couldn't face the thought of going into some fancy restaurant and paying a small fortune for a fork full of food and a bottle of wine. Hang on. I almost did when Janet had me in the net in Chateau Gontiere. I am sure that much of it is down to snobbery, as it is with wine, so it is with food. It's getting as bad with coffee. Now people boast about being called and known as coffee snobs. For Christ sake, it's getting worse. We're levelling out as a society. Of course, the old class system is disappearing a bit. Not completely, and it never will. But another far worse form of snobbery is taking its place

The year I met up with Janet and Keith, I had picked them up from their home in Chateau Gontiere. We set off around Italy via Chamonix, pulling onto the car park below Mont Blanc. We spent the evening meandering around the town before getting a night's sleep. Our plan, to get the cable car the next morning and spend a few hours on Mont Blanc. We had arrived on a warm, clear sunny day. Typically, the next morning was overcast, and the visibility almost zero. The cable car up Mont Blanc was cancelled. We had to get another cable car up the opposite mountain and not to the very top. As we arrived in the cable car, we saw skiers setting off and down from the first and second levels. Still being a bit overcast, we called into the restaurant overlooking the mountains and had some lunch. I don't think either one of us was particularly hungry. It was just to soak up the ambience and the atmosphere. To take it in, savour the atmosphere and say we had done it, lots of pictures to boot. Satisfied and sated, we then set off into Italy through the Mont Blanc tunnel. At some eight miles long and fifty plus quid for the privilege, that in itself was a tad nerve-racking, one of the highest mountains in Europe, and we were driving underneath it?

The following year I had driven over to France with my lady friend named Val. Calling in to say 'hello' to Janet and Keith. Val loved Keith's farm. Still, it wasn't long before Val got her knickers in a twist and had a falling out over Janet sadly. Unfortunately, Val was an alcoholic. She just couldn't leave the wine alone. Even the vodka, really, when I left any around. Worse, as I started to discover, Val had a massive inferiority complex. She quickly resented Janet with a vengeance. The next day we had to drive off, this time heading to Narbonne and then Gruissan. Sober, Val was a lovely girl, her marriage broke up, her husband had been having a long-standing affair with a woman with looks and money. After 25 years of marriage, Val fell apart and never got off her sofa for four years. When she did, she had already hit the bottle. She knew Narbonne and Gruissan well, having travelled extensively to France with her husband, who had French relatives. Stopping on a campsite in Narbonne, Val was quick to point out the difference between crabby sites in England and those here. Amazingly, every pitch had its own toilet. Not every site had those facilities though, it was a revelation. Most sites in Europe were far superior to England and for less money. Having put her ghosts to rest, I had clocked that she had visited these places with her husband and wanted to put the memories to bed. We then set off down into Spain and Benidorm, Val hitting the bottle increasingly more.

Val was an intelligent girl, but I was starting to see where the problem lay. On getting married, she and her husband had started to make a nice life for themselves, both having nice jobs with good incomes and raising four decent, respectable kids. But like a lot of people I've seen over the years, they also wanted to live a nice lifestyle. Expensive meals out over a bottle of wine, nice clothes for the kids, holidays abroad. But when the proverbial hits the fan, we find there is nothing in the pot. I have seen it too many times, the same with pensioners. We go blithely along in life, and understandably so, until retirement stares us in the face, and it hits us like a brick wall what we will have to live on for the remainder of our lives. From that point on, we start dying slowly, accepting the inevitable.

Reading an article once by a middle-class professional lady, with a high flying job in the city, pinstriped power suit, a nice rented apartment, nice clothes, money in the bank, she had heard the expression of being only two paychecks away from a park bench but just let it pass. Until she lost her job. Unable to get another job, her savings went, her nice apartment went, and then she found the park bench.

I wasn't cleverer than anyone else. I was born in the so-called slums of Birmingham, Summer Lane and Nechells, and whilst my dad was a clever man earning a living as a barrow boy, he spent it enjoying his life. There had been a war every twenty years involving England. He and my mom were determined to have a good life. Others were not so lucky. I wasn't bothered about Val having no money. But I just couldn't handle her constant drunkenness. Coming back from Spain, Val was getting worse by the day. Maybe it was the memories of her marriage breakdown, but things didn't improve once we got to the Italian Alps. The experience should have been amazing. Driving through some beautiful villages, we drove into a pretty medieval village called Arenzano. Pulling onto a small open car park, we decided to stop the night. Walking around the town mooching up the little alleyways and nooks and crannies, we clocked this skinny topless guy. I had seen more fat on a chip. He looked like a concentration camp victim. But then, astonishingly, in perfect English, completely unexpected, he asked us what we were looking for. It turns out he was a chef in the local restaurant which he took us to, but unfortunately, it was closed. Whilst he was Italian, having worked as a chef in England, he had met and married an English girl and was now living in this little village with his own restaurant, where his customers were god only knows. But seeing how skinny he was, he was either working flat out or starving. After a pleasant chat and a bottle of his wine, we headed back to the camper, where we spent the night. We set off into the Alps the next day, Val, as per usual, knocking the wine back.

The Alps were stunning, cutting through them by the time we reached La Grave, La Meije, on the French side, Val was again out of it. Under La Grave was a large and free Aire, brilliant. Yes, those French do cater to the motor homers. There were plenty there. Calling in, we pitched up for the night and spent a few hours in the local bars. The next morning, I was determined to get the chair lift to the top of La Grave. It was something that you had to share. Val did not want to come. Where she hid her secret stash. I never knew, but again, she was out of it. With or without her, I was going up that mountain, again I asked her but still, no. The cable car cost me some 22 euros, but I thought it was well worth it. The view was spectacular, amazing. No words can explain it. I was literally on top of the world, seeing a few other sightseers. I asked them to take my photo. The other mountains acted as the backdrop to my picture, doing the same for them in return. Yet again, I had to enjoy the experience alone, knowing Val was at the bottom of the mountain, lying drunk in my motorhome.

Yes, sober, Val was a nice, intelligent girl. She couldn't cook to save her life. "I do a mean corn beef stew."

"A corn beef stew? What's that?" It would just disintegrate. I do a mean chicken chasseur. Well, my wife Bet did a fantastic chicken chasseur. Sadly, Val's didn't fair too well before she got drunk yet again, and I had to finish it off. But I didn't mind that, I can cook my own dinner, like my dad I eat simply. Val was also bone idle. I didn't mind that either. She would never wash or clean up, but I put that down to us only seeing one another spasmodically. Maybe, if we got together, she might shake up, but her constant drunkenness? I couldn't handle it. Her inability to handle money was beyond belief. I had never come across a woman of her age not being able to handle money. I knew I was never going to be able to trust her with a bank card.

The experience of La Grave was beyond words. Like many other experiences, it was something that should be shared. My sweet and dear wife, Bet, is no longer here to share it with me. I thought there was a possibility with Val until I saw her constantly hitting the bottle. La Grave was quite literally the grave for our relationship. With no fixed or set timetable, I slowly started to form my next plan of action, my next attack target. Recalling my trip over the Alps coming back from Italy made me realise how little I knew about the Pyrenees. In all, I think I have traversed the Pyrenees some four times, not stopping in or amongst them once. How stupid of me, I had looked at the Pyrenees simply as a means to get through France into Spain or vice versa. Maybe stopping off in Andorra for a bit of duty-free.

It's surprising what is around the corner when it comes to travelling in the motorhome. We pass through somewhere and say we have visited it. Morocco was a prime example. I was amazed at how many people would boast that they went on holiday to Morocco, but many of them never ventured far from the hotel. I'm not entirely blameless. I had dismissed Switzerland from any future itinerary I had in mind purely because it was constantly covered in ten feet of snow, right? Wrong.

A couple of years ago, I had set out to visit a few countries heading over to Bulgaria before turning south and down into Greece. My route from Calais took me through Switzerland, so I decided to explore the country. How glad that I did. Switzerland was stunning, mainly populated by Germans who most likely did a runner there after the war to escape the turmoil. Driving through lush valley's with beautiful log cabins and the obligatory ton of logs stacked up outside, I couldn't believe how clean, immaculate, peaceful and serene everything was (Germans, see?). Mile after mile of magnificent scenery, stunning mountains and equally stunning waterfalls at every turn. I would constantly stop in a village just to soak up the atmosphere, even popping into one little shop for a bite to eat. A lump of cheese, a small chunk of bread and a little gherkin. Was that it? The old lady with the stern face who served me just took my three euros and walked away. Oh well, maybe that's normal fair over here. No matter, sitting outside that little shop left me with an experience never to forget.

Calling into a campsite overlooking Lake Lucerne, with my trusty ACCI card, of course, I wasn't disappointed. Again, clean and immaculate commenting on the tunnels I had come through, the stern-looking lady booked me in. They all looked stern. Said in that Germanic tone, "ahh zes. Ze tunnels, I zink Switzerland invented ze tunnel." She didn't smile either. The next day I set off for the capital Bern, again a beautiful city with lots of character and outdoor seating areas. The ten feet of snow I was expecting was nowhere to be seen. The climate was mild, with people walking about in short sleeves.

Bern wasn't a big city, but it made up with it in price. Everything was so expensive, food was expensive, clothes were expensive, the famous cuckoo clock was beyond a joke. I had planned to buy one at the back of my mind, here in the heart of cuckoo land. I was thinking maybe forty quid for the genuine article. Walking along the main cobbled high street, I saw a shop with dozens of cuckoo clocks hanging up outside. Wahey, Mazda. Until I looked at the prices, the smallest ones started at two or three hundred pounds rising to over a thousand pounds. Inside was no different. The walls were filled from floor to ceiling with clocks, hundreds of cuckoo clocks. After I had got my second wind, I walked out in shock and disappointment. I didn't mind paying a bit over the odds, but this was ridiculous. I didn't see too many walking out with one, either.

After a short walk around the town without even stopping for a coffee or ice cream, I decided to set off for Chur, a few miles away. Many people are far cleverer and more diligent than me in researching where they are going, me? If I see something in a magazine or national paper of interest, I will cut the article out or copy it into my little book of places to visit. I have sections devoted to Italy, Spain, France. When I visit the area or city, I try to remember my little book. One such event was the Bernini express, a unesco registered train ride from Chur in Switzerland across the Alps into Tirano, Italy. Across the Alps, indeed. I had read it in some article and decided to try it if ever I did visit Switzerland. Now I had, in contrast to the rest of Switzerland, Chur was a bit of a disappointment. It was a grotty little rundown town with nothing appealing about it. I found a neglected little car park in the centre and parked up, making sure I kept right in the centre after deciding the outer limits didn't look too clever. Locking up, I found the main Bernini express train station some half a mile away to check the availability and prices. The ticket cost me £120 return, and as I had to leave my motorhome here in Chur, I had no choice. Arriving early the next morning for the ten am start time, I made my way to the station platform. The Bernini train was a lovely sight, bright red with glass roofs, so you didn't miss one second of the magnificent views. The train was packed with excited tourists, all of us jumping up and down, taking pictures non-stop.

To traverse the mountain took some three hours and did so in a deliberate zig-zag fashion, slowly and steadily. As well as completing the journey, it also allowed us all to take in the scenery from both sides of the train. Stopping once at the top of the mountain for a break and refreshments, we then set off into Tirano across the border and into Italy. Tirano was a pretty little town with plenty of restaurants and shops selling ice cream and meals. With only a two-hour stay, trying to get into one of the restaurants was a bit of a waste of time. I pictured the image of the town just dying a death as soon as we had left on the train, much like the Caribbean islands after the last ship leaves. Some people spent the night or longer in Tirano, so getting back on the train, I felt I could see many unfamiliar faces.

The journey back was a tad boring, merely looking at the same ice packs, mountain lakes, and the tips of the mountains, which just made it very hard to believe that we were at the very top of the Alps. Certainly, it was a sight and experience well worth seeing. The £120, like the snow, melted into nothing after the journey. I was so glad I had done it. It was an experience again, never to forget. But it was also giving me a taste for the Alps and the hidden gems that lay in wait to be discovered. In my ignorance, I initially thought that the Alps were a group of mountain ranges stretching from the Atlantic and across to the Mediterranean Sea. And shared between France and Spain, well, technically that is correct, with the little country of Andorra also stuck between and shared between the two, originally a nondescript independent country that no one wanted, Andorra was now ruled by Spain and France, somehow. But the Alps? Well, they were something else, in all about five times I had travelled through or across them to get into Spain or coming back into France, sometimes going through or into Andorra to visit or spend a night before travelling on. Not being a skier, Andorra held nothing for me at all. In truth, I just wondered why people, anyone except skiers, would want to spend time there. A dreary looking place.

VENTURING FURTHER AFIELD

But the Alps were, in actual fact, more beautiful and stunning than I even realised. There were dozens of villages, lakes, sulphur springs and baths. Different languages are spoken in different parts of the range. It was something I was desperate to look more deeply into. I loved it here in Gruissan. The Languedoc region in itself was beautiful, but I knew there was just so much more for me to see and do. Tomorrow I am going for a walk around the harbour and village of Gruissan. On the recommendation of Colin, a place I had not visited yet, I will head out to one of the first of many Castles. The Castle or Chateau Cathar Gruissan, The castle is derelict, but it doesn't matter. The history will be there of one of the last bastions of defence for the Cathars as they were hunted down and eliminated by the catholic church, usually by being burnt alive as a warning to the others not to join. Men of God, eh? I suppose I'd get burnt, alive, for choosing to be an agnostic. Yes, it's easy to see how we in England, being a protestant Christian country, were at war with the frog eaters for all those years.

It had been raining overnight, and early morning, so after a coffee, I set off for my local internet bar and another coffee whilst catching up on my emails on my main laptop. I then set off down to Gruissan harbour at my leisure, round to and across the bridge to the 'The Village.' For some reason, I assumed 'The Village' was just another section but a separate part of Gruissan itself. No, 'The Village' is the old original part of Gruissan, for the most part medieval. As I passed under the second bridge and followed the canal that opened into two small lakes before opening up to the sea, I then saw the Castle, or Chateau, Castle Gruissan.

As I entered the town, I could immediately feel its antiquity, walls with bits of render falling off, shutters in need of a lick of paint that seemed to have been there for hundreds of years. When these streets were built, the car had never been thought of. Small narrow alleyways cut through them off one another. Then I heard the bells. The bells, coming to the base of the chateau. I noticed the bell tower and the church below, along with the crowd of visitor's waiting patiently to be allowed to enter the castle. Well, it is popular, but how long is this going to take. Ordering a coffee, I asked the girl how long she thought it might take for the crowds to filter through? She didn't know. Sitting down with my coffee, the bells going again, I decided to give the castle a miss. Well, a castle is a castle is a castle. Soon, the crowd started filtering through into the doorway, Gendarme on hand to keep an orderly eye on things, security in black suits to keep everyone in check. For a few seconds, I debated tagging onto the end of the crowd. It's a good job, I never. It was a funeral procession. Phew. Once they had disappeared, I made my way up to the side of the church and the now almost empty stairs.

Getting to the top of the castle was a bit daunting. I was glad to see I wasn't the only one gasping or sneakily stopping to get my breath back, but I was baffled. This seemed to be quite familiar. It was only when I got to the top I realised why. Yes, I had been here before, with Val. We had just come in from a different angle. Val had brought me in from the swamps on the southern side of the castle. From the top, I could see out towards the sea, the swamps and the Flamingos that Gruissan was also famous for. The views were absolutely stunning. Amazing, breath-taking, to the sea, miles across to the north and the La Clape. To the south, Gruissan and the port looking out over the Mediterranean, below, the rooftops of the old village.

The castle was built in the 10th century on the orders of the archbishop of Narbonne as protection against the continuing hordes of invaders trying to get into and plunder Narbonne. The townspeople were terrified of the constant attack by Muslim hoards who were utterly ruthless. You almost get the feeling that the archbishop and his cohorts in Narbonne didn't give too much thought to the inhabitants of Gruissan. And why should they? They were a good few miles away. Eventually, there were arguments between the archbishop and others, resulting in the castle being split into two. It was eventually left derelict by the 15th century. The castle and the surrounding land had stood alone for centuries until it was abandoned. From that point on, the locals started taking all the stones and building their own houses that are still standing below, now only the circular tower remains, showing the skill and originality of the French builders.

I didn't want to leave, moving from one spot to another, taking photos before slowly, I headed off back down the stone steps, this time a lot easier. Having seen the castle, I now had a walk around the narrow allies and streets, passing the many bars and bistros, stopping for a croissant which I ate outside, savouring the moment until the funeral cortege came past me. Weary but exhilarated, I made my way back to my local bar, enjoying a burger at the local fast food bar than a coffee at the bar. The history of France, to me, mirrored the history of us in England. We were just as barbaric. Well, our feudal kings were, they didn't give a hoot about us peasants. We were taxed to the hilt to keep them in power and luxury, left to starve if we nicked a loaf of bread or had the audacity to kill one of the king's deer. We either had our arms chopped off or were tortured and killed. No wonder Robin Hood was so popular. Come to think of it, I don't think things have changed too much.

My knowledge of the history between the two countries was and still is scant poor education, you know. I knew a little bit about the hundred years of war. But that was all about those same kings who were mostly related anyway, fighting over lands that they were stealing on the west coast of France. I think everyone is aware of where the two-fingered salute comes from. Our longbowmen were famous for their skill and accuracy. The French were terrified of them, so much so that when they were fortunate or lucky enough to catch any of our bowmen, they would chop their two fingers off. It then became a game of taunting whenever the French and English came face to face in battle. The English bowmen would give the French the two-fingered salute to tell them they had still got their two fingers. Can you just picture the scene?

CARCASSONNE, LAGRASSE AND OTHER MEDIEVAL VILLAGES

My time here in Gruissan has been thoroughly enjoyable and satisfactory. It has been relaxing, interesting, and by its very offering, educational. It would be very easy to stop another day, then another day after that. I'm in an absolutely pleasant spot just yards from the sea, restaurants and shops. Ok, ok, I know I keep repeating myself. But it's the truth, I could literally stop here all summer, but I know, beyond that nearby road, there is lots more for me to see and a lot more adventures to be had. There is Carcassonne to visit again, even just for the day. Then the medieval village of Lagrasse. Recognised as one of the most beautiful medieval villages in France in the top ten. Termes, another on my wish list with its Chateau Arquess? What's there is for me to find out, that is before the Cathar castles down by the Pyrenees, Chateau de Queribus, and Chateau de Peyrepertuse. The last of the Cathar strongholds. All this before hitting the Pyrenees themselves.

I got to Carcassonne about 12pm, yes, it's only forty-odd miles from Gruissan, but I'm not rushing. The drive through the Languedoc was pleasant, with mile after mile of vineyards, little villages selling wine by the bottle or by the case. It was market day in Narbonne, but try as I might, I could not see anywhere to park up with my camper. Narbonne is a beautiful, attractive city with tree-lined avenues and a river running through it. I suppose the only way to see it properly is to camp up outside and get a taxi into the centre. It looked difficult enough as it was. What irritated me is it looked a bit of a cut above your usual market selling the usual tat next to the fruit and veg. I saw antique's, works of art, the lot. Ah well, another day. Carcassonne, the medieval city, is breath-taking it's an awe-inspiring living piece of history, pulling on to the car park in front of the main entrance with the imposing walls, castles and turrets in front, the ditch in front of the medieval drawbridge stuns you into silence as you take in the enormity of it. What must it have been like for the local inhabitants five, six hundred years ago? What must it have been like for those invading armies who came and tried to penetrate it without success? In front and to the left of the castle ramparts was a graveyard. I decided to go in there first, view and pay my respects to those dead, some quite recent, some hundreds of years old. Visitors are still coming in, paying their respects to relatives, some long gone.

Yes, we had our castles in England, many from the same period. Unfortunately, with our harsher climate and our governments' lack of short-sightedness, ours were left to fall apart and decay. This almost happened here. The French tried to demolish the site, in 1849 causing an uproar in the city. Fortunately, a restoration project was started in 1853 by Eugenie Violet-Le-Duc, a famous architect of the time who totally restored it. The site now relies on tourism. Amazingly, there is no entrance fee into the castle or the city, due to Covid it was also a lot quieter and more organised than during previous busier times. Carcassonne is just not something you rush through. You just can't. Every single brick seems to have a story, with the atmosphere emanating from every groove. Much of the frontages throughout the site are made up of restaurants, sweets, souvenirs or other goods. This must be, presumably, how the city funds itself and makes a profit. The rental income from all the many and varied businesses. What a great idea, something that supports itself, why can't we do that in England? Get the royals out of Buckingham Palace and Windsor Castle. Our properties, us plebs. Fill the surrounding outer grounds with respectable, suitable and attractive shops, all making a fortune of course, and indeed paying a fortune in rent, going forward a bit, think how many derelict castles we could restore? Someone will think about it one day, probably after reading my book.

I could never get fed up with visiting Carcassonne castle, reading and soaking up the history of it. Having had a good leisurely walk around the shops and ramparts finding it quite easy to try and imagine what it must have been like to live within those walls, after a few hours, I sat and enjoyed a nice soup in one of the many restaurants before heading off to have a look at the torture chambers. God only knows how their minds worked in those days to carry out such evil acts, but I suppose it was consistent with the times. During the Albigensian crusade's when the city was a Cathar stronghold in 1209, the crusading army forced its citizens to surrender before burning them alive at the stake. Yes, they loved burning them alive, did those medievalists. I think a forward to one of the many books on Carcassonne might say it far better than me.

Here all at once, the traveller forgets the cars, the crowds of holidaymakers, the frantic haste of his contemporaries; time stands still. He discards his tourist dress and quite naturally discovers the spirit of these innumerable people on foot or on horseback who, 7 or 8 centuries ago, trod the dusty roads of pilgrimage, trade or war. He sees the very same golden walls that the shepherd saw as he drove his sheep to the razes or the black mountains. The canon was on his mule as he rode to the bishop's council. The Cathar, on his way to the friendly castle of some nobleman well disposed towards the heretical preachers. He gazes at these walls and towers from which rise the clamour of battle, the neighing of horses and the whistling of arrows. He sees the knights galloping through the gates, the banished burghers fleeing in their short sleeves along the stony hillside.

THE CITY OF CARCASSONNE
AND LAGRASSE

I think the above says it all for me. Certainly, I don't think I have seen such an imposing fortress/castle. It is easy to see why it was never penetrated. The only way of defeat was to starve them out or stopping their water supply, which happened once in history. I wanted to stop in Carcassonne for longer, but I had other goals to fill, other journeys to make, other places to see. My next destination is Lagrasse, the medieval village. But first I wanted to visit the Canal Du Midi, maybe even spend the night. Heading out of Carcassonne, I headed for the canal crossing the River Norde, which runs parallel to it. I saw a camper by the River Nord. But reaching the Canal Du Midi, I could find nowhere to park up. After a few tries without success, I gave up, stopped the camper and put Lagrasse into my sat nav. Low and behold, didn't I then pass the canal with a great big parking space to the side. Ignoring my sat nav, I pulled in quickly and did a couple of turns like a dog in his new bed, set up right by the canal with my passenger door wide open and facing it.

I could not have been happier. In my oil tot, I switched the cooker on, did myself a nice English breakfast, sort of. Then settled down for the night, a bottle of wine cracked, sorted. Lagrasse tomorrow. Only I didn't make the morrow, well I did, but much later than I thought. After a peaceful night's sleep, I woke to find the canal life building up. Boats were passing up and down. Cyclists and walkers were passing by along the bridleway. The canal was certainly being made use of. After my usual wake me up cup of coffee, I tidied the van up, ready for the off. At the top end of the car park, I noticed two other campers had pulled in. I wondered why the place wasn't so popular. Maybe they called in late last night?

Pulling up alongside them, I decided to pop across and ask them a question. Walking between the two campers, I debated left or right. Left won. They both had their awnings out and were sat on their chairs, the table in between seeing the French flag. I said, "bonjour," and we started chatting. The wife's English was non-existent, but the husband spoke quite well. It took me a while before he pointed out he wasn't, in actual fact, French but Danish. The next couple were Spanish. After a few pleasantries, he asked me how old I was? Why do some men have to ask this question? Is it a man thing? "I am seventy-two." He got in quick. "Ahh, you are very old. How old are you?" he asked again. "Sixty-five?"

"No, no," I said, "I am fifty-five, a lot younger than you." His wife made a disapproving sound, and he just kept saying, "you tell lies, you lie." Well, it broke the ice, but he didn't like it too much when I said I was the same age as him but looked much younger. They were all set up for the Tour de France.

The Tour de France? I hadn't got a clue. I vaguely remembered someone mentioning it earlier. Where is it passing? Here? Right on the island that the car park was alongside, the Tour de France was not something that overwhelmed me. Watching a mob of cyclists racing each other was not on my priority list in life. The couple followed them all over France, travelling along the route and then also watching it on the television. I didn't know what to do. My engine was still running, and it was only 11 am. Getting to Lagrasse by lunchtime. The cyclists would be passing us at around 5 pm-ish. Sitting in my camper, I couldn't make my mind up. Then finally, I did. The Spanish couple were tucked in behind the Danish couple. There was just enough room behind them for me to also tuck in without impeding on the car park pulling in and reversing up. I backed up close. Getting out, I walked around and put my thumbs up, indicating where I was and seeking their approval. Walking across the Spanish guy, looked at my camper and gave a big friendly smile and a nod of approval. There was a raised bank in front of us, so setting my table and chairs out, I then noticed each had got their own country flags up. Going into my camper, I brought out my three-foot union jack flag, waving to them. I unfurled the flag. If you can bring your flags, I can bring mine. The atmosphere was relaxed and friendly, the Spanish couple inviting me for tapas. On the back of their van, they had signage. The 'Tour de France.' Pointing to it, the Spanish guy told me that they were tour officials. This is getting better by the minute. Setting out my cheese nibbles, I sat down to enjoy the day, reading my newly acquired book on the Cathar religion. There was little hope of that, the activity building up bit by bit. First, the council workers came to cut the car park off. Then the police arrived to set up roadblocks. I couldn't get out if I wanted to. All around the island was the sponsorship signs SKODA in large letters.

First, the cars started coming round at speed, then a couple of cyclists, presumably to check the terrain. Then more cars, then rows of Skoda cars all packed with people shouting, waving and bawling. The excitement was building up nicely. By now, the crowds were building up nicely all around the island. A German couple in another camper further down behind us. Other cars parked around us. All were getting into the mood of excitement.

Standing by the island, the Spanish official and now my friend tried to explain to me that I must be prepared for what was coming. Next, he just couldn't translate the words he was trying to find into English. After a few failed attempts, I then guessed that he was trying to say some kind of carnival? Yes, yes. I was bobbing up and down like a yo-yo. Getting on my chair, then up again as someone came whizzing past, down again, up again. Eventually, I could sense a build-up with plenty of shouting. It started, coming from the direction of Carcassonne, the flotilla of carnival trucks, the first one throwing loads of stuff out. It took me a while to catch on. T-shirts, and Tour de France hats. The trucks are made up of all kinds of figures, some with cyclists on the back, others with figurines, all advertising their goods, of course. Every other vehicle was throwing goodies out, pencils, biscuits, bottles of water, T-towels, more T-shirts and hats. I was having a field day, full of excitement at the little prezzies I could give my grandkids. The excitement of being able to say, my granddad brought this back from the Tour de France. I don't think I was alone. Kids and adults alike were fighting to grab what they could. I thanked the Spanish guy for reminding me of the event.

Next, more sponsorship cars, more police motorbikes, then eventually the Spanish guy started giving me the count down. They are five kilometres, then three kilometres. My knowledge of the race was zilch, so I didn't know what to expect, surely just a load of fit guys whizzing around like lunatics. Eventually, the first of the cyclists appeared from the far side of the island, 10? 20? 30? Then the backup cars laden down with bicycle's on the top. Dozens of them? How many bikes do these guys go through?

I thought that was it. But no, after a few minutes, another wave came through. Another load of backup cars with yet another load of backup bicycles on the roof, after what seemed like a dozen or so waves, then the odd straggler came along to a few hearty cheers. I was that elated and excited I kept crossing from my video to my camera on my phone, getting my thumb caught and spoiling the shot a few times. Thankfully I took plenty of both, my little fingers going like a dervish.

Eventually, it was finished, slowly it started to filter through that all the cyclists had gone through, all the sponsorship vehicles had passed, the cops started slowly to disappear, the council workers came to take the barricades down, the sponsorship hoardings away. The Spanish guy came across to shake hands and say goodbye. They were a lovely couple, and it was a pleasure to have spent a few hours in their company. Now they were off to the next stage of the race, something else I didn't realise, it was heading down in stages into the Pyrenees and Andorra. Where I was eventually heading. Should I follow them? For now, I was heading down to Lagrasse, some twenty-two miles away, the medieval town.

Although Lagrasse was only a short drive away, it was a pleasant drive through the Languedoc region. Passing through acres and acres of vineyards, this was the home of the Sauvignon Blanc and Merlot wines. One of the bonuses of avoiding the tolls is that you get to see so much more of the country and the natural beauty. Leaving Santander some weeks ago, I had accidentally got onto the toll roads, heading for Marseillan. I'm glad I did, as it enabled me to get there much quicker. Now I wanted to slow down and savour everything in more detail. I reached Lagrasse by 7pm, too late for any supermarkets. I could kick myself. Why didn't I stop at the Aldi store outside of Carcassonne? Now it was too late. I had fancied a nice couple of chicken legs chased down with a bottle of wine to round off the day, a bottle of nice Merlot to show my support for the region.

Lagrasse has one of the most beautiful Aires that anyone could ask for. Set just before the town, it sits in an olive grove, to the far corner a tipping point for wastewater and cassette, plus a water tap, what more could you ask for, all very civilised, yet again the French have a very kindly attitude to the motor homer. Most of us will spend some money in the town. Finding a pitch amongst the other happy campers, I set up and got all my windows open before locking up and heading the few yards to the town and a shop. I knew Lagrasse didn't have a supermarket as such, just a couple of small shops. All were closed, except the wine shop. Obviously, it was a couple of bottles of wine and a Fray Bentos mincemeat and onion pie. After a pint in the local bar, I set off to my little camper, sated and ready to tour the town and abbey tomorrow.

Maybe Lagrasse isn't everyone's cup of tea. Certainly, I think it's one of those places you put on your tick list if you're able. To me, I like soaking up a bit of that history. Lagrasse itself, the name coming from 'grassa,' meaning fertile, came out of the abbey, which goes back to before the end of the 8th century. Even before it was known that a monastery had been on the site, the dwellings came later beside the monastery where the graveyard is now. Later it moved to the other side of the river in about the 13th century.

The abbey grew tremendously over the 9th and 10th centuries and had property as far as Spain. By the early 12th century, Lagrasse owned about a hundred churches and ten monasteries. Yep, those monasteries knew how to turn a profit without a doubt. Its fortunes declined in the 14th century when it was decimated by the 'Black Death.' Eventually, it was sold at auction in 1796 and split into two. Where it made its living from crop and livestock farming, it also lived by crafts and trade. It was noted for its cloth, its market, which still stands today in the centre of the town was the biggest in the region. Today its main income comes from tourism.

I found the 'Abbaye Sainte-Marie' closed due to covid on both occasions I visited. Still, I wasn't too fussed. The walk alone across the ancient bridge to the abbey and the cemetery was quite enough for me. However, I did enter and visit the private section of the monastery to the left. Coming back across the bridge and viewing the houses sitting on the banks of the river, I couldn't help but wonder how some of them were still standing. Heading into and around the village listed as one of the most beautiful villages in France, it was amazing to see these picturesque jumble of buildings, its narrow streets giving onto tiny squares with many of the frontages ranging from the middle ages. I just found it so difficult to envisage anyone living in these dwellings and/or what kind of people they are. Another thing I just can't get my head around is the French insistence on the shutters. Here maybe I could understand a bit, the streets are that narrow you could spit from one side to the other, no one likes their neighbours gawking in through the windows, never mind us long-necked gawking tourists. But haven't they heard of nets? Crikey, we all grew up with nets. That stopped the neighbours nosing in, but shutters? Do they all live in darkness?

There was a concert going on in the old market hall built in the 14th century, a crowd sitting there enjoying the concert pianist, a French man was giving an introduction before the pianist would give a recital, I couldn't understand a word of French of course, but it didn't stop me enjoying the music. Sitting there underneath its ten stone pillars supporting its wooden timbers whilst listening to that pianist was magical.

Saint-Michel's church sits in the centre of the old village, a typical example of late gothic style. It was built around 1359. Unfortunately, it was closed. Carrying on to the main high street, through the road, I popped into one of the many café bars lining the route, all looking busy, not many paying too much attention to the socially distancing covid rules, ay, I bet most of us have had the jab. Well, I have. I sat at a small single table nearby a couple at the next table. As it was only about 2pm, I only wanted something light. As per usual, it was all in French. Looking at the ten euro menu, I recognised the word jambon, ham, and pate, also olives on the one item. When the waitress came across, nice friendly smile on her face, I ordered that without the olives. When the plate came, I was staggered. I only wanted a snack. That's what I thought I was ordering. This was a massive plate full of different hams, aubergines, pates and toasties, plus a basket of bread with plenty of butter.

Trying to explain to the French couple at the next table, I asked if they wanted some, no, no, no, when I saw their meal arrive, I understood. They had gone in for two courses.

The French couple started talking once the meal was finished, and I didn't need much persuasion. Telling them about the Tour de France, they asked how I had got here. With the Covid regulations, I explained that I had cheated by coming through the back door via Santander. After a quick flurry on their phone to check where Santander was, they then told me they were from Dieppe and were touring the south of France, stopping at hotels or gites along the way. They were a lovely friendly couple, again just a spontaneous conversation with a couple of strangers who I would never meet again. Heading back to my camper, I started thinking about the next stage of my little tour. Termes

Before setting off from Lagrasse the next morning and following a relaxing cup of coffee, I drove over to the service point, dumped a bit of rubbish and topped my water tanks up. Being Sunday, there was a bit of an antique market being held in Lagrasse, so I stopped to have a meander around before setting off. Driving through the countryside and small hamlets of the Languedoc was a delight. It was only as I was driving through Termes that I realised my blunder. Castle Termes was built on the top of a mountain, well, quite right, as are many of them, but as I drove into Termes itself, I could see it was quite a high mountain. Oh well, let's persevere.

Driving into the small hamlet of Termes, I couldn't help but be impressed with how pretty it looked, a couple of pavement cafes looking very inviting. Driving through, I was directed to the parking area outside of the village. Inside and on the boundary was the information board. There a small charge to visit the castle, which was in ruins. Worse, it pointed out the climb to it. Weighing up the odds, I didn't consider it worth the effort. There are lots more castles. I decided to make my way to the next castle or château. In Villerouge-Termenes, just a few miles further on. Only on pulling into it did I realise I had visited it only the year before driving back from Spain.

Pulling into the village, I got my bearings and headed straight to the car park.

How these people get on in these small villages for food and shopping, I don't know. When I asked, it had no shop, only the post office, a small bar that served food and a restaurant in the main chateau. I called into the bar first, asking about food. I hit a brick wall. No one spoke English. I couldn't speak French, leading me outside the lady owner introduced me to a customer who could speak English. In the main, the menu was quite straightforward. Omelette, with salad and frites. Entrecote with salad and frites. I decided to have a walk around the village and chateau first. The village, as with many of these villages, never fails to have an effect on me. Who lives in these places? They are so quiet, hardly anyone is moving about, how do they lead their lives, do they ever have arguments. What do they do? Where do they work? Surely they are not all OAPS. I couldn't imagine leading my life so quietly. The only sound is the church bells.

The village is your typical little medieval village built in a cluster around the main castle that overlooked it. It is imposing now. How imposing must it have seemed in the 14th century with its four massive corner towers? Walking into the courtyard and looking around, I could see bales of straw to one side, the office to the other and the rotisserie restaurant above it. Looking at the menu and its prices, I decided to give it a miss and eat at the local bar. Ok, I shouldn't be mean, but I always feel places like this are taking advantage of their very existence by charging 25% more to eat in the chateau. Maybe it's me, maybe I'm a bit of a cheapskate. But the bar overlooks the beautiful village stream and the castle itself.

Villerouge-Termenes was owned by the Narbonne Bishops in 1321. The last known Cathar, Guillaume Belibaste, was, as was the norm, burned alive in the castle courtyard. Today, for some strange reason, bales of straw sit against the wall. Hmm. Is that the leftovers or a reminder? And what about the villagers? Did they know this was going on? "Something rum going on up in the castle, me duck. I can smell burning?"

"Ay, well best keeps yer gob shut then, or it could be you."

How barbaric were these people? What was their mindset to burn another human being on a blazing fire alive? In the hundreds. And what about the inquisitions? Now that's another one, "are you innocent or guilty?"

"Innocent, my lord."

"Well, we shall see, tie him up and dip him in the river. If he dies , he is innocent. If he lives , he's guilty." And these people were followers of God. What did Saint Dominique say? "I have preached for years, where benediction is useless, punishment will prevail." And the other one, "kill them all. God will know his own." When the priest got Mel Gibson on the rack and said, "repent my son, repent and die quickly." Well, I thought it was just a film, a bit of made-up history, with William Wallace being drawn into quarters and distributed about the city. It brings you up with a start to know that it was the truth. And we were just as bad. Our lords and masters, how come they never learned any of Christ's teachings. But there again, look at Hitler, look at the Germans, look what they did to the Jews and others, and that was only a few short years ago. I ask myself what the royal family would do to us if they had the power. Let the peasants eat cake.

The rear of the castle had an exit point that overlooked the stream and the bar I had been in earlier, stone steps leading down. Walking the short distance to the bar, I ordered the entrecote steak, frites, and salad. And very nice it was too. With the restaurant, I assumed the chateau was privately owned. It wasn't. It was owned by the commune. This must be a good thing, everyone within the community benefits. Driving from Termes to Villerouge-Termenes, across the mountains, I had passed a cut in with a large parking area to enable viewings across the valley to the mountains behind. Ignoring other more local Aires near the village, I made my way back to it. With my recliner set out, a bottle of wine on the table, I sat back to enjoy the sunset and spend the night in such a heavenly place, bliss.

After a peaceful and relaxed night's sleep, I woke to find the sky overcast and rain trying to get through. It looked like it was succeeding. The tops of the distant mountains were lost in cloud. Looking through my Cathar country book, I decided to filter the chateaus down a bit. Well, by their very nature, many of these castles are built on the top of sheer cliffs, climbing to the top of Gruissan castle was bad enough, some of them, like Padern Castle or Puilaurens Castle you had to be very fit or have a helicopter handy. I'm not so fit, and I didn't have a helicopter. I whittled it down to Arques, Coustaussa, and Puivert Castles.

My first castle or chateau was Arques, situated just a short distance from the village of Arques near the Rialsesse Forest. The castle didn't seem like a castle to me, nor a chateau. In fact, it looked more like a wealthy country house, built on four floors with four corner towers, the one tower containing the circular stone steps rising to each floor. The ground floor contained the granary or grain store, which held the food supplies. The second and third floor was the masters or servants quarters, and the soldiers lived on the top floor with clear visibility to all corners of the land from the four watchtowers. To keep warm and sleep, they would spread straw on the floor. They would eat, chat and sleep in this room, all the while looking through the watchtowers for any approaching enemy. The whole castle is surrounded by a high curtain wall. Unusually, the castle was built so far away from the village, as though the master Pierre de Voisins, another ally of Simon de Montfort, didn't want to be close to them. Nonetheless, the commanding position of the castle would have made it a very nice place to live. My next port of call was Coustassa castle. Coustassa castle looked very impressive, perched on top of the hill opposite the small village of Chateau Rennes. But having got to the top of the village via a very narrow and twisting road, I wasn't all that impressed. From there, I followed to the Chateau at Rennes just a couple of miles away. This wasn't in my Cathar books, but I decided I must see it as it was so close.

Chateau Rennes seemed a whole different set-up altogether. This wasn't the normal stand-alone castle-like Arques, nor was it like the awesome Carcassonne that had a whole host of shops, cafes, bars and hotels whilst still retaining its medieval character. Chateau Rennes wasn't just the Chateau or about the Chateau. It was a whole small village set around and a part of the chateau itself, the whole place being a living, breathing museum. I just couldn't help but wonder where the past finished and the modern started. Shutters were barely hanging from the windows, render flaking from the walls, yet next door would be an artisan shop. A restaurant. The village extended back from the Chateau, all higgledy-piggledy blending in yet strangely at odds. Gites were being advertised for lettings, so it must be a thriving little destination break. I walked around the Chateau and its grounds before calling into the equally small medieval church. It was very dark, with rows of candles lit in memory of those passed. I lit a candle for my lovely wife, Bet, and said a silent prayer.

From there, I set off for the castle Puivert which looked very impressive, dominating the village of Puivert itself. The distance was only 15 miles, but my plan was to pull in somewhere suitable and welcoming for the night. It didn't take me too long or too far. Within a couple of miles, I pulled into the town of Quillan that sat on the banks of the River Aude, yes, that same river that passed through Carcassonne. That in itself wouldn't have stopped me, but on the banks of the river, I saw a party of motor homers. Before them, with all flashing lights, was a small fete. Doing a quick turn on the opposite side of the river, I returned and pulled in next to the other campers. The fete was only small but brilliant, kiosks all around serving all kinds of food from Moules with frites to wines. Tables and chairs filling up, and a live band warming up. I had arrived just in time.

Again, it raises the question or thoughts of campsites and paying their, sometimes extortionate, fees. I am on yet another Aire here in France, this time right by the town and river. And it's free, how can you put a value on that I am spending money in the town that maybe I wouldn't spend if I was on a campsite, so it's a win-win all around. Last night I felt that comfortable high up in the mountains I never even locked my doors. Mind, I wouldn't recommend doing that often, but I had had a bottle of Languedoc wine. I have the sound of the River Aude gurgling past me. Bliss. I have been in France for over five weeks, and I have not paid for a site once or felt the need to.

Waking up to an overcast and rainy morning, I just hoped it would be worthwhile travelling to view the Puivert Chateau fifteen miles away. Puivert Chateau dominated the town of Puivert and the surrounding area. At some 12,00 feet and surrounded by mountains, it overlooked the area for miles. It must have been magnificent back in the 1200s when it was built on a promontory. Again, the drive was very pleasant and relaxed, driving through beautiful, peaceful little villages dotted about through the countryside. The Chateau was visible for miles. It was easy to get to until I got there, then I lost it. Driving into Puivert village and then back out again on a different route, I saw the sign of the museum. So carried on until I saw the Chateau signs again. After six miles, I did an about-turn until I saw the turnoff that I missed the first time. Sometimes I wonder who puts these signs up. Within a space of a few hundred yards, I saw big signs. PUIVERT CHATEAU. Then I missed the very small sign pointing up the hill that was single track and steep, but there was no going back once I started. I'm just glad it was such a rubbish day, and no traffic was coming down. Eventually, I got to the car park, if you can call it that. The Chateau was in private ownership, and I wondered if it was the guy in the hut who took the 7 euros off me and was supposed to live in the Chateau.

The entrance to the Castle was very impressive, exactly what you would expect a Castle to look like and to me as one of the ones I had seen with Russell Crow in Robin Hood. The entrance opened up to a big grassed area the size of a football pitch. It was easy to imagine the different animals being kept around, horses, chickens, ducks etc., or maybe the occasional jousting session. The main living quarters of the chateau were spread over three floors living quarters, the music room which features sculptures of figures playing instrument's for entertaining privileged guests and above that the chapel, presumably this would be where the lord of the manor and his troops would go and pray before killing all those Cathars. The chateau was given to the De Bruyeres family after their loyalty in the battles.

The drive up to the chateau had been bad enough. I'm just glad I had got a 2.8 turbo diesel. The walk up from the car park was just as bad, along a steep and uneven path. The chateau itself was another matter. The only place you could visit inside was the main keep at the end of the chateau grounds. Some 35 meters tall, the only way to reach the three floors was by steep winding stairs. After each one, I had to sit and take a breather. Getting back to my motorhome afterwards, I was glad to think that this was the last of the chateaus to visit for this year. I swear another chateau would see me off.

After visiting the Chateau Puivert, I drove down to the outside swimming pool just below the village. I would have happily spent the night and had a dip, but it was raining cold and overcast. I set off for the Pyrenees some 60 miles away, in particular the small village of Dorres, just outside Andorra. Dorres reputedly had the best sulphur springs in the Pyrenees. Together with the lakes, I was prepared to try a few out. I always put in my sat nav, no toll roads. Most of the time, this works out great, giving you the opportunity to see the real side of the country, but sometimes it can lead to either crappy terrible roads like in Italy or places like Albania. Or it can be the seat of your pants driving like I was to find out. The rule is with the sat nav is to trust it, but not too much.

Keep your eyes peeled for the narrowing roads or rivers in front of you. Many a time, someone has trusted their sat nav only to find themselves stuck in a river. I have had to back out of narrow allies in Benidorm old town and once drove across a mountain track to reach a beach. Not only does that give me nightmare's still. I cannot believe how stupid I was to go along a mountain track. It all seemed quite clear this time until I followed the instructions to take a left turn onto a single track road. There were the bridges. These were no ordinary run of the mill bridges that we are used to seeing at home. No, some giant from a time long ago had just gone at these with an axe, chopping and hacking at the roof. Oh, go on, get stuck in. it's a tunnel, isn't it? I had to drive through an inch at a time. That happened three times, three tunnels.

I had driven through a few medieval villages and always wondered how the inhabitants, the French people, led their lives. I was born in the slums, row upon row of terrace houses with no front garden, the front door leading straight off the street. In many cases, no gardens either, maybe a small back yard and I don't remember anyone who liked it or was happy there. Most were desperate to get out to a nice house in the suburbs, but here? The French seemed happy and content, some having not left for generations, and then there are the shutters. The French love the shutters. Is it to keep the unbearable heat out or stop nosey neighbours gawking in? Surely it can't be the weather. OK, I appreciate it can get hot in the summer, hotter than our summers, but we are not talking about the Sahara here. Even detached houses out in the country have their shutters, so it can't be the nosey neighbours there. And they all seemed to be elderly, so one minute I'm driving through tiny little villages, streets so narrow the neighbours can spit across to one another, dreary and miserable looking, the next, wide-open streets attractive more modern looking houses, some tree-lined but still no front gardens. It is only when you get out into the country you see front and back gardens, and even then, the French are growing grapes or vegetables in them.

The Parisians, like Londoners, live the same. They must, on the whole, be quite wealthy. Yet, they buy or rent very expensive apartments on the top floors, and how do they get their furniture in? Why does the removal company carry ladders, of course? You will see them outside apartments, big extending ladders up to the tenth floor, shunting wardrobes up by pullies. It's strange how many of us choose to live, really. A television documentary showed the parking problems being experienced in London. In one cul-de-sac a mile or so from the centre, the residents were up in arms because people were commuting from outside London then parking in the cul-de-sac to get the underground to the inner city. The residents were trying all ways, leaving notes on windscreens etc., to no avail. One bloke got that worked up. He had a heart attack in the street cameras still filming all over a parking issue. He could have sold his mid terraced house in London and bought a mansion up north. A famous comic was embroiled in an ongoing heated row with his neighbours because friends were always parking outside his multimillion-pound mansion, to the detriment of other neighbours. Why would you want to live like that?

It wasn't just the dodgy tunnels and narrow streets or single track roads I had to navigate. Those were bad enough in my camper with no visible signs of any cut-outs for passing by. It was also the overhanging rocks. It was scary enough seeing the falling rocks and boulders signs. In any language that was easy enough to understand, no, it was that giant again, brought in to clear a path through to the hacked out tunnels, swiping away at them just to give enough room for a car to get through. Obviously, the thinking behind it was it was only a little dirt road. Let's not waste money on it. Well, I had to drive at 3mph, using the whole road to avoid slitting the side of my van from front to rear. Getting back onto the main road was a blessing.

DORRES AND THE FIRST
SULPHUR BATHS

I reached the beautiful skiing and toured the village of Bolquere in the Pyrenees around 4 pm. I had been driving that slowly, partly enjoying the beauty I never realised how time flew. I had passed through villages that were clearly reliant on tourists, as evidenced by signs for La Grotto, with huge hotels closed and shuttered. While Bolquere seemed quite busy in comparison, a lot of hotels and chalets were still closed. Truly, I'm just glad I'm not in business anymore, well, not running a hotel or being in the leisure industry.

Leaving Bolquere, I got to Dorres at about 6 pm and settled down for the night with the cab door facing the fields and a very friendly grey horse. This was yet again another free Aires for campers and other visitor's, thoughtfully, as usual, with a tipping point for the cassettes and fresh water. A group of bikers had pulled onto the car park, so I asked them if they were here for the baths. A lady biker said they were, but it was now too late, so they would return the next day. She had been here previously and considered them the best sulphur baths in the Pyrenees, which perked me up.

The next morning, I set off for the short walk to the sulphur springs, up the road that way, and turn left. Right, so up I go, turns left at the sign Baines de Romaine, ahh, that's got to be it. Another steep incline down to know where I did an about-turn after fifty yards. Where are these sulphur springs? I was in the back of beyond. Thankfully my guardian angel turned up in the shape of a French lady in her car. Waving her down, I asked her where the springs were, she didn't know either but was heading for the same place, she spoke very good English and offered me a lift. I was glad to accept. It was only a few yards further on. Parking up, we made the rest of the way on foot. Although I had read the warning signs on the board, 70degrees rising to 100 degrees natural thermal sulphur springs that came up from the Pyrenees, they were supposed to be beneficial to anyone suffering from allergies, like bad skin, asthma etc. It warned if you had a weak heart or other problems not to go in. Great, quite discriminating then. I thought maybe my luck was in with my newfound friend who was here to help cure the asthma she suffered. She was in a clinic for a month undergoing treatment. She had come here to further it, having heard such good things about it.

At the reception, she explained to me the procedure, which the receptionist couldn't. She simply explained it was what I had read in English on the board. If I had a heart attack and died, they were not responsible. Understood. Set out before us were the pools, three in all, with varying degrees of heat, surrounded by grassed areas with recliner plastic chairs and benches. All this for 5.50 euros, and no time limit. The longer I got into it, the more I appreciated what a bargain it was, free parking, and only 5.50 euros for the day? I might spend a few days at this. As I only had a shirt and trunks on, I headed straight for the pool, my newfound friend, to the changing rooms.

Getting into the pool, I was pleasantly surprised when my newfound friend got in beside me. I definitely thought my luck was in. Her name was Marie, and she had worked in management for a hotel chain in Windsor, hence her good English. It was advised that only 30 minutes at a time were spent in the water for safety reasons. I didn't see why but Marie watched the clock like a hawk. A big clock is fully visible from the pools. She was a very nice lady Marie, knowledgeable and able to talk on various subjects, without taking offence or being offended. I find in life that many people consider themselves intelligent, but very few, in actual fact, have much common sense. We were able to talk about the religious persecution of the Cathars whilst also recognising the obvious cruelty of our own royal family in England. We enjoyed a very pleasant day. While she had a break, I decided to join two elderly ladies in the top higher heated pool. After a few minutes, the one lady gestured to me to eat? "Sorry, I'm English. I do not understand." She then leaned over to the fountain where the water was rushing in and drank from it. Drank from it? I'm trying to understand and from their gestures and the rubbing of their stomachs that it is good for your belly, your inner self. Her friend agreed with her. Gesturing, I pointed for her to have a drink. She did, leaning over a putting her head under the faucet. She drank from it and rubbed her belly. Well, I hadn't got a problem with my belly but thought, oh well, let's give it a go. Whether those women were serious or not, I don't know. Had they really drunk the water? So over I goes, and like the proverbial idiot, I take a sip. Thankfully only a taste. It was disgusting. Water? Full of sulphur? I still don't know if they were having me on.

Inviting me to join her on the next sun lounger, Marie told me that she had three boys, two grandchildren, and was divorced. She had a boyfriend but didn't live with him and would never get married again. Kindly, Marie offered to give me a lift back to my camper as we had both decided to end our session at about the same time. I was extremely grateful. I just didn't fancy that hill climb back. In gratitude, I invited her for a coffee in the site bar afterwards. For three euros, I feel I got off cheap, Marie dropped me off right next to my camper, and after showing her around, we shook hands. She left, back to her clinic for further treatment. What a wonderful lady, kind, decent, friendly, intelligent, a nice conversationalist. I'm only sorry I never exchanged numbers, just as friends, but that's a difficult one.

Marie understood my dilemma immediately. Without knowing the history and with no written or printed guidance, I didn't know where to go next or the best places to go. The Cathar Castles or Chateau Cathars are very easy to understand, up to a point. However, they still don't tell you the essentials, the nitty-gritty. Only an experienced tour guide can tell you why that village is famous? The history of that village? Seriously, someone, someday, might have the brains to put together a history, in detail, of every place of interest around the world. Dead simple. You call into a country, you are given detailed information. You visit a town you are given more detailed information. Because I tell you, most of what I see is crap or useless.

Marie understood, but have you visited Targassonne? It is famous for its ice crystals that, over the years, have turned to stone? So ok, I put in my sat nav to Mont-Louis knowing it would take me through Targassonne. Up to and into Targassonne, I could see these interesting and majestic rocks, but was that it? A clump of rocks? And Targassonne? Sorry, so I drove on. Same for Mont-Louis, so my next port of call is Evol, a UNESCO recognised village in the Pyrenees, known for its beauty. But just before the turn off for Evol, I see the little village of Olette. Now, this looks interesting. Seeing a car park, I pull in quick, no charges, and pull over to the local bar café.

TAKING THE MOUNTAIN TRAIN ACROSS THE ALPS

The family who runs the bar are amazingly friendly and show a keen need to understand the questions I'm asking. What time do you close? I'm gagging for a drink, around 8 pm. Where can I park my camper? They pointed down by the train station. What time does the train arrive tomorrow? Don't know, sometime during the day, maybe five or seven times. My plan is to get the train somewhere on a return ticket getting a good look at the Alps, hopefully, in an open carriage on a nice sunny day.

After a couple of drinks and a very nice ham and tomato baguette, at six euros, I thought was good value (I'm getting brainwashed into the higher prices here.), I left for my van and had an early night. I didn't want to get up too early for the train, but I didn't want to leave it too late either. In any event, I was up for 9am. It took me a bit to ascertain that the train was arriving at 10:15. The people in the bar told me that normally you get on the train and the ticket collector comes and takes your money. As the ticket office was closed, that seemed logical. The train came in on time, the little yellow tourist train, three carriages were closed, two open. Naturally, I jumped into the open carriage. Well, there is no point in locking yourself away in the carriage when the sun is beating down and you're being taken through the Pyrenees. Oh no. On cue, the ticket collector came over, and as a way of explanation, I pulled out my map. I wanted to go as far as

Bourg-Madame. I was on the wrong train. This train only went to Mont-Louis. Confused and embarrassed, I got off only to realise within seconds that Mont-Louis would have suited me. I only wanted to have a tour of the Alps by train. After some effort, I discovered that the next train, the collector had mentioned, was at 10:30. Wrong advice. It was 11:15. At 11am, a smartly dressed couple approached and asked when the next train was due, well tried to, but as soon as they realised I was English, they both started talking in perfect English. As I explained it was due in at 11:15, we started chatting. They were French, from Paris, Parisians, the city of sophistication. They were a very nice couple, and we chatted on a whole variety of subjects, from the state of Brexit to Covid, to the threat of the Chinese.

"Hmmm, what do you do?"

"I'm a journalist," he replied.

"Ahh, you're just the guy I need, someone to help promote my books. I was on a loser there."

He agreed with me when I explained how I had set out to write my books without realising that thousands of books were being printed every day, new books, new authors. He didn't help my confidence too much. He himself had written a couple of books, bound to, he's a journalist. One on the subject of the middle east. He was somewhat of an expert on the subject and another on the Muslim population. In the meantime, his wife was on the phone with someone and informed us that the train was 45 minutes late. The journalist from Paris then took the opportunity to tell me in great detail what he thought the Palestinian/Israel conflict was all about and how the Jews, given the past history, felt that they were always being persecuted. Without a doubt, the guy was very knowledgeable but seeing his wife edging away a bit, I think she was getting a bit bored.

Eventually, the train turned up, and in a rush to get on, we both got into separate compartments. This time, no doubt because it's later, the train was jam-packed, I had no choice but to sit inside. Oh well. Probably just as well we separated. He had quite strong views on Brexit and felt in the current circumstances and potential threats coming in from other parts of the world, we needed to stick together in Europe. While I agreed in principle, I didn't think we had to be in a dictatorship, which is what I saw it had become with all of us losing our identities. That started him off again then about what is our identity. He was a strong believer in the fact that we are all the same under our skin colour. He had spoken to all kinds of people of colour in London who spoke perfect English. Of course, I was glad to get on the train.

Sitting down in the carriage, I was glad to rest my weary legs after standing about for nigh on two hours, but as the train set off, I noticed the odd passenger get up and stand on the small platform outside. As soon as I saw the opportunity, I went out. Logically there was only room for about two passengers. In the event, five came out in all. The train was a small gauge electric train consisting of five carriages and two open decked sitting areas. I don't think the views were quite as stunning as the Bernina express that crosses the Alps in Switzerland, but we were in the height of the summer here.

Driving my camper, whilst enjoyable, means I miss out on seeing a lot as I have to concentrate on the road. As I said to my French friend, Marie, I could do with a tour guide to show me around France. I know I'm missing out on so much. The castles are fairly straightforward, with a bit of history in the guidebooks. But on the bigger picture, I'm stifled. I plan to visit the small village called Evol, a few miles from my little camping spot by the train station. It is described as the most attractive village in France. Now that's really going to be interesting. But it may turn out to be a damp squib.

The problem is without properly knowing beforehand makes it difficult to judge. Coming here to Ollete, I called into three little villages that looked very pretty and interesting. One, I could barely get in or turn around, never mind finding a parking space. It was also completely quiet and locked up. I would have felt like an intruder. Bolquere seemed a busy and thriving place. Even though it was out of season for skiing, it was not going to be my scene. The last, a village just before Ollete, looked very interesting and quite some size. At the first opportunity, I did an about-turn. The first road was a no entry. A half a mile further on, I came to the second road in. I had to do a very sharp U-turn to get into it. I hadn't gone very far before I realised my dilemma, this village was built before the car was thought of the roads were narrow and twisting, the houses built into the cliffs above and below me. I realised very quickly I had made a mistake. I decided to take the road ahead and get out. The road got narrower and narrower as the buildings on either side closed in on each other. My bottle was well and truly going. It took me a while to realise the road I was on was a one-way system exiting out where I had seen the no-entry signs. I didn't realize this for a bit as I was feeling like a nervous wreck driving under overhangs as well as keeping my eyes peeled on my mirrors, both sides barely missing the walls. Another car in front was blocking my access before the lady driver came out, saw me and got in to drive off. By the time I got out, I had to stop and take a picture just for the record of how narrow it was. The other added problem I was finding was that a lot of these villages, pretty and attractive as they are, are private residential places. They are not for the gawking tourist. The village of Arques, just along from Castle Arques, was a case in point. It had no café bar, no shops to speak of, just the one patisserie, and that was closed. When I enquired at the castle if there were any shops? No. Was there a cash machine? No. Where on earth do people do their shopping then? The next town. Well, if it's the one I hit next, it was about six miles away. If I had stopped to look around, what would I be seeing?

The idea of the train and the sights was to give me an overall impression of the towns and villages we were passing through and to enjoy the scenery. The Parisian couple were on a three-week break. Having gotten the car to a nearby town and rented a house, they got a hire car and were touring the area. They were as new to it as I was. They were going to Mont-Louis about seven stops along and a third of the way to the final destination. This was simply and specifically a tourist train. I didn't know where I was going, I didn't care, anywhere will do that I can return from. The journey gave me a good opportunity to see the surrounding towns and villages across the valley. We saw beautiful log cabins, chalets with grass roofs between the mountains, small farms, and Swiss-style chalets. Beautiful and diverse. I also saw some of the Aires, dozens of them indicated on the map. From the train, I could see many were in beautiful scenic positions. I made a mental note to remember where they were, right within visual range of the train.

Thankfully, most of the passengers got off at Mont-Louis, leaving the open carriages almost empty. Everyone's cameras were clicking like lunatics at every photo opportunity. By the time I got back, my phone was flat. I was quite happy to get to Bourg-Madame. The final destination was two stops further on at Enveitg, that's when the train came to a dead end. It was now past two o clock, and when I enquired with the ticket collector, the same train would be leaving on the return journey at ten past three. I had an hour to look around, barely having a coffee at the little café bar next to the station. Reaching it, I could see many of the passengers had the same idea, most having a snack or a meal, I decided to follow suit.

The staff were well geared up and utterly efficient. This was their main source of income, I guessed, so when that train came in, they ran around very quickly and efficiently to make sure everyone was fed and watered. I was impressed. Also, at how friendly they were and at how reasonable the prices were, pitched just right, I'd guess. I just about had enough time to eat and pay for my meal before getting back on the train with five minutes to go.

I wasn't looking forward to the return trip too much. It was quite lengthy and having gotten up early, I was a bit tired. But in actual fact, it wasn't so bad. For one reason or another, most of the return stations were missed out. I estimated the train was travelling at about 20mph, so our journey was probably longer than 30 miles, even allowing for the few stops. It took over two hours to get back.

Getting off the train in front of me at Ollete was the Parisian couple all smiley and happy. Greeting them, I expressed my surprise, expecting never to see them again and assuming they would be much later. They had enjoyed their day, and following me round to my camper, we wished each other a continued happy holiday and said our goodbyes. It's nice to find and say hello to such a diverse variety of people from around the world. Tomorrow I shall be visiting the prettiest little village in France, Evol, and after that, or in the meantime, I'm going to re-evaluate some of my next destinations.

After some six weeks in France, I'm chuffed to note my leisure and main batteries are keeping well topped up. My 100w on the roof has been doing its job now for over two years. The main battery had then become of concern. Hindsight is a wonderful thing. I forever have hindsight. With hindsight, I should have had a 200w installed and feeding the main battery also, that would completely put my mind at ease, but ignorance is bliss. It was in Bulgaria that the first benefits of the rooftop solar panel came into their own. Checking my instrument panels every day, I was pleased to note the leisure battery was well topped up. But my anxiety then transferred to my main battery. I had found a very nice hotel that I had parked next to in order to get internet. Within five minutes, security was out to tell me I couldn't park there. But I have just bought Wi-Fi connection.

"Ahh. You are a guest in a hotel?"

"Well, I couldn't blatantly lie, well...."

"Ahh, you have friends in the hotel?"

"Yes."

"Well, that is no problem." He then took me around to the land to side of the obviously owned hotel and told me to park there for as long as I liked using the hotel facilities. Well, I did, and I did. It was brilliant.

But after every couple of days, I was becoming paranoid about my main battery. If I disconnected it, then my alarm and locking system didn't work. So, after every two or three days, I would have to take it for a run, topping my water up as well. It was the only downside. I was getting up in the morning, going into the hotel. I used the toilet and washroom facilities and then spent the day around the pool, getting the rays on my little body. I bought a 20ah trickle charger solar panel with four suction pads that could attach to the windscreen. This I found was fine if the sun was shining, not so good on a miserable day. Most days in England were miserable. Here in France, every day was a sunny day. It was working well. When I get back home, I will consider getting another 100w and a direct feed also to my main battery. The confidence it gives me is unbelievable. Even more so now that I was spending more and more time touring. Whilst I was lucky that I had a nice house in a nice area, I couldn't anticipate living full time in a camper, no matter how luxurious. Course, the downside to that is the more luxurious the motorhome, the more expensive the maintenance costs etc. No, I was more than happy with my Cheyenne Autotrail. As Bet, and I found, it was plenty big enough (for two). Whilst it was a six berth and great to have the kids for the occasional break, two could live comfortably. The length was right, the height manageable. Until I came to some of those low cut ceilings. Mind, I have seen people with bigger vans and the problems they encounter getting into sites or narrow passages. As for the small transit-type campers with the pop-up roofs, I just can't get my head around them. We had seen them on sites struggling to keep occupied. If the weather is rough, we've seen them huddled up at night playing cards around the little table, passing the hours until bedtime. In the morning, we've seen them sit outside in crappy weather, heavy-duty coats on, drinking a cup of tea. As a teenager with a constant supply of nice female nubile bodies, great. Once a certain age is reached, it's about comfort. Well, I've reached that certain age and I like my comfort.

The other downside is the price you pay for them being, in the main, custom-made and the facilities. No toilet, maybe a sink. Some of the horror stories I've read don't bear thinking about. In the country, you have to think about digging a hole maybe. Yet all I hear them boasting about is, "ahh, but we can get in under height barriers you can't." Oh, yippee do. No, ok, it's everyone to their own, and it's what suits us as individuals. We considered the bigger Chieftain, but we didn't think it was worth it for the extra six feet or so. Everything inside was just stretched a little bit longer. No, I feel we made the right choice. Even now, on my own, I'm content with it. One short term lady friend tried to get me to change it for a different model, but I guessed that was because she knew it was my wife's camper as well. But she was short term.

MORE MEDIEVAL VILLAGES AND THE LAKES

All I had read was that Evol, in the commune of Olette, was voted the prettiest looking village in France. Well, France is a big place, and there are a lot of medieval villages. I had thought Lagrasse had been voted the best looking medieval village. But then, I'm a bit of a cynic. At any rate, I set off for the village of Evol. But not before filling my water tank from the free tap inside the station. If there is one thing there is no shortage of here in the Alps, it's water. Evol was only a short drive of some two and a half miles, but unexpectedly it was all uphill with some very narrow and tight bends. I just hoped it was worth it. Evol was to the side of the mountain road, and the road into it was just far too narrow for me to risk it. Again, this village was built before the car was thought of. Probably the horse and cart too. Driving on, I saw a car park to the left, but that looked a little too full. It was only as I drove past, I noticed there was a spot, but I couldn't turn around. Further on was another car park. Turning around in it, I returned to the first one and got in the very end.

Walking along to the small road turning off into the village, I wasn't overwhelmed. My first thought was, why on earth doesn't a small village like this have a little café bar? The village was pretty, in a medieval way, the houses very individual and higgledy-piggledy. Halfway up the hill, I noticed a chap sitting on a small wall. In front of him and to the right was a little shop/bar of some kind. A short walk further on, the road levelled out and opened up to a fair-sized seating area with a group of people sitting eating a meal, perhaps family. I asked the guy on the wall where he had got his beer, and he pointed to the small doorway I had passed. Just then, the owner came out and asked what I wanted. Not being really hungry, I just asked for a drink, directing me to the bar. She appeared a few minutes later and gave me a carafe of water, how much? Free. In truth, I could see why, water was coming out of every pore and orifice. There were taps dotted about with no regulator, a watercourse to the side of the road was gushing with water from the mountains. No one here would die of thirst. I felt a bit guilty drinking free water, what with all this Covid and pandemic going on, so I ordered a coke, paying her three euros. Outside, the guy on the wall started chatting as soon as he realised I was English. His first thought was to ask if I understood the menu? "No." He explained it was all salad with jambon, which is ham, or salad with cheese. I asked if she could do a nice jambon and tomato sandwich, but basically, I got the drift from her that it was the meals as of the menu or nothing, said with a smile, of course. Feeling petty, I decided to have what the French guy was having, jambon with salad, though I would have preferred cheese. Now maybe I am a cheapskate, I certainly don't like paying through the nose for something, but I had seen prices of 14 and 15 euros on the menu board. Now whichever way you turn it around the way the pound is to the euro, I put it on level pegging. So, to me, that's 14 quid. Oh well, I give up. I'm just going to go with the flow. The village was lovely, the ambience was even lovelier.

The proprietor, waitress, whatever, was a cheerful and attractive soul named Audrey. She knew her business, she was very friendly and efficient. I was to see how efficient later. Sitting myself down at an outside table, Audrey soon came out with a table mat and a knife and fork. A few minutes later, she reappeared with my meal, jambon and salad. Straight away,

I noticed the plate was full, salad buffs up really big on a plate, the ham or jambon wasn't in slices or laid flat, which I consider the normal way. No, it was bulked up loosely to make it look bigger. Difficult to figure out what actually was on the plate. I wasn't particularly hungry, but I had to eat the bread to fill me up. But fair play to the girl. I could see what the method was. The menu had all of three choices, one jambon, one cheese, and another I didn't get round to figuring out, all with salad. It would take her minutes to prepare and serve up on a plate. Normally this is served up as a starter, entrée, for about six or seven euros, even at decent restaurants. When I went in to pay my bill, she hit me with a big smile and 17 euros. I just about had enough to pay her. Only as I walked out, I realised she had charged me for the drink I had already had. And paid for, I recon, up and running, that girl does a good little trade there. The French man, his wife and two kids had a meal. I wonder if he queried the bill? No, I reckon those French are used to paying the prices. Sometimes you have to take a Loss. I continued up into the village and past the medieval church and the chateau, seeing what looked like a hotel boarding house with tables and benches outside. I could imagine under normal circumstances, this little village could make a very nice living for one or two people. The track led onwards and eventually back onto the little mountain road where my camper was. After a quick mental debate, I carried on instead of returning through the village. It was a pleasant and enjoyable experience. Certainly, I could have spent a lot longer. Reaching my motorhome, I saw the Frenchman and his wife and kids heading for his car next to mine. Saying our goodbyes, we both departed.

To be or not to be, as Shakespeare said. To have a guide or not have a guide, that is the question. Once on a cruise and stay in Egypt, Bet and I were treated to a few inclusive guided tours around the valley of the tombs and Luxor, including one to the obelisk, Cleopatra's Needle. This was below the Aswan dam. If anyone ever goes to Egypt and visits it, you will see we were guided to what seemed like a cut-down mountain, with its rim maybe some 20ft above ground level. Without the tourist guide explaining, none of us would have had a clue. The engineers of the day had picked the mountain as a suitable source for an obelisk. Putting the men to work, they chopped down the mountain using the blocks for other building work. Eventually, they reached the required base of about 100ft in diameter. They started cutting down until they got the shape of the obelisk. They had cut it out right to the base, even boring holes every foot or so before realising that finishing the obelisk was a no go because it had a fracture in it. To release the obelisk from the floor, they inserted dried hemp into the bored holes and then flooded the canyon. Nature would have then finished the work and cracked the structure releasing it from the floor. The next step is to get it on rollers (don't ask me how), chop down the sidewall of the remaining mountain and simply roll it out to a waiting barge. But where was the Nile? It was half a mile away. Well, originally, the Nile came within feet of the mountain, but the dam had diverted it, all very simple, really. None of us would have a clue without the guide, which was my dilemma.

The guide books were quite limited at each place I visited, and mostly in French. You can pull up to a beauty spot, Aire, or picnic area overlooking some mountains, and the board will tell you it was a sacred mountain to the Catalan people etc. Now that's great and very informative, but when you reach a small town or village, the tourist office is either closed or has scant information. Gruissan was a case in point. Gruissan was a beautiful harbour town and resort with a very interesting medieval village, including the chateau. Yet, the tourist office had no information in English.

My internet was limited. Ok, the little village of Evol was self-explanatory, but I knew nothing of the chateau. If I had,

I might have visited it. Now, leaving Evol, I was looking at the map and more or less taking pot luck. Which, of course, in itself is part of the excitement. This part of the country was very exciting and had so much to offer, you could almost stick a pin in the map and say, let's try there, which of course I was doing. I was in the Parc Naturel Regional des Pyrenees Catalans as I left Evol, turning right and following the route of the little yellow tourist train as I headed for one of the first of many lakes in the Pyrenees Lac De Matemale. Well, who knew that the Pyrenees had lakes? The Pyrenees are mountains. You can't have lakes in the mountains. How ridiculous. But there are, and to my amazement, some you can swim in. I wanted to see and try a few. To the left are the swimming pool and sulphur springs of Saint Thomas Les-Bains. Those were for later, according to what was around the corner.

Around the corner with some 6 miles to go were the lakes, but turning the bend in the road, I saw a whole host of activity cars, people pulling in or milling around then I saw it, a great big imposing building set back from the road. Thankfully the French must have anticipated this and put an ample slipway into place before the main road in. I had enough time to pull in sharpish and turn into the car park that led on and on to an Aire with a few camper vans in, now this looked interesting. It was the citadel of Mont-Louis. I had been made aware of it, and it was on my list to visit Mont- Louis anyway, but I didn't expect it to hit me in the face so quickly. Following the request of King Louis XIV in 1679, a guy named Vauban, who was a minor royal and the superintendent of fortifications, conceived of the plan. Spain had recently handed back some of its French lands, but in doing so, the King had to marry the daughter of Phillip IV. At first, King Louis wasn't interested but quickly realised the importance of a military stronghold. Vauban was the man. Vauban saw some places near the border towards Bourg-Madame. But it was on his return from Perpignan that he stopped in the small hamlet of Ovenca. It was from there that he saw the hill of the future, Mont-Louis, which allowed easy access for all materials. The only problem being labour. But Vauban solved that. It was in a time of peace, and King Louis had the biggest army in Europe. They will serve as the workers, dead simple. The work was completed in the main 29 months after starting. There were 37,000 soldiers and workers, stone cutters, masons, carpenters, blacksmiths. He couldn't go wrong. It was France's last southern military border with Spain, the city was buried in the ground, and outside only small sections of the wall were built behind the drawbridge. The tunnel is closed by a series of heavy doors. It was also protected on three sides by the mountains.

The citadel is a city within a city with its own church shops and hotels. It was planned to accommodate 2500 men in the 17t century, but it has never had more than 500 inhabitants over time. Today, the second section of the battlements or citadel still acts as a military base for the first regiment shock for the national centre of training commandos. The main entrance is on the road leading to Lac De Matemale. It was a fascinating place to visit. Beneath the ramparts and through the archways carrying the main traffic into the battlements was the Aires. What a fascinating place to spend the night. After a quick little tour around Mont-Louis, I drove into the Aire for the rest of the day and night, having a little walk around the citadel and up to the barracks. My plan is to enjoy another little tour on the morrow, maybe have lunch as well. Settling in for the night, I noticed an official-looking guy outside scribbling notes on his clipboard and taking details of the van next door. It wasn't long before he knocked on my door asking for 7 euros for the night. 7 euros is a fair price. I just wish they had put it up more clearly on a sign somewhere. The next morning coming out of the citadel after a nice coffee, I returned to my camper via the stone stairs on the other side of the bridge, the entrance side. There in front of me, that any idiot could see, was a big enough sign about two-foot square, setting out the price. From May to September, it was free, gratis, between 6am and 6 pm, after 6pm it was 7 euros a night. I could kick myself for not seeing the sign, and very generous it was too, I thought. I might stop a couple of nights.

With my wife, Bet it was quite easy and straightforward. Florida? Fine. How about Morocco, she loved it, we went a few times in our motorhome we would just say where shall we go? Spain, Portugal? Then off we would go. We never really had any arguments because Bet hated confrontation. But now, I realise what a beautiful shrewd woman she was. Today I don't think I will meet anyone as compatible. I think this will apply to most married couples. I like to think so anyway. Today I wonder if many marriages are like battlegrounds, what with all these equal rights. Val, the alcoholic, was a fairly intelligent girl, quite knowledgeable about France. When we visited, I bowed down to her superior knowledge. But many other things were a battleground. All of six stone, ringing wet, it felt like she always had to argue about something, maybe it was from her marriage, maybe that's why her husband had run out for another woman after twenty-five years, but if you said the wrong thing, she would jump on you to show you how intelligent she was. Fine and great, but not in a relationship. For Christ's sake, I don't know how people can live within a volatile marriage, fighting and arguing every day.

Touring in a camper or motorhome is all about enjoying the journey and scenery. Touring is all about the comfort, joy, and ambience of sharing. Until that right person comes along, I shall remain content in my own company and the memories I shared with my wife. Being on my own means, I can live as expensively or cheaply as I wish. This will no doubt be equally true to anyone with a camper. I can afford to eat out every night. That is the comfort blanket I have around me, but having come from nothing and having had nothing, I tend to treat money with a bit of respect. I suspect a few others do. Many more don't.

THE PYRENEES SULPHUR SPRINGS AND LAKES

I don't normally eat early anyway, but about lunchtime, I had decided to go up into the citadel and have a coffee and maybe a bite to eat. Having the coffee first, I had a bit of a walk around before seeing a small shop. I got a tin of old oak ham and sought out a nice bottle of wine, then a baguette and two tomatoes. Excluding the wine, I think it came to all of two euros. Back to the camper, and I had a really nice ham and tomato baguette. I couldn't have wished or asked for anything more. I wasn't cheap skating. I was eating exactly what I wanted, such as the beauty of camping. I suspect many other couples in campers or motor homers live the same way. Each and every one will have their own methods and budgets that they work on. Judging by the number of solar panels on the roofs of motor homes around me, I suspect they are all seasoned travellers.

Ok, so where shall I go today? First, I wanted to go to the little yellow train station at La Cabanasse just down the road. Did I see the Aires there? So off I go. No, it's not that one, although there were campers at the station. It must have been planes, but no Aires are showing on the map, ok, let's try it. Off I trot, but before I know it, up pops the sign of saint Thomas Les Baines, the Sulphur Springs with the swimming pool as well. I do a sharp right turn, but after ten minutes wondering if I'm on the right road, the road leads first downhill until I come to a fork in the road, campsite to the left, a little sign pointing to Saint Thomas Les Baines, besides the wording a little figure that looked like an umbrella, or by a stretch of the imagination, could be a spring. It was pointing uphill and into the mountains. Ok, first gear all the way up into the mountains on a single track road. More edge of my pants driving, overhanging rocks to the right mountain chasms and gorges to the left with a nice steep drop to the bottom. I was silently screaming that no one was coming the other way. If they did, someone would have to backpedal. It was not going to be me. After nearly a mile and a half, I reached it. I think a little crappy car park opened up before me, and a young couple were getting out of their car. Bonsoir? Sulphur springs? Swimming? Yes, 300 meters ahead, the top car park is full, full? But the single line track is empty? And there is only one way in, oh well, getting to Saint Thomas, it all started to open out before me.

Saint Thomas Les Baines was amazing, I've been to a few swimming pools in my life, but Saint Thomas Les Baines is out of this world. The sulphur springs of Saint Thomas Les Baines is a natural phenomenon that occurred 500 meters upstream from the hamlet of Saint Thomas, three sodium sulphur springs at an altitude of 1,300meters, almost a mile sprang up in the wild the villagers were the only ones who knew about the springs and used it up until the 19th century. From then on, when it became more widely known, people used to travel to Fontpedrouse by stagecoach, then walk the rest of the way by foot for the cure. The automobile and yellow train added to the boom. The Fontpedrouse Municipality then bought the bathhouse and opened it up to the general public, making it accessible to everyone.

In the 1990s, three organisations got together. The baths of Lio, Dorres and Saint Thomas are located in the heart of the regional natural park. They decided to put these benefits within reach of everyone. The hot sulphurous springs that come from the Pyrenees' depths along faults have beneficial healing qualities and have been used for ages, traditionally for respiratory diseases, rheumatic or muscle pains, and skin and hair care. The place was packed, well it was a Saturday, but it also explained why the road was empty. Most French people treated this as a day out, spending the whole day bringing drinks and food in to eat. It was slightly dearer than Dorres, at 7 euros, but who can complain. I had forgotten my mask, so I was hit for 50p. Utterly ridiculous because as soon as you got through reception, you could take your mask off and get into the three pools with everyone else breathing our germs and Covid over each other. The other thing was shorts were not allowed, so I had to pay another 1.50 euros for a very nice pair of trunks, 9 euros in all. But the experience was delightful, and I would recommend them to anyone.

I personally think the French are still trying to keep it to themselves. Buried deep in the Alps, the Germans would never have found it. I had a job. It's like once you get in, you can't get out. Seating has been set into the mountains like a circular roman amphitheatre looking over the three pools. It was brilliant and well worth the money. After a few hours, I set off back to Mont-Louis, a drink in the citadel and the comfort of the night within the walls of the battlements. Tomorrow, maybe, up in the lakes. There were another three more lakes within the area of Lac de Matemale, Lac Des Bouillouses and the Etang Du Lanoux. I was feeling in the mood to have a pop at all three.

LES ANGLES AND
THE SKI SLOPES

Les Angles took me completely by surprise. My first intention and aim were for Lac des Bouillouses, which was to the south of Lac de Matemale. I had tried visiting Lac de Matemale a couple of days previously, but I think I had approached it from the wrong side. Beautiful as it was, I couldn't see a way down to the shore or lakeside. I then decided to visit Lac Dec Bouillouses, but I could only see to get to that from Les Angles. Setting off, I duly put Les Angles into my trusty little pal, Tom-Tom, and set off.

Les Angles was 8 miles further up into the Pyrenees, more climbing. Again, it was a quiet and pleasant drive. Being a Sunday, I think all the tourists were hitting Mont-Louis as I was leaving. The roads up into the Pyrenees were almost empty. Some four miles out of Monte-Louis, I saw a turning to the left for Lac Des Bouillouses. Doing an about-turn quick sharpish, I followed it. After a few miles, mysteriously, I came to a dead-end. One road was a no entry. The other was barricaded off. Seeing a sign for a campsite past the no entry sign, I decided to do an about-turn and try Les Angles again. There might be a turn off from there. Pulling into Les Angles was a bit of a jaw-dropper, to say the least. From the map, I could see it was a ski resort, also that it had an Aire's campsite. But as the town came into sight, the first thing to hit me was the circus tent animals and lorries on the car park to the side. Three other motorhomes were already parked up and settled in, the one driver giving me a friendly smile. Pulling in behind the lorries, I backed up to one of the motorhomes, settled in and turned the engine off. I knew immediately this was more than a one-day stopover.

I had called into a few ski resorts in the Pyrenees (there are a few ski resorts in the Pyrenees). I had called into Bolquere with the intent of maybe spending a couple of days. Still, after looking around, I found it totally uninviting, except for the skiing, of course. Still, there were none about it. It is the height of summer, all the hotels bar the odd one was closed up along with all the apartments, French shutters closed tight, and guess what? There was no snow. On every available space was the big circular sign, a motorhome with a cross through it. Verboten. It had nothing to offer me anyway, nothing of interest. Making my way out, I called into the supermarket, bought a bit of food and carried on. Font-Romeu-Odeillo seemed the same. I'm not knocking these resorts. For the skier, they will probably provide everything that is needed another time. In my younger days with a nice income, it might have been different. But here in Les Angles, it immediately gave out a totally different vibe. It was pretty, attractive and nestled comfortably within the surrounding mountains and landscape, nestled in on three sides.

Just below and to my right was Lac de Matemale, with its stunning view to my right and in front of the many mountain tops and ski runs. This was definitely asking to be explored. Locking the camper up, I made sure I had my bank card with me. Normally, I only ever carry my credit card. I pay for all my fuel on my credit card as I think it gives me better security, in any event. Before I left England, I exchanged 700 pounds for euros. The girl behind the post office counter persuaded me to take out a post office cash card. What a con. I can't get a readout of my balance, and most places won't accept it. It may cost me more. I still can't figure it out, but I prefer to use my cash card as and when I need it. If I have a meal in a restaurant, sometimes I prefer to pay with a card. Today was Sunday. I had my baguette in the fridge for a meal, plus my trusty Fray Bentos pies. After being caught by the ticket collector for seven euros at Mont-Louis, I only had one euro left in my little purse. Here I knew that was not going to do me until tomorrow. Walking over to the circus first, I gathered the next show started at six. It was ten euros for the show, which I presumed included all the animals that were grazing in a paddock directly opposite me, horses, goats, camels and long-horned bulls. I got clicking away with my fingers on the trusty camera, seriously debating going in for a showing. Tomorrow night was the last night. Making my way into town, I could see, Covid or no Covid, life was still going on. A building to my right looked lively. Going in, it opened out to a great-looking little bar. Stairs leading off and down signalled a spa room. Outside, overlooking the lake, was a big Jacuzzi. As a family came walking out, I gave it my best bit of French. "Scuse-moi, is that the spa?" Straight away, they guessed I was English and spoke to me in English. Yes, it was a Jacuzzi and steam room. For 8 euros they felt it was good value for money. Yet another little potential. Further on, a little outdoor market selling bric-a-brac, antiques, and object de art took me by surprise. On one stall were five beautiful figurines of old French characters', officers, a napoleon type figure and a French lady, all in the 17th-century costume. Picking them up, I thought they were lovely. But I had no money. Carrying on, I came to the village. The village seemed to be the skiing resort accommodation, from hotels to apartments, to gites. It looked very quiet. Making my way back, exercise duties over, I was starting to feel a bit desperate. Didn't this town have any cash machines? Calling into the patisserie, I asked the girl behind the counter, "Bonjour, Madame, do you know where there is a cash machine?" That word is understood in any language. Pointing her arm down and to the right? "Closed Madame, kaput?" Laughing, she then used both arms to indicate, left?

Then, right? Then on the right? I got it, "merci beaucoup Madame." I'm getting good at this malarkey, alright.

Making my way back, finally, I saw a cash machine. It worked. I drew out some cash and made my way to the market. The figurines were still there. The kids might hate them, but I thought what a nice memory for them of France, where granddad had visited. Especially the Cathar castles and all the period evoked. The guy sitting on a stool behind the counter with his wife or daughter didn't look the happiest of people. Picking up a figurine, I said, "how much for all four?"

He clocked on straight away, "you English?"

"Si." Now I'm thinking maybe ten euros will be a bargain, but at first, I thought he indicated with his fingers twenty. Then maybe twenty-three. I'm just about to throw ten fingers at him to begin the negotiating, when he then jumps in with a three and a 0, meaning thirty. I hardly thought it was worth haggling. Yes, I would have gone to twenty, maybe. But I think he'd had a bad day, I think they all had. Oh well.

Flush with my newfound wealth, I called into one of the many bars and cafes along the street. It wasn't packed, so I didn't have to fight for a prime seat overlooking the mountains. Ordering an orange, I asked the young waiter when the season started, November he told me, ten feet of snow will sit on the mountains. Indicating the chair lifts at the bottom, I asked what was going on. I thought people were queuing for a cash machine. Les Angles catered for everyone. There was mountain biking, the spa and the Jacuzzi, then there was the mountain chair lift. I had seen someone hurtling down a slide at breakneck speed in what seemed like a toboggan. It was a toboggan. The waiter explained for 18 euros, you go up to the top of the mountain by chair lift and fly down on the toboggan. Well, I thought I would have a bit of that, but I will leave it until Monday and avoid the Sunday crush. I was beginning to love this little town. Mind, I was beginning to love a lot of these little French towns. How much could my little ticker take?

Going into the village and the tourist office, I asked if they had anything in English. No, if you come here, you almost have to speak French. The French are rigis in speaking their own language. Their attitude is, if you want to visit France, learn French. That is fine, but they even fill their tourist books with French. Where's the brains behind that? If I had a direct and exact itinerary of where I was going, what place, then maybe I could do some homework, but I just don't know where I'm going next. I almost feel like one of the early pioneers. Oh, ok, that's probably exaggerating a bit. But it's almost like trial and error. I have just seen the sign for an animal park, Le Park Animalier. I shall have a look at that. In the meantime, I went over to the ski lift booking office to book myself a chair lift to the top of the mountain and a toboggan run back down. I know I will regret not going for it. I left it until late for the crowds to die down before going over. Hitting the language barrier again, the girl behind the counter brought her colleague over who went to work on the mobile phone. Her English was worse than my French. I couldn't go up because it was too late. It closed at six, but it was only five? Yes, but at the top, there is a two-hour queue, ahh, now I understand. I'll give it a bash tomorrow. Walking back to the van and passing the circus, I decided to have another look. The booking office closed. How do we pay to get in? Earlier I saw another lady looking perplexed. But the side panel was open. Music was coming out, but it looked empty. Walking in, I had a look around. Yes, there were a couple of groups of kids there in the back seats, so I guessed the show was about to start. Walking back out, I again looked for the ticket office, closed. This time I noticed a fixed setup entrance tunnel into the circus. Walking in, and with no one around, I found myself a seat at the front. First up was a young girl doing a few gymnastic moves with a couple of hula hoops. She got a round of applause at each turn until I looked around and saw the average age was about seven. She then did a few turns with a hula hoop raised a few feet off the ground. More raptures applause. After that, Mickey Mouse came on, then Minnie mouse, she was followed by Donald duck. By now, I'm getting ready to slit my throat with boredom. None of this would have got past the first round of Britain's Got Talent. But maybe it's all the result of political correctness and the cruelty against animals brigade. I didn't expect the big top as we had back in the days when I visited the circus, but I did expect a bit better than this. I suppose the animals outside gave it away a bit. The kind you see on the local countryside campsite that keeps a few sheep, ducks and pigs to keep the kids entertained. But what about the gorilla? A big picture of him outside? I suspect it was Mickey Mouse in his next role. Next on was the little Shetland pony that I had seen in its enclosure. What a sad little fellow he was, head down trotting around the ring, the Ringmaster with his whip letting him get into his stride, then his female assistant came to the edge of the ring with a five-foot hoopla ring, moving around the ring, so we all got a look. He circled the ring raising his front feet on the stand in front of the audience, asking for applause. For one of the first times in my life, I felt sorry for the poor little guy. He didn't look happy at all, very sad, in fact. I suppose like us, he's got to earn his crust of bread and chunk of hay. After all, he only had to perform for a few minutes, maybe twice a day. I suppose he was a reluctant little film star. Well, star, circus star. After another ten minutes, I decided I couldn't take any more. The sun was still shining. I'd got a nice couple of chicken legs in the fridge and a bottle of merlot to go with it. Another day awaits. I wouldn't recommend it, but quite a few times, I felt so secure I didn't even lock up at night. I've just got to make sure it doesn't become a habit.

Last night my inverter packed up. What should I expect? It's a Chinese make off eBay, 2500 watts. A bit over the top, I think, but my 300 watt wasn't much use. And I felt for some 25 pounds it was worth the risk, with two plug sockets and four USB points, I thought it might be too good to be true. But it worked a treat until last night. I guessed it was to do with the Sargent control box. The guy who fitted my solar panel suggested bringing the power in through the control panel. After taking it all apart, he realised he couldn't. In doing so, he buggered my control panel. In the end, I had to send it back to Sargent to be returned. Now, whoever I got to fit it back didn't set the plugs in securely enough. Through trial and error, I discovered that by unscrewing the panel underneath and wiggling the cables, it would come back on. The only problem was I just wasn't sure which cable was to the lighter socket. Last night I wiggled what I thought was the lighter socket plug only to find it popped out completely. Now I'm really in it. I've got no power inverter or phone charger. Worse, it seemed the plug was the main power source for my control panel. Now I had nothing, no lights, no water, nothing. Having drunk a few glasses of wine, I didn't fancy attempting to try anything, so I left it until in the morning. Psyching myself up for it, I had either got to find an electrical engineer or attempt it myself. Anyone with experience of the Sargent panels will know how difficult it is. To me, it's frightening.

First, I had to unscrew the Sargent panel, then lift it up high enough to get underneath and push the plug back in. It was almost an impossibility with my chunky hands and fat fingers, all whilst trying not to pull the other plugs out by a miracle. I don't know how, but I did it. That's when I discovered the plug was not to the lighter socket at all, just the control panel. I found the lighter socket plug was another one. Trying to push that in further did the trick. I now had the power all around. Switching my inverter on and plugging my laptop in produced a fairly loud screaming sound. That's it, kaput. The USB chargers worked but not the plug sockets. I was still in the doodah. I decided I had to carry on with my plans for the next couple of days at least whilst keeping a thought on finding a new inverter from somewhere. To those new to motorhoming (and we all start off the same), all these little trials are sent to test us. It would be great to carry a little magic wand, but in truth, it's all really a case of suck it and see. Nothing in any of the guidebooks or instructions could tell me how to rectify the above faults. All I could do was make things good on the hoof and get an expert once I got home. I don't see it as a major job, more that I am not an electrical engineer.

I was steadily starting to formulate my short-term plans to visit Lac Balcere, Lac des Bouillouses, maybe spend a few days then call down to the Dorres sulphur baths and spend a few days there before making my way steadily down to Spain, maybe via Andorra. I had seen the sign for the Balcere lakes, and whilst it didn't look anything like the size of the other two lakes, I felt it was worth a visit. It's one of those places or situations you can very easily decide to give a miss. I had seen a sign for a restaurant in the guidebook but hadn't a clue what to expect. Following the signs that I had seen earlier, I just followed the mountain road up, higher and higher, much more of this, and I will be perched on the mountain top. Seeing two camper vans pulled in off the side of the road, I turned in to ask the lady outside the bigger camper where the Lac (Lake) was. As I pulled in, she came out waving her hands frantically. Obviously, she didn't want me spoiling her view, which was fabulous overlooking Lac De Matemale. She gave me the directions to Lac Balcere, which was just further along, though she pointed out it was only a single narrow track, at this stage, I was not going to turn back. Surprisingly the lady was all alone and on her own. Bravo for her, I say.

Driving on, I found she was wrong about the track. Yes, it was a single track, but there were plenty of pull-ins. I reached a camping car parking zone buried deep in the Pyrenees Forest in just a short time. I mentally noted it as a great place to spend the night. There were plenty on it. Further forward was banned for campers. The lake was some 100 yards further on. Another fifty yards brought me to another car park, just for cars. Fifty yards further on brought me to the lake. As the land opened out in front of me, I was stunned by its sheer raw natural beauty. Ahead of me and facing the lake was the restaurant. Well, it was more like an upmarket café really but spread across two areas it looked very colourful and inviting, flags and bunting flying in the breeze. One section was undercover, the other section outside, the smell of barbeque smoke wafted over the whole area as the food was being cooked on a B.B.Q. It was brilliant, but first a walk around.

Lac is a lake I know, and I've seen a lot of lakes. We have three lakes in Sutton Park, where I live, but this lake was something else. It was absolutely stunning, beautiful, and so peaceful. The peace emanated from it. Lake Matemale below was very nice, beautiful with a nice view, this lake was far more. The lake seemed empty, yet there were dozens of people, hikers, families, just walking about. Fishermen were dotted around. I don't think they were really there to catch fish. That was just the excuse. They were there to just enjoy and soak up the peace and serenity. Many were with their wife's just enjoying the day. If anyone spoke, it was in whispers, everyone too awestruck to speak loudly for fear of spoiling the atmosphere. I was so in awe I had to keep sitting down. We were almost at the top of the mountain. Even though I could have a bash at climbing to the top, we were at some 1756 meters. Mountains were surrounding the lake, trees densely covering the mountains down to the water's edge. Calling back to the restaurant, I was out of luck for an outside table. Sulking a bit, I ordered a jambon salad. Sitting at a table overlooking the lake, I was in my oil tot. It was so beautiful, calming, peaceful. My only immediate regret was the thought of how much I knew my wife Bet would have loved it. It just wasn't the same without her.

My fellow hikers, walkers sightseers, were all French. One couple I spoke to from Perpignan. There were hiking trails signed all over the mountain. Small hikes to major walking hikes over the mountains. Finishing my salad and cup of orange, all in plastic cups and plates, I decided to make my way back to my camper and then back to the lady's camper and the other and squeeze myself in between so I could enjoy the views also. But first, I saw the little sign, Tour de Lac. I thought I was having a bit of that. The walk around the lake was possibly half a mile or so, steady and exhilarating. I'd got the wrong footwear on, for starters, sandals instead of my hiking boots. Well, I didn't expect to be doing any hiking. The sun was shining, and the lake was flat placid. Passing a couple of fishermen and their wives, I asked the one elderly couple if they had caught anything, pointing he knew what I was saying, no, no fish, I don't think they looked too bothered. I kept stopping to sit on a log or a rock to have a rest and take in the scenery. I still don't know which reason it was. I didn't care.

I had taken a picture from the café of a building halfway up the mountain on the other side of the lake. I assumed it was a house and wondered how nice it would be to live there. When I reached it, I realised it wasn't a house but a travellers/pilgrims rest hut. Concrete built, it consisted of two separate rooms containing a fire, a table and bench for sitting and a double bed. Presumably, only couples come up in the mountains to climb. I had heard about these mountain rescue huts, now seeing one brings them more to life. Getting back to the café, I noticed it had emptied out a bit, as had the car parks. Looking up at the clouds, I could imagine why. The thunder started slowly and quietly. By the time I found a water supply, it was belting it down, my shirt was soaking wet within seconds. Well, it was due for a wash. Getting back to the two campers, they were not happy to see me or have me share their little pitch. There was plenty of room for me, but their attitude was threes a crowd. I crossed over the road in front of them to the local picnic spot and pulled in. As I did, the heavens really opened up. I hadn't heard thunder like it since I was up in the Greek Albanian mountains.

Marie, the lady in the Dorres sulphur baths who I befriended, had spent time in London as part of her job running a restaurant. She felt that all English people disliked the French. I could see she meant it too. I hoped I had put her mind at rest when I made it very clear that that was not the case, but it did make me wonder. Growing up, I got used to this dislike of the French but dismissed it as not very friendly banter. Even the papers have had a pop at them for years. We grew up calling them froggies because of their fondness for the little croakers. In return, they call us the 'beouf eaters' for our liking of roast beef. The first time I drove into France, I thought it was an unappealing country, apart from Paris. But over the few years I have had the pleasure of visiting France, I never fail to be impressed with how friendly they are. They have a very relaxed and laid back way of looking at things. Yet, I have noticed on various Facebook camping sites I'm on, whenever someone asks a question about France, whether it be touring or camping, those little voices keep coming out in unison. Watch it, those French are horrible, the police worse, they hate us Brits, even to lying in wait inside roads ready to bash us with a heavy cash fine for doing three miles over the limit. Well, maybe I've been extremely lucky.

Whilst trying to find the Lac des Bouillouses. I came across a large car park in the middle of nowhere, pulling in to get my bearings. Twice my sat nav had told me to turn right across a dirt track, and ignoring it, I found my distance had shot from 11km to 17km. Obviously, I should have followed my sat nav and crossed the fields. There were a lot of cars in the car park but no people, just a few buildings. After a short nap, well, I had had another hike around Lake Balcere, I decided to get out and have a little nose. Nothing. Seeing skiing signs, I guessed there were more hikers trails about. There were hiking trails all over the place. By one noticeboard and looking a bit lost was a Frenchman, "bonjour monsieur. Do you understand a bit of English?"

"Yes, a bit."

It took me another five seconds before, "hang on, you are English? You sound very posh. Whereabouts do you come from?" He had that southern accent. The rather tall guy with the posh voice said, "well, I come from Geneva, but I've bought a place in France." After telling me, he had pulled up for the very same reason as me. He wondered what was going on, he started to extol the virtues of living in France and what it had to offer. We were both talking about what France had to offer compared with England. The weather, for starters. When I mentioned the comments by another Englishman I had spoken to a couple of years earlier, who compared it to England of the fifties, that excited my newfound friend completely.

"That's exactly right," he said, "it's very laid back. The French have an easy-going lifestyle and attitude." Well, there is a little matter of size and numbers. France is twice the size of England with fewer numbers, we can barely breathe in England, but the gist is the same. Here in France, it's a pleasure to drive on the roads and the Aires. While being respectful, of course, it seems the attitude to the camper van is totally different.

Yesterday I went for another walk around the beautiful lake Belcere. After two stroppy motor homeowners refused to share their little plot of land with me, I decided to get a tank full of water and parked up directly in front of them. But across the road, at a picnic area directly overlooking Lac Matemale. A very nice sleep I had too, until, enjoying my second cup of coffee, I heard the bus pull up behind me. It was the bus driver, "bonjour, you cannot park here. It is a bus stop." He was almost apologetic in his friendliness. Apologising, I asked if I could finish my coffee. "Yes, yes, no problem," with that, he left. Now ok, I'm not getting soppy about it, but can you imagine that in England.

Les Angles continues to surprise me. It's a ski resort, right. There are dozens of ski resorts all over the Pyrenees. You can't turn a mountain without hitting a ski resort. That's why people come, right? To ski. But Les Angles is a lot more than that. Les Angles is a complete holiday resort with plenty to do besides just skiing for anyone who likes plenty to do and fresh air. The townspeople had given a lot of thought to improving the place and giving variety to the tourists in or out of season, for skiing the season is winter. For the sun lovers, there needs to be a bit more. Les angles have given it some thought. I was already aware of its proximity to so many places of interest, the Grotto de Fontrabious, Cathar castles, little yellow tourist train, fortress Mont-Louis, fortifications of Vauban, and the sulphur baths at Dorres and Bains de Saint Thomas. But there were more. The Zavatta circus had just left town when within 48 hours, the Apollo Circus posters were being stuck up advertising their arrival. Les Angles is a tourist destination in its own right.

Returning to my little parking spot opposite the now empty Zavatta Circus spot, I woke up with my first coffee, door wide open, when a little head popped in and said, "I wondered what an Englishman was doing here." Well, I nearly spilt my coffee.

"Your English?"

"Yes." The guy had a house further down towards Lac Matermale and had just brought his motorhome over to park up in front of me. I had seen it previously and, with its French plates, wondered where the French owners were. No, this English guy parked his motorhome here because the track to his house was too narrow for it. After a bit of chit chat, he mentioned that there were a couple of Aires down by the lake, or lac. Well, I had wondered how to get down by the lake. Giving me directions up into the village, turning right and right again, he told me that there were two Aires. One free and one to pay with electricity. I promised to go down and visit. Then he mentioned another Aire at the top of the mountain near the ski station. Water and electricity were available and a nice restaurant nearby. Another car park further up that motorhomes stopped on. I decided to first visit down by the lake and then pick the best between the two. Well, turning right, I hit another steep mountain road, down into first gear, up and around, twisting and turning, I eventually came to the Aire. Pulling in, it had a water supply, electric hook up points and nice views. Below there were several vans on the site, most new and modern, some just big van conversions. Truly anyone can tour even on a tight budget. A couple of them looked semi-permanent, maybe gipsies. But hang about, how much is the site? Asking a couple of French lads, well, there are no English here, they told me it was eleven euros a night plus another three for electricity which seemed very fair. Driving out, I went up to the top car park where there were another few motorhomes, all parking up for free, even better with great views over the lake below. I was puzzled and couldn't figure it out. Driving back down to the official Aire, I asked the two French lads why they paid when the site just above was free? Laughing, they replied, "we don't know. We are just tourists." The pay point machine was by card, so it occurs to me no one is putting their cards in, especially those older vans. Who is going to come up and check? I might have to spend the night there and try it out, but I had already filled up with water, so I was grateful for that.

Driving out, I then drove over to the other car park for a little snoop. This was fairly packed. A bus parked up and several cars. Driving over to the far end near the ski station, I noticed the restaurant, parked up and went in and looked at the menu while ordering a coffee. Surprisingly the prices didn't look too bad. Walking out after finishing my coffee (right underneath the ski slopes, which must be brilliant in the winter), I picked up a couple of brochures, one advertising the Parc Animalier des Angles. The animal park that I had kept seeing the signs for walking over. I could see the price was 15 euros for adults, well why not? Going back to put on my hiking boots. (Recommended – well, I am up in the Alps.) I went back and paid my fifteen euros and was given a map in English. She'd clocked that then. She gave me instructions that the yellow route was to the left. Of course, that covered the whole park with seeing almost every animal. There were five routes, the long circuit. Yellow, of some 3500m, the short circuit 1500m, then the trail footpath, the prehistoric footpath and the botanic footpath. I was trying to figure out what 3500m was and an altitude of 1800m.

So off I set, turning to my right, I followed the little yellow arrows. The park seemed to cover half the mountain, most of it going uphill. After a bit of level walking, it was more uphill. After fifteen minutes, I felt like I was dying. Fortunately, there were plenty of rocks or benches to sit on. I sat on plenty. Fortunately, again it looked like I was just taking in the views instead of avoiding the onset of a heart attack. The park was set up in 1994, the idea being to take all the natural wild animals that live in the Pyrenees and keep them in this almost wild but captive state. This included the bear, red deer, fox

and badger, wild boar ibex and marmot, roe deer and the
wolf, plus many more.

The beauty of it is they are all in their natural habitat, in
the wild, in the Pyrenees. I used to think Twycross Zoo in the
west midlands was a good zoo as against, say, Dudley Zoo,
but here in the Pyrenees, I was impressed. Although one or
two of the animals looked in poor shape. Most of the animals
were behind wire fencing, some just roaming free. I took
advantage of the situation and took many photos, putting
them on Facebook with the caption just some of the wild
animals I see in the Pyrenees. Well, I'm not exactly telling
lies, am I?

By the time I had finished the
circuit, it was gone at 7pm, and
I was well and truly done in.
I had had a glimpse of the
prehistoric footpath but decided
not to go the whole length.
Though somehow, I seemed to
have ended up on the botanic

path coming back. My only thought was that it was a pity
they didn't have maybe a little café halfway along. They had
plenty of picnic tables, and I noticed many of the visitors
had brought their own little picnic hampers. It was a most
enjoyable afternoon, and any family coming here could
easily spend the whole day getting lost in the atmosphere
of the place.

Driving back to the free car park at the top of the mountain, I edged nicely in front of another motorhome which placed me directly overlooking lake Matemale, absolutely wonderful, reading for a bit, I got into bed at around ten pm. Not having the best of sleep, I guessed I had got overtired. I still quite hadn't had enough of Les Angles. For anyone with a family who wanted a bit more than the bucket and spades holiday with plenty of variety, I don't think there would be many places that could beat this. You had sport, culture, history and health-inducing sulphur baths to boot. What more could any family want. Certainly, I would love to come back in November and see the contrasts. If I can get up the mountain, of course.

It's funny how we change as we get older, see things differently. Coming from the so-called slums and back streets of Nechells and Summer Lane Birmingham, you carried your bank in your pocket. I well remember how my dad and his mates would pull out a roll of some 300 or 500 hundred quid. If you were skint, you kept schtum and flicked out enough for your drinks, and that was it. You were respected by how much you carried in your pocket. But it's funny really because that's all they had, such was the reality of growing up in poor surroundings, you were very self-conscious of it. If you worked in a factory or the mines, you would flick a quid out before handing the wage packet to the wife. To your fellow workers and mates in the boozer, you'd rather die than let them know what you earned. Usually, the same as all the rest. Ruth Smith was a music teacher at our school and used to invite me to her home to do a bit of gardening. One day whilst talking, she said, "Tommy, you do keep going on about money. Why does it mean so much to you?" Well, it took me some time to figure it out. Ruth was an English music teacher, an only child, brought up in a comfortable middle-class background. Whilst being taught to be careful with money, she had never really had to worry about it. Leaving university, she then trained as a classical pianist before becoming a teacher. When her parents died, she just, well, automatically inherited the house, as you do. Now here she was giving me a lecture because I kept going on about money. Course, when she had to go into a nursing home, and her money was haemorrhaging, and she had to sell her house, her tune changed a little bit, bless her heart.

When Bet, and I first started in business and bought our first house in Sutton Coldfield, I was very conscious of living hand to mouth. No regular paycheck when you work for yourself. You have to live on what you earn or lose your house. For the first couple of years, we couldn't afford to go out. When we did, we went out with enough for a couple of pints, and that was it. I think that applies to the majority of people, whether self-employed or not. After a bit, because people kept going on and on, I tried a different tack. People would say, "how much have you got?"

In the end, frustrated, I'd say, "I'm skint, I've got nowt." But it had the reverse effect. The more I said I had nothing, the richer people thought we were.

This came home to me yet again in Gruissan a few weeks ago. Talking to a nice guy named Colin who lived in the town, we got talking about money. Bringing out his wallet, he showed me he had about £300 in notes. When he paid the waitress, he made quite a show of flashing his wallet and bringing out a fifty. I was reminded of my dad and his pals all those years ago. He couldn't believe it when I shuddered and said, "oh no, I couldn't do that." I'm always losing money, for starters, and if I went out on the bevvy, I'd lose track of it. No, if I'm going out, I estimate what I'm going to spend and take that with me. In this case, some twenty euros plus loose change from the last notes. If I decide to have a meal and haven't got enough, I bring out the trusty credit card. I'm just so in the habit of it. Abroad, and for safety, I never use my bank cards, relying on my credit cards for everything. At the end of the month I go online and clear my cards.

A couple of days ago, I went into the little mini supermarket in Les Angles and bought four cobs and a loaf of bread amongst a few other things, far too much for a single person. Now I can't take the loaf back, can I? It was over two euros so I couldn't throw it away. No, there is only one thing for it, I've got to eat it. So, I used up two of the cobs with two little pork chops. Yesterday I fancied eating out at the fancy restaurant under the ski lift but having paid fifteen quid to go into the animal park I knew it would be wasting money when I had bread in the fridge, so I used up the two other cobs toasted with a bit of cheese on them and a couple of eggs. Today I've used up half the loaf with a packet soup. Tonight I might have beans on toast and use up some more bread. I don't mind throwing a couple of slices away. So, with a coffee yesterday, a glass of juice today, I've only spent six euros. In three days, I've spent 30 euros, without even trying. Tomorrow I shall push the boat out and have a nice meal, maybe. Yes, I'm getting to be like that, Ruth Smith. Sad isn't it.

I know I must seem like a cheapskate at times but actually far from it. My years in business had taught me the value of money. I can afford to eat out at nice restaurants, and quite often, I do. But spending money unnecessarily goes completely against the grain. On a Caribbean cruise ship and at the Captain's dinner, we were presented with a fifteen-course meal. Fifteen courses, how are we going to get through that? The first course was a single prawn with a squirt of fancy sauce. By the time the main course came, we were both still hungry. To my wife, I said, "you do realise if we were eating this at some fancy Michelin-starred restaurant, we would be paying some £300 for this?" Neither one of us was impressed.

Today we live in an age of impress. It's a sign of our standing, how much we earn, and how affluent we are. I have been to restaurants and had a well-cooked, well-served meal for twenty pounds. In others, I've paid that amount for a starter without being impressed. Sadly, snobbery has entered into eating out today. To many people, especially women, it's becoming the norm to boast about how expensive your meal was the night before. With a motorhome, the joy is in what you see and where you go. Eating comes low on the list.

Coming up to the weekend, I'm formulating my early future plans. I've enjoyed and am still enjoying my time in France. I've been to the Riviera. I've travelled a fair way around the country to see beautiful little villages, medieval towns, and the Cathar castles. Now I'm feeling the need is coming on for a change. With that in mind, I will have at least Monday at Dorres sulphur baths. I shall take some magazines and spend the day there if I enjoy it so much, I might spend a couple of days. From there, I'm going to click Benidorm into my sat nav some 400 miles away, stopping off at a couple of nice little towns and villages as I go, Martell being the first on the list. I'm in no rush, probably coming back through Andorra, getting a bit of duty-free before hopefully seeing a few littler French towns as well as seeing Les Angles under snow. That's also, of course, not knowing what the ludicrous situation is in Europe and England, over Covid. I know we all have to follow the rules, of course. Who am I to think I know better than the guy next door. But come on, let's have a bit of common sense, ay? Whether on your own or with a partner, you can't self-isolate as well as you can and do in a motorhome or caravan. I know there are guys on social media gagging to come to France but are not allowed. Why is no one screaming about this? And let's face it, when the President of the United States suggests drinking bleach to destroy the infection, you have to start questioning the brains of the people who are leading us. Frankly, the older I get, the more I trust my own judgement.

Well, tomorrow is now today, and after a restless sleep, I was up at seven, a first for me for a few years. The sun was shining brightly in a clear sky, a complete change to yesterday, which was overcast for most of the day and night. This is the one downside that I see to the Pyrenees. The day before was nice and sunny, but with gale-force winds that came in heavy and unexpected gusts, one being so powerful I thought my roof light was going to blow off. I closed it quick sharpish. A few nights earlier, the heavens opened up. Thunder and lightning came down like it was the end of the world. How must our ancestors have got on in those times? Imagine leaving the south of Spain heading north, "ay Pedro, look at those big hills. Why they are so big we could find some wood and build a house, no enemy would be able to attack us." I bet they would have been scared witless out of their straw beds at the first good night of thunder and lightning.

Definitely, when you come here, you don't come for the sun. Oh, the sun is here alright, except you hardly feel it. In fact, I realise I'm about the only idiot walking about with shorts, swimming shorts at that. Everyone else is in trousers, puffer jackets and hiking boots. I thought they were the idiots when the sun was shining. No, the Pyrenees is not for sun worshippers. It is for the actively inclined, and to be fair, there is lots to do. But I feel I have gorged myself on culture with the Cathar castles. I thoroughly enjoyed seeing and being around the Alps, walking around Lake Balsere. If I'd had company that was into hiking, it would have given me the incentive to do a bit more. Whilst I enjoy my own company, I can sit for hours meditating, contemplating nature at its most peaceful, enjoying the sheer beauty and tranquillity of the lakes and forests. I can only take it for a limited time. I'm not Buffalo Bill.

Skiing is something I'm not into. It's a younger man's thing really. Ok, if you are older and have been doing it all your life, but I never had the money or the inclination. Truly it's a middle-class hobby, but what so many people see in it, I don't know. You ski down the piste, get on the chair lift to take you back up again. "Wow, I say, chappie, you did a brilliant turn on that second corner," then spend all night getting sloshed whilst boasting about how great you were. It's a bit like golf, really, I suppose. I tried it once, and the guy who kept pestering me to have a go said he always cheated. Walking around the course banging a ball about, picking the right iron for the right section. Yes, I can understand the under-pressure businessman playing it to cut off. Great, one friend of mine used to bore the pants off everyone harping on about how he almost got a hole in one. He's now an ex-friend. But that's the beauty of being different. It would be a boring world if we were all the same, like robots. So no, whilst I've thoroughly enjoyed my time here, I think it's time for a change.

Hence, it's down to the supermarket first on my way to Dorres and the sulphur baths. If I pass anywhere interesting on the way, I shall have a little meander around. If I like it, I shall stay for a night or so. Calling into the main supermarket in Boquerón, I got myself a nice couple of chicken legs for dinner together with a tin of mixed Petit pois and carrots, a little cauliflower and some cheese. All for under ten pounds. The chicken legs I shall have tonight with half the tin of veg. The cauliflower I shall cook tomorrow night with a big chunk of cheese on two slices of bread and the rest of the vegetables. I know Dorres has no shops or cafes, it's a quiet little hamlet with a nice Aires and the sulphur springs, and that's it. I just don't feel in the mood for one of my Fray Bentos pies. Good as they are as a backup, and I started out with a few, they tend to be a bit sickly with the soggy wet pastry.

Looking at my fellow campers, I don't think many think differently. Here in the Alps, I notice more than one or two just treat the motorhome as their home or second home and just enjoy the beauty of their surroundings. Like the lady who wouldn't let me onto her little site, apart from seeing her in the town doing a bit of shopping, she just spent her time around her camper. A couple opposite me were doing the same, perhaps going for a little stroll. The guy in front has a car on the back. Each day I've noticed he sets off with his wife and two kids for the day, coming back at night and cooking up a meal. The couple who pulled in behind me yesterday was later doing a barbeque. Frankly, I would book into a hotel if I want service, failing that a rented cottage and eating out most nights.

A site is great I feel, if you have family, kids. Though the guy in front is saving quite a lot of money by not going on a site. In all, it's how you feel yourself. I've stopped on sites and saw the benefits, I've also seen the pitfalls, if I couldn't find a suitable place to spend the night or a few nights, then I would certainly go on a site rather than demean myself by sleeping in a side road or noisy lay-by. A site is fine if you want to put your awning up. Needed with the English weather. If you want to put your chairs and table out, cook like you're at home, yes, we've done that also, but the more I wild camp, the more I enjoy the freedom. Before I came away, I took the kids on a three-day break to Rhyl and Barmouth, with no hygiene problems. We had enough water on board to handle all things.

I find we don't need the awnings out in France or Spain, except in really, really hot weather. Still, in Aires, you can do that. If you're wild camping, you can't. In Spain, you can park by the beach but not put your chairs out. Fine, you're right next to the beach like I was in Gruissan a few weeks ago, pick your deck chair up and carry it over to the beach like dozens of apartment holders do every day. I watched them. They had further to walk than me. More and more people are seeing the benefits of owning a motorhome, and it doesn't have to be a big expensive monster. Yikes, no thanks, I see no pleasure in that at all except for major movie stars. I see some amazing and interesting things that people travel in. Some I take pictures of to show others that it's not all about money or big fancy motorhomes. One opposite has converted a big seven tonner, which looks like a removal van. Standard wooden doors must have two 500 watt solar panels on the roof, massive. In England, it would stand out a bit on Barmouth seafront. But here, in France, I don't think people give a hoot. It reminded me of that first time my dad took us out for the day in Jacky Willis's big van, table and chairs inside. a wonderful day and a wonderful memory. Today there is too much snobbery. After the war, people used to have to move their furniture by hand cart, poor as we were. Today it's all about snobbery. Yet logically, and I had to see it myself before I realised it, when you're in the sun, in Spain or Morocco, you're only in your camper to sleep, you get up in the morning, sit outside, or go down to the beach.

HEADING SOUTH FROM LES ANGLES

I am fortunate that I can afford a nice motorhome that suits our tastes. But I don't knock anyone looking for a nice or better quality of life with what they can afford. I see more and more people making conversions, buying second-hand campers. We all want the freedom a motorhome or camper gives us. Soon I can see a battle, already starting between the campers who want their freedom at a reasonable price and the campsite owners who want to stick us for as much as they can get just to park on a clump of grass. I suspect the site owners might win unless the government wake up to how the French look at things. Again, I think many campers damage it for others with their attitude and lack of respect for everyone else.

Setting off from Les Angles made me wonder if I was doing the right thing. But then I've had that feeling at every place I have left, from Marseillan to Gruissan to the Cathar Castles. Each time I felt that I wasn't getting or having enough of the place. At Gruissan, I felt I could stop half the summer. In Les Angles, there is just so much to see, so many places to hike. Setting off from my comfortable little pitch high up above Les Angles, I first filled up with fresh drinking water. First, my 5 gallons and one-gallon plastic water bottles, then my tank, which I never drink out of. After that, I set off first to Bolquere, where I knew there was a good supermarket and the casino. From there, I set off for the ski resort of Font-Romeu-Odeillo-Via. I guessed I had been here before on my way to Dorres but couldn't recall it. I soon realised why. Romeu-Odeillo-Via seems to be split into two sections: skiing, golfing, hiking and activity resort. With Aires to boot, as you approached the town, I assumed that was the town. When I saw the Aires and all the activity pulling in, I sat back a bit before having a look around. There were 4 or 5 other vans pitched up around me. When I got out, I saw the golf club, kiddies play fair, pitch and putt, and an all-terrain bike track. Everywhere was pristine and well kept, but something was puzzling me. This didn't seem a destination point just for a game of golf, surely. Then I saw it. The main town and ski centre was a few hundred yards further on. It was bustling. Hotels, shops, ski shops, coffee bars, then more shops. It was vibrant, bustling, alive. Skiing or no skiing, I hadn't missed it the first time. I had simply driven straight through it, unable to find anywhere to park up. I was desperate to stop and explore. I simply hadn't put the first part, with its camping Aires, together. This time I was determined to spend a couple of nights here.

Here, Covid or not, recession or no recession, this, like Les Angles, was/is a prosperous town. Here again, they had got it all. A round of golf after a day on the piste, kiddies golf and cycle activities for all the family. I reckon the townsfolk must pray every day to whoever came up with the idea of turning those mountains into ski slopes. It seemed people could always find the money for golf and skiing. I had a very nice two days just meandering around the town during the day, people watching with a coffee on the sidewalks. From a simple chicken dinner to round off the night, Dorres can wait another couple of days.

Arriving at Dorres, the free camper van Aire was almost full, with one space left and plenty of cars. The sun was trying to break through. It was struggling. I snuck in on the end of the line and said hello to a couple of people around. As always, I find these sites relaxed and friendly, people ready and willing to say hello and have a chat. Up to yet, in all my time in France, I've only met two English men. Settling in, I cooked myself a simple meal before settling down to read a magazine or two. I don't have the time to read the Sunday magazines that come with the newspapers at home, so I quickly learned to save them. Any other magazines that came along, the articles in them are timeless. They can be read from one year to the next. I also carry a couple or more word search magazines, ideal for passing the odd hour or two. In my cupboards, I carry a few puzzles, draughts, and snakes and ladders.

I was awake for 8:30am the next morning. The weather was dull, the sky overcast, so I just sat reading and drinking a coffee, enjoying the moment, looking around. I reckon I was the only one up so early. Slowly, one by one, the others got up with some leaving, including one with an amazing piece of kit that looked like something out of WW2. It was a monster, wheels like lorry tyres and raised about four feet off the ground. When it started, it sounded like a tank. This was a monster and clearly made or adapted for heavy-duty terrain. With limited language, the two Frenchman conceded, Africa, meaning built for the African terrain. But really, how well suited for the Pyrenees, it wouldn't certainly go where I couldn't. But that's the beauty with some of these motorhomes or adaptions, here abroad, in the sun, no one seems to give a fig. I could imagine the comments with that popping up on a campsite in England, mind, I could cringe at the fuel consumption of it.

Dorres literally meant springs and was discovered by the Romans over 2000 years ago. Though people were no doubt using them thousands of years previously, the sulphur comes out of the granite rocks at a temperature of some 140 degrees. It's warm. The baths or wash house was carved out of granite in 1842. Originally the villagers used to wash the sheep wool and hog casings in its very hot water. The baths of Dorres now enable tourists and local people to enjoy the benefit of the sulphurous waters after a bit of skiing or hiking in the mountains. Setting off up into the village and then down to the bathes, I realised how well hidden it was. Talk about discreet. Here you have a very small unobtrusive village, in the back of beyond, so quiet and laidback you would never know it existed. It was only noticeable from very small discreet signs saying, Romaine-Les-Baines, Roman baths. You continue on down a little country lane that seems to go nowhere when it appears in front of you. Once inside the entrance, it drops down onto two levels, the café and reception inside the gate, then the lower level containing the three pools, or sulphur baths and the bathhouse containing two roughly shaped granite baths, in a granite enclosed bathhouse, this is where the villagers used to wash their sheep wool, marvellous.

Being my second visit, I was feeling a bit cocky, "Si, Si," when he started talking, obviously asking me if I had read the warning signs, "Si, Si." But he wasn't. He was asking if I had had the injections. That's why the two French people in front of me walked away. So, in two weeks, the rules had changed yet again. Thankfully, I had waited to have my two jabs. Chatting to the French guy in the camper next door, I asked him if he had been down to the bathes. "No," he replied, "I have no trunks."

Then he asked about the jabs, "yes, I have had mine."

"No, I have not." Ahh, that's why he hasn't been in the bathes. His wife kicked him out in favour of her new boyfriend, I couldn't figure out if she gave him 30% or he still has 30% whilst she retains 70%. Either way, he is living in his camper, he doesn't care if something happens to him, but he will not have the jab. He looked quite sad and miserable with his lot. I can't imagine much worse than being kicked out in your twilight years for a younger model. He was 68. Now I wonder if he doesn't just go from one free Aire to the next, passing his time on his pension. Well, the Aires are free, and like this one has free water, tipping facilities etc., what more could a man want? Just a wife/companion.

Cooking the cauliflower was simple enough. It was just that it was French cauliflower (you'd think all cauliflower was the same), took ages to cook, and was as tough as old boots. Putting the shredded cheese in after made it like super glue (French cheese). Oh yes, it tasted like cauliflower cheese when I eventually got it off the fork. Now I've got to wash up, regrets. After a couple of enjoyable days in Dorres, I decided to visit a place called Porte-Puymorens, further up in the Alps and close to the Andorra border. Please don't tempt me to go in. My interest lay in the fact that the little yellow tourist train ended at a little town called Enveitg. But another train carried on from there just the short distance to Porte-Puymorens. Why? The farthest point for a ski resort may be that it also has free Aires to stop overnight before heading to Martinet and then to Spain. In the current covid situation, I don't fancy driving into Andorra from the French side then encountering trouble from the Spanish trying to get out.

It's funny how losing someone can affect us in different ways. My wife wasn't a flashy woman. In fact, she was painfully shy, but her home and kids came first. In our early days of struggling to build up a business, she would scrape by on pennies to feed us. One day, I gave her a few extra quid, not a lot, but told her to treat herself. What did she do? She went out and bought a few packs of knickers for the kids. When I told her off, she said, but I have bought myself some knickers, it was so typical. The year she passed away, we had just gotten into our stride, having little mini-breaks around England, a week's break in a nice hotel in Scarborough, a Caribbean cruise. She had just started buying better, nicer quality clothes. Still, she remained quintessentially the same.

We had booked a month's cruise to the Caribbean. Typically, she brought a simple, cheap little Rasta man fridge magnet with dangly adjustable legs from a bar in St Kitts. On the cruise back, I bought her an Oriana watch celebrating its maiden voyage. She was very proud of that. I bought her a lovely silver charm bracelet from a noted lady designer. She loved it. Knowing she was never going to wear it, she gave it to our daughter, Louise. In Spain, she bought a cheap, tacky little market stall watch, a pink plastic bracelet connected and held together with plastic. She loved it. When she left, I treasured it. I still keep it in my motorhome. Sadly, it's stopped working. So did the Oriana watch.

Whilst going through one of my little boxes of all sorts looking for a screw, yes, you never know when you might need a screw, elastic band, shoelace, or a cotton reel. People go on and on about weight in a motorhome and exceeding the weight limit. Some are obsessed with it and go into real technical detail such as how much weight is a gallon of water, don't overfill your tanks, don't carry too much-tinned food etc., etc. Proper Einstein's some of them. I keep it dead simple. I've got a six-berth motorhome. I'm carrying the equivalent of one full-grown man, sorted. Amongst the dozens of little things, I picked up my wife's Oriana watch. Obviously, it had stopped working, and I had put it away. After finding a screw and realising I didn't need it, I decided to have another look at my wife's watch. Taking the back off, I went back to my trusty little box, put the screw back and brought out a few packs of the spare batteries I carry. Yes, you never know when you're going to need a spare battery, key fobs, watches, controls, half a dozen packs from the pound shop. Anyway, I pulled out the little battery, put a new one in. Hey presto, magic, it's working, is she looking after me, I wonder? At any rate, I've put it back up in the pride of place above her sofa, chuffed to bits. Silly, stupid little things, but they give me some comfort. I'll have to try that market stall pink watch again.

Setting off for Porte-Puymorens, I found the roads clear. Again, very little traffic, it was 13 miles to Porte-Puymorens, and the land was lush and green. It was a delight and pleasure to drive through. Coming up to Porta, a small village a few short miles before Porte-Puymorens, I almost passed it before realising that I must visit it, maybe have a coffee. Bit of a mistake, doing an about-turn, I pulled into the road leading into the village, approaching the almost medieval village houses. I realised my mistake. Again, the road was getting narrower and narrower. It was getting to squeaky bum time. I could see ahead a bit like the very narrow lanes and village houses. Soon my side mirrors were scraping the walls of the houses, built before the car was thought of, probably before the horse and cart were invented. Thankfully, after a nerve-wracking little drive, I could turn into a wider road at the end of the village. That's it, I've had enough, I'm getting out of here, the village was beautiful, like so many, I swear some of them were invented before God's dog. Carrying on, I soon came to the mountain range and the village of Porte-Puymorens. This time, the roads were a lot wider. The village was bustling with life, with a couple of cafes or restaurants. This was obviously the main destination point for skier's and hikers alike. It was very pretty. Driving around, I came to the Aire, which had a gate across it, that meant a charge. Maybe it wasn't the Aire on the map. I decided to travel on a bit. Leading out of town, I was looking for the mountain road leading up one of the biggest mountains when I came to a barrier, a little hut to the side and a security guard. Thinking I was heading into some private estate, I pulled in to turn around. As I did, another car pulled up, words were spoken, and the guy handed over some money. The guard let him through. I couldn't understand him enough to find out what was on the other side of the barrier. Returning back the way I came, I carried on past the village until I saw what I thought was the mountain road. it was. Driving on was no problem until I came to traffic lights and workmen in the road. For some stupid reason, they had put two-foot-high blocks on either side, creating narrow lanes, squeaky bum time again. With inches to spare, I tore a chunk out of my rear tyre guard. I couldn't go back. My only way was forward. Thankfully I made it but dreaded the idea of travelling back.

Travelling onwards and increasingly upwards, the land opened out, and I was met with the most stunning views surrounded by mountains. I was almost at the El Pas de la Casa and the N22. This was obviously one of the higher ski runs. Judging by the length of the runs as I drove up, they seemed a hell of a lot bigger than the ones at Les Angles. These were for the big boys, I reckon. Seeing that the road went up even further, I decided to carry on up, safe in the knowledge that the one I was leaving was good enough for the night, here the ground opened up again to a massive big car park. Pulling on, I backed up to another smaller camper, obviously with the same idea as me, overlooking stunning mountain views. I was ecstatic. The views were positively overwhelming. I've heard of people using the term orgasmic to describe food. Well, this was orgasmic. If I've ever seen such stunning views before, I can't remember, Switzerland? Les Angles, yes, but here there was no comparison, no houses, no shops. If anyone has been to Porte Puymorens, then you will know what I'm on about. It is completely untouched and unspoilt. The only people about were visitors who came to soak up the ambience and hikers. There is an abundance of hikers. I had enough food and water on board to allow me to spend at least a couple of nights here. Putting the kettle on, I poured myself a coffee to take in the views. After the coffee and without locking the van up, I started taking a walk up the track in front of me. It was a few hundred yards before I felt it a bit prudent to get back to my unlocked motorhome. Back in the motorhome, I used the other half tin of beans on some toast, put my feet up for an hour before deciding to go for another, this time longer, hike.

I felt energised, stopping every few moments to take in the view as well as getting my second wind back. I could feel my lungs opening up. I think I managed about ten miles before coming to the couple who had just passed me in their car. What were they doing? Going over, I could see immediately, they were collecting water from what must have been the highest fresh water spring in the mountains. They had gallon containers in the boot of the car. Taking a picture of them, they were happy to try and explain how excellent the water was. I believed them. Ok, I never walked ten miles. I think I managed a mile before turning back. Well, it felt like ten miles. Bikers were passing me, coming uphill, then I saw what must have been about forty young hikers heading towards me. Was this a mountain trail to Andorra? As the first group approached me, I could see it was a mix of young men and girls all looking red and sweating with the exertion. Pointing uphill, I said, "bonjour, Andorra?"

"Yes." Ahh, so this was the mountain trail to Andorra. When the next lot came close to me, I said, "Andorra closed, kaput." It was too late. I saw the look of despair and utter frustration on their faces as the one turned around and shouted to the rest. I knew what he was saying. Quickly I said, "no, no, I was joking." I don't think too many of them saw the joke. Well, I estimate they had got a circa twenty-mile hike in front of them. Me and my big mouth. Getting back to my motorhome, I put the kettle on and a vegetable Balti Fray Bentos pie in the oven. Across the road was a very substantial building that looked like a former hotel and restaurant with individual cottages, now all blocked up, the roof burnt out, obviously from a fire. Another sad story of a business hitting the skids, what sad tale lay behind that I wonder, sadly we will never know. The business has its good points and its risks. I've been in business all my life. But sometimes, the risks can be heavy.

After two nights, I felt it was time to move on again. There was something almost spiritual about these mountains, the peacefulness, the simple serenity of the place. Like in Gruissan and visiting the Cathar castles, Lake Balcere, I always felt a bit of a reluctance to leave, a tugging feeling, have I seen or done enough? I just knew I would love to have done that Andorra trail hike, to experience that feeling of being in a group or alone, as one with nature. I consoled myself with the fact I couldn't just up and leave my motorhome stuck on top of the mountain for a few days. Waking up to a beautiful morning, mist hanging over the mountains from the sun drying out the rain from the night before, I sat down with a coffee for one last moment of enjoyment before moving on. Each time the mountains presented a different appearance. At night, in the dark, malevolent, silent, brooding. During the day, a freshness, awesomeness inviting you to climb it, each season would hold a different view. Already people were pulling in, on motorbikes, cars or vans, parents with their kids undoing the bikes off the back to go trekking along the trails. Who were these people, I wondered, locals? Coming to make use of what was on their doorstep? Certainly, the two ladies looked local, the daughter brought her elderly mother out whilst she had a little walk a few paces up the mountain, I watched her stop, and spend some minutes in deep meditation, was she, like me, thinking of a lost one?

There were only two ways off this mountain, a left turn onto the N22 into Andorra or a right turn back down the way I came into Porte-Puymorens. I was dreading it, first one short barrier blockage, I'd forgotten that one, then the big one, I'd already passed an artic coming from Andorra. Stuck. Too big to get through, too big to turn around, he was crackered. I decided to approach it from a different angle at the big one, getting my driver's side as close as possible. This time I grazed the wheel arch over my rear driver's side. I just couldn't understand the stupidity in using such wide blocks. It was ridiculous. Thankfully the damage is repairable, but until then, I've got to drive about in my beautiful but knocked about motorhome. Maybe I can repair it in Benidorm, a bit of filler will soon sort it. I decided to carry on past Porte-Puymorens and make my way straight to Martinet some thirty miles away. I hadn't had anything to eat and was feeling peckish. The only problem is I've still not got the hang of what the French call a breakfast. Not for them a good wholesome full English, no it's a croissant, maybe with a bit of jam. Effectively it's a choice of maybe something with frites, and I'm just not keen on frites for breakfast or lunch. Then I saw the Carrefour.

I pulled into the car park doing an about-turn, got my little carrier bag, and picked up a few items, a bit of meat, a baguette, cheese spread, and a small butter. It was only whilst

I was shopping, I heard the phrase, "Gracias," before realising I was in Spain. Carrying on from the supermarket, I realised the police hold up that I had passed just a few minutes earlier was the French Gendarme on the French side checking all occupants of vehicles, no doubt for the vaccination jabs, now I'm doubly glad I never went through Andorra. Mind, I don't think the Spanish are too bothered. They just want our money and fair play to them. You can always tell, guaranteed, that when you cross that border into Wales, the heavens open up. Often, I would say to Bet, "get the kids ready. I'm getting paid today," and set off on a nice sunny day. So, it is when you cross into Spain, or thereabouts with no border. Although the sun was struggling to come out in the Pyrenees, it was still overcast with the threat of rain. Here, in Spain, the sun was shining, hot. Driving into Martinet was almost like visiting an old friend. This time approaching it in reverse order, I recognised it immediately. The last time I visited was in October. With Covid, it was very quiet. Now it was relatively busy with people eating out at the sidewalk tables. The Aire was full, with motorhomes parked anywhere they could get in. There was one space that I backed into quick sharpish. Clearly, these Aires are very popular, but it's a two-way street, the motorhomes bring in much-needed revenue, in return, we are provided with a good-sized and discreet place to park, with cassette emptying facilities, water, showers and toilets. What a great trade-off. I couldn't wait to lock up and get out for a little mooch and a coffee at the nearest bar and patisserie. There was a mix of French and Spanish on the site. The family next door trying to keep their kids occupied were Spanish. At first, I thought they were a bit gipsy-ish, seeing as the wife looked quite scruffy and unkept with scruffy looking trousers. Big mistake, a bit later she came back from the shower with a skirt on that small I couldn't take my eyes off her tiny figure. She was a little beauty.

Saying hello, she asked if I was English and from what part.

"Birmingham."

"Ahh yes," in good English, she explained that she spent six months working at Birmingham airport. What a coincidence. Her husband had got a flight booked for the next day not too far away on a glider trip, for fifteen minutes it was 110 euros, for 45 minutes it was 160 euros. Naturally, he went for a longer period. So would I. I was tempted to ask if he could book me in and let me tag along, perhaps not. But it was something I would love to do, even sat in the cockpit with a pilot gliding it, wonderful. I was still trying to get my head around the cultural difference. This morning I was saying bonjour, merci, now it's ole, gracias. Before pulling out of the Aire in Martinet, I filled up with water and punched La Seu d'Urgell into my sat nav. A friend had suggested it was a lovely town to visit. Dave was an ex lorry driver and knew Europe like the back of his hand. Whilst travelling, he kept a friendly eye on which route I was travelling. Just out of Martinet, I saw the sign for Montella, 3 kilometre's into the mountains. Now, whenever I click on Martinet, it comes up as Martinet Montella. I couldn't understand why. The drive up into the mountains was breathtaking. These were the Spanish Pyrenees. Finding the village of Montella, I couldn't help but be impressed with its natural beauty, a small village/hamlet at one with the surrounding farms. Intending to drive through, I came to a full stop. Oh no, not again. Narrow little streets getting narrower by the yard, no thank you. I did a sharp backpedal and made my way out. d'Urgell was about thirty miles west below Andorra and into Spain. Pulling into d'Urgell, I wasn't immediately impressed. d'Urgell wasn't really a town, it was more like a city, and I just don't like cities. Arriving in the centre, I pulled up before three cops and asked where I could park up for a little sightseeing. They directed me to a parking space just a few feet in front of me in a very open and friendly manner. Getting out, I had a little mooch about, pulling into one of the many open coffee bars along the pavement. It was nice to be met and greeted by such consistent friendliness. After a short hour, I got back in the van punching in Cambrils, just south of Barcelona Tarragona and Salou. Barcelona didn't even come into my line of vision. Some people like big cities. To me, one big city is much like another, with lots of people running around. Lots of shops wanting you to spend your money, and in between, you've got the pickpockets. Barcelona was notorious for them. Tarragona was a major big industrial fishing port. The places I could see to camp up for a few nights did not look very inviting, neither did the characters shuffling about. The cleaner, nicer, more salubrious part where I could have stayed had no place for camper vans. Oh well, on to Salou or Cambrils.

From d'Urgell, I had driven and stopped at a few enchanting little towns and villages on my way to Tarragona and Cambrils. Villages like Solivella, Huesca Monzon are beautiful, peaceful, whilst very different to the medieval towns and villages in France. There was still a lot to see. Unfortunately, because of Covid, it was difficult to get a full picture or feel for the place. I reached Cambrils, a beautiful and prosperous seaside resort with a long fine grainy, sandy beach that stretched from Salou. As with all destinations and resorts, I have to spend the first hour or more looking for somewhere to park up. It didn't take me long to find somewhere. Leaving Salou, and just as you drive into Cambrils, I clocked the slip road to the right, opposite the beach and fronting onto a large green open space. It was a one-way system, so I had to turn back towards Salou, take a left at the island then into the long slip road. Towards the end, a full line of motorhomes all settled in. Mainly French, with the odd German. Where were the English? The couple in front were French, and the wife was sitting nicely as you like in a deck chair on the grassy parkland. Behind their motorhome, they had got an enclosed trailer and a very nice motorbike. Hubby was going for a spin leaving his wife to enjoy the peace and quiet of the afternoon on her deck chair. She confirmed to me that all this was included in the price of a ticket from the machine a few yards away. I was happy to bung my few euros in. Hungry, I set off over to the beach and bars clustered along the sand. Normally, I find these places a bit of a rip-off and only selling drinks, but who can blame them? Trebling up on a can of coke makes more sense than slaving over a stove to earn a few quid, but I don't like the thought of being ripped off. Two bars along, surprise, surprise, was a bar, and it was serving food.

Sitting down, I tried to understand what the waiter was telling me. Not many English come along here, that's for sure. I was having difficulty. Until he mentioned sardines. Sardines? With frites? That's me sorted, and a can of Fanta orange, please. You can't really go wrong with sardines. They are what they are. Sardines, well, I was expecting maybe 2 or 3 sardines, about six inches long and plump. When they came to the table, they were about four inches long, not plump, but at least there were about a dozen of them. They looked very appetising. Cutting their heads and tails off, I enjoyed the meal, impressed with the presentation from a beach bar. Sitting there watching all the activity on the beach, people playing volleyball, surfing or doing a bit of sailing on the sea, the sun shining and the blue sky, it was hard to imagine there was any kind of a pandemic going on in the world.

No one hardly used the slip road, which seemed to have very little purpose except for parking up. This suited me fine until I got my head down for the night. The main coast road adjoining, I think it fed the whole coast road from Salou to Benicasim, was busy. Not that I couldn't sleep, of course, when my head hits the pillow, that's it, but when you wake up with the birds in the morning, you know you're near a fairly busy road. Two nights was enough for me, I would have stopped longer, but I was at the far end of the beach. The main shopping and tourist area were a mile further on and the hotels further back the other way. I know I needed the exercise but hiking up and down along the resort didn't appeal to me too much. I know what it was. I've been spoilt. In France, there are pull-in sites on every corner, Aires galore. Even in the Pyrenees, there are seemingly places to pitch up with a welcoming sign everywhere. I liked Salou and wanted to spend time there, but I couldn't find anywhere to park up as big as it was. Clearly, Salou, like Cambrills and other popular resorts, has made their fortunes and killing on the tourist industry. They simply didn't need campers. No run-down hotels and resorts here, oh no, this was a million miles from Blackpool. When I made a couple of enquiries, I was pointed to the side roads and back streets. After a couple of runs, I decided to throw the towel in. Side roads? Back streets? I'm not lowering my standards. Don't ask me to explain it. I can't, but there is a line we all draw. Each line is different for us all. When we first bought our camper, our plans were quite clear, short breaks around England, wild camping as we went, then longer breaks in the sun abroad. We are self-contained. We don't need to pay for electricity or a toilet on a crappy little grass field. So, one year, we called into Brixham, South Devon. Brixham has a lovely little fishing harbour. But after spending the day there, we looked for somewhere to park up for the night, well I did. Eventually, after what seemed hours of searching, I found a very nice, quiet, little industrial site. Pulling in, we settled down, closed the curtains and went to bed. Oh my god, the next morning, did I feel embarrassed. The site and units were swarming with lorries, vans, and workmen. Did I feel a d**khead? Clearing up and opening the curtains, we got out of that place quick sharpish. Never again, Bet never said a word. But I can guess what she was thinking.

Most times around Europe, you just don't feel that you are imposing or intruding. The French are used to it. Vineyards, Cheesemakers invite you to stay in their free Aires, hoping you will buy their produce in return. They just pull up, get out and explore. I've now got into that habit. In England, you are made to feel like an intruder, an unwanted gipsy. But there is a line and a limit. On some sites, fellow campers will recommend the layby at the side of such a road, a bit noisy. But it's safe, or it's fairly quiet until the lorries start revving their engines up. Christ almighty, I don't want to spend my touring and travelling times putting up with that. Oh no, the side road in Cambrils was fine for a couple of nights. Maybe I could have spent a week, but not much more. The other thing was, and I knew it, I was secretly yearning for Benidorm. I hadn't had a proper meal for over two months, whilst I'm not knocking the French, it's everything with frites. Moules and frites. Escargots and frites. Entrecote and frites. I was yearning for a nice English breakfast, a good fry up, a well-cooked traditional

Sunday roast on any day of the week. And in Benidorm, I'm almost embarrassed to say, there is one on almost every corner.

So, I set off. I had two choices. I could spread it out, pulling into different resorts along the way like Benicasim, Villareal, Gandia Denia. Each resort had a different appeal to me and was a place with different memory. Benicasim was a major resort that drew recording artists from all over the world. Denia? We had visited a few times. The last time we had bumped into a jeweller named Chatwin from Birmingham. Chatwin had built up a small chain of shops in the jewellery quarter dealing in gold, but the more successful he became, the more demanding his wife became. This is a regular occurrence in the jewellery quarter. Everyone thinks jewellers or gold dealers are millionaires. The truth is it's a very vicious environment. His wife wanted a nice house, he got a nice house, and she then wanted their kids in private school and into private school they went. Eventually, it got too much for Chatwin. At the end of his tether, mortgaged up to the hilt, he decided to do a runner. Very shrewdly, he built up a good credit line with his suppliers. He was very well known and respected. Then he hit the lot of them, wallop. He hit the suppliers between the three shops for over a million quid's worth of gold and jewellery. Then did a runner to Denia. The only problem was he never allowed for the uproar and publicity. Oh, so you nick a million quid's worth of jewellery, and no one's going to notice?

Chatwin knew Don Fewtrell from the clubs and his club, Pollyanna's. First, Donald, who had an apartment in Denia with his floozy, Nina, sensing a few quid in the making, suggested Chatwin leave a sack full of the jewellery in a telephone box, ring the cops, the cops would find the jewellery and call off the chase. Donald was never the brightest spark in the Fewtrell family. Neither was Chatwin in his. The cops never stood for it. Bet and I were in Denia at the time. Don asked me if I could help his pal out by getting a buyer for his jewellery. Chatwin was in a right state. He had never done anything dishonest in his life, now his whole world was falling apart. By the time I had made a few phone calls, that was it. He caved in and threw himself into the police. He cited all kinds of ailments, from his poor eyesight to everything else. In truth, the poor b*****d had had a mental breakdown. He ended up doing a couple of years in the clink, his kids were taken out of private school, and they were all given a little council house on the Kingstanding Estate. So no, Denia was not one big happy playground for me. I decided to carry on to Benidorm.

The roads in Spain are a delight to drive on, more than twice the size of England and with only some 40 million people there was always the feeling of plenty of space with far fewer cars than our over-packed country. The only problem I found with Spain is my sat nav couldn't keep up with the major road-building schemes. The Spanish were building new roads like there was no tomorrow. One minute I'm tootling along nicely, my little car zipping along on the little red road. The next, I'm in an empty space, a field, and the little red road is going off in the same direction but a mile to the right or the left. The first couple of times, it was panic stations as I wondered what the hell I'd done wrong, where had I taken the wrong turning, before realising not to panic and just carry on, eventually the little red road and the car on it would merge back with my little car on the track. My suspicion, driving around the country, is that some bright spark pointed out to the powers that be in the government, that with all the money that was awash in the European Union, now was a good time to borrow billions and spend it on the infrastructure and new builds dotted all over Spain. Little villages and communities were springing up all over the place. In their greed and eagerness, many were being built without planning permission.

But no one seemed to care, the banks, being even greedier, less so. Then, the bubble burst, the recession hit, the builders disappeared, the banks grabbed all the new builds, the part builds, and the start builds, and they spent the next few years trying to get their money back. In Turre, a small village outside Mojaca, the new in-place, awash with finished and part-finished houses and apartments, I offered £22,000 on a very nice two bedroomed flat that was less than half its real price. A lot of people were grabbing bargains. The plan was that with all the new roads and new builds, the Germans, British and other Europeans would all come stampeding into the country, buying these lovely properties and bringing billions into the economy. Sadly, as the economy slowly started to pick up, creaking and groaning, the pandemic hit. Even before the pandemic, the roads were a delight to drive on. Now, in the pandemic, even more so.

The Italian roads are terrible. Many of them are still in the Middle Ages, with mile upon mile of cobbled stone or tarmac with potholes all over the place. After a few miles in Italy, I tend to break it by going on the toll roads. France is different again, with the many and varied beautiful medieval villages and towns. Not forgetting the chateaus, the roads were a delight to drive on. For speed and a never-ending round of putting your hands in your pocket, then the tolls can be the way to go. My only reason for ending up on the tolls in France is by mistake. By going on the tolls, you just miss so much of the natural beauty of France.

Leaving Cambrils, I soon headed onto the main highway N332, south. it was a straightforward 200 miles to Benidorm, so I decided to do it in one full gallop. I FOUND the N332, well known for its prostitutes spread out along the way and other main routes leading out of France and into Spain. It took me a bit to clock what was going on, naïve as I am. Sat on chairs on the side of olive groves or vineyards. At first,

I thought they were selling wine or olives. One to the left on the opposite side of the road in a bikini and a body to die for was doing stretch exercises to show off her limbs, and very nice too. My curiosity was getting the better of me. Eventually, I had to find out. At the next stop, I slammed on the brakes. When the girl at the side of the road said, "hello," I asked her what she was doing here.

"Vorking," she replied in her eastern accent. Seeing my puzzled look, she repeated, "vorking. f*****g, I vork."

"Oh really, and how much do you charge?"

"30 euros," she replied. Fascinated, I got my camera out to take her picture but crying out, "no," she turned her back. Unfortunately for me, I had a lady friend with me who was very embarrassed. "I can't believe you stopped and spoke to a prostitute."

"Well," I said, "we have been driving past them for the last hour, and whenever I kept asking you what they were doing, you refused to answer me." She just wasn't very happy at all.

The fact is, I was simply curious. I had heard about prostitutes most of my life. Of course, in Birmingham, we had the notorious Varna Road where they would sell their wares. I had heard about the red-light district in places like Amsterdam, but it never entered my mind or came within my vision to pay a prostitute for sex. It seemed so cold. How or why would you want to do something like that with a stranger? If my girlfriend had told me they were prostitutes, I would not have stopped. In any event, she couldn't believe my stupidity in not realising it. Oh well. When I mentioned it to my friend David who used to be a long-distance lorry driver, he told me it was rife. They were run by the Bulgarian or East European mafia. This astonished me, and when I asked, he proffered that the police probably don't do anything because they get paid in kind for turning a blind eye. Last year I noticed row upon row of them carrying the same yellow umbrellas. A clear enough sign, I think that they are run and handled by the same cartel. This time around, I noticed, just out of curiosity, of course. No yellow umbrellas or ladies of the night were sitting around. Obviously, the pandemic had put paid to that little pastime. I mean, who wants to risk getting Covid from a quickie in the olive groves?

BENIDORM

It was around 2 o'clock in the afternoon by the time I got to Benidorm. It felt like I was returning to see an old friend, this time, I knew which turn off to take to get to the Levante beach and the Levante med hospital where I knew there was a large car park to the side where I could park up for free. Unfortunately, it was all locked up. Judging by the groundwork that had been carried out, it was obvious some kind of planning permission had been granted for something, either for the hospital or maybe yet another hotel. Benidorm was awash with high rise hotels.

For a bit, I was completely lost. Driving around, I just couldn't think where was the best place to pitch up. I have been free camping or wild camping for the past two months. When you realise the benefits of wild camping, it's quite hard to accept paying to go on sites. I am 100% self-sufficient.

I have a solar panel, inverter to convert my 12 volts. I have adequate water. I just don't need to go on a site. If I had company or a girlfriend, I'd go on site. I know others work it in different ways to suit themselves. Many couples will wild camp for two or three days then go on a site for a night to shower, fill up with water and empty their cassettes. We all have different ways of doing things. One couple I met on one very nice site paid 15 euros a night, just over £100 per week. Plus, electricity mind. Now I thought that was very reasonable, but they were there for some seven months. Worse, they mostly sat outside on their chairs, just having a drive out on their twin-seater scooter or popping up to the bar for a drink. I don't think they ever sat around the pool. After a few turns around the block, I found a temporary park up in a reasonably quiet side street until I could do some figuring out. There were another couple of motorhomes spread out. A large free car park opposite a kiddies park was just a few hundred yards from the hospital. But I felt this was a bit too far away from all the action. Where I had parked was convenient to all the hotel's, bars and restaurants like the corner bar that did a nice line in traditional English cooked food. All I wanted was a nice brekkie, a traditional roast dinner and a very nice hotel swimming pool to work it off.

Because of the pandemic and Covid, most hotels and caravan sites were increasing their prices or doubling them. It's bad enough in England, where they have an increasingly captive audience. Years ago, when we were kids, a local farmer would let you pitch your tent up for free or just a few quid. In some rural areas, you still can if you hunt around a bit. But today, in the main, it's a different story. In England, you will pay 40 quid a night plus for a pitch on a soggy bit of grass, 240 quid a week. Here in Benidorm, they wanted 30 to 35 quid a night, plus electricity. 210 quid a week plus electric. If you were a family, fine, but even then, that's only for two people. It's extra per person after that. If you're happy to pay that, fine. I've owned a caravan site, and yes, if I could get away with it, I would charge it, but it doesn't alter the fact that it's a bit over the top.

Last year whilst I was heading into Benidorm, one of my daughters informed me that she had booked into a very nice four-star hotel. The hotel was very accommodating and allowed me to call into the hotel, have a coffee or a drink and use the toilets. I think this covered the hotel swimming pool as well, which was exceptionally nice. Many hotels or campsites will let you use their pool for a small fee. I considered this very good value.

A few years ago, whilst in Benalmadena, I caught onto the benefits of what a good hotel has to offer. We were in a car park just a few yards away from the seafront, walking along the front one day Bobbie, my granddaughter, wanted to use the toilet. Looking at the public toilets along the seafront, I was horrified at the thought of what they must be like looking at the queues outside. No, no, no, Bob. Look, this is what you do. First, we found the biggest four-star hotel along the front, walk-in as though it's your hotel, don't look at the receptionist just walk in and find the hotel toilets, floor to ceiling with marble, pristine clean with a cleaner in three or more times a day you can guarantee a throne to sit on and a lovely posh sink to wash your hands, she soon caught on. The rest of the day, we spent around the hotel's swimming pool paying just a small fee of one pound when the attendant came over.

I got chatting with one girl in the gym one day. She was in every day, keeping herself to herself. I happened to see her one day on the campsite I went on later, a mile further on up the road. She had got a caravan on the site with a swimming pool but no gym, savvy girl. Many hotels also have sister hotels within the area, so allow you to use the facilities of each, should you wish. I thought this was a brilliant idea. My plan for a month at least was just to relax, chill by the pool, build my tan up and dip in and out of the pool. It doesn't take long to get into a routine. Up in the morning, go for breakfast and a glass of pop or water for four and a half euros. Then a day around the pool, maybe a light snack or evening dinner for another five euros. After that, a cabaret in one of the local bars like the Showboat or Sinatra's. It was quickly obvious I was only using my motorhome for a coffee or two in the mornings and to sleep at night. I was in a quiet enough spot, so I decided to stay where I was. Benidorm has been the go-to place for us Brits since the early 60s. Kiss me quick, stag do's, drunken kids spewing up all over the place. The Spanish cops were having a field day bashing their poor little bonces all over the place. Sadly, that's what gave the place its bad name, and it stuck.

Today it's improved immensely, but it still has that air of tackiness about it, which is a shame really. For all its faults, Benidorm is a great place to relax and chill, have fun. Levanter beach is spectacular with its sparkling blue sea and seven miles of beautiful soft golden sand surrounded by sky-high multi-story hotels from one end to the other. After a very nice traditional cooked breakfast at the corner bar, £3.50, proper bacon and egg, sausage, tomatoes and even a bit of black pudding, I would be set up for the day. A short walk to my favourite little hotel, sunbed out, lashings of suntan oil on and let the rays do their work, bliss. In between catching the rays, I'd dive into one of the pools for a cooling dip before hitting the sunbed again.

The one thing that never fails to amaze me about Benidorm is the amount of boozing that goes on. It's almost like you can't have a holiday without a pint of lager. Not just at night. Go over for breakfast at 9am, you will see them sitting there with the traditional in front of them, with a pint of lager close to their wrist. Even the wives will join in and have a pint or two. They will boast about their pickled liver like it's a badge of honour. Even worse, since the series 'Benidorm' was made with Madge whizzing around the pool on her little mobility scooter, fag in mouth, it seems everyone now trundles around on a mobility scooter. There are hundreds of little and big Madge's. Many of them are on double scooters, which is the rage in Benidorm. Now you can trot out of your hotel or campsite, tootle the mile or so down into town, get pickled, then tootle back, many a time with the spouse flat out on the back. No one sees the irony of imitating a programme that takes the pee out of the British holidaymaker. There is a thriving trade in scooter hire and sales, with many of the hotels equipped with charging bays.

The campsites amaze me even more. Stopping at one the year before, I felt it was like God's waiting room. People had bought a mobile home or caravan to retire to and live their great dream. But you would see them slip into the routine of getting up in the morning, down for breakfast, washed down with a pint or two of lager then out on their mobility scooters for a little meander around the town, lunch down the corner bar or some other favourite little place, another couple of pints then a leisurely tootle back to the campsite. Maybe a nap before freshening up, then down to the bar for a game of bingo and maybe a little karaoke. Then it would be off back to the caravan another couple of cans whilst watching Corrie or Eastenders before popping off to bed before starting the same routine tomorrow. But there is far more to Benidorm than just that. There are some beautiful and interesting places around Benidorm, including the old Benidorm itself, at the far end of Levanter beach. Narrow streets, charming little shops with a quaintness all of their own. People will often walk or tootle down on their scooters from the new to the old town for a few hours. Some people even prefer the old town. Then there is the natural park overlooking Levanter beach and the whole of Benidorm, the Sierra Helada Natural Park. This beautiful area stretches from Levanter beach to the far end and past Benidorm with breath-taking cliffs and mountain walks. From a short trek to a major hike, there was something for everyone and a sure way to clear the cobwebs out of your system along with the lager. I did the shorter 3-kilometre walk, which nearly killed me, but equally was quite exhilarating. I spent over a month in Benidorm, thoroughly enjoying my stay and barely spending a lot of money. Truly, at 1.50 a pint of lager and 3.50 for breakfast, Benidorm is a cheap place to holiday. But I felt it was time to move on. My next destination was Poland and the concentration camps 1800 miles away and some £4-500 in diesel. I had decided, stopping off as I felt along the way, my next stop not too far away, on Altea a few miles further along the coast. I would be passing through some 6 or 8 countries, a marvellous adventure, but I was not rushing it.

ALTEA

With some reluctance, I had decided to leave Benidorm, when I got here. It was quite busy, but not, I quickly came to realise, with Brits. It was the Spanish holiday month, and the town was full of them, very nice, very friendly. Still, it was clear that they kept to themselves. I enjoyed the thought of some English speaking company, but it was very few and far between. The fear of Covid plus the ever-changing policies of the governments were having its effects. It was pleasant to watch the Spanish and the way they interacted. It was clear that they were very family orientated and doted on their kids. Whilst they were friendly with each other, spoke to each other, they did not socialise with each other as we Brits do. Maybe not so much today. The other interesting thing that struck me was their tendency not to drink so much. They will enjoy a bottle of wine or water around the table followed by a leisurely walk around the town, but that's about it. At night the bar was empty. The other thing that intrigued me was their attitude to the sun. Normally the Spanish have a permanent tan. True to form, the majority of the Spanish will disappear for siesta, leaving the pools and sunbeds empty whilst leaving their towels out, of course. But when they reappeared, still at the hottest part of the day, some would disappear under the shade, which begs the question, why come out at all. Then you had the others spraying on the oil and soaking up the rays like me, which then makes you ask what the point is. They are already a nice shade of brown, a colour I am trying to achieve. How brown do they think they are going to get?

By September, and as the Spanish started to disappear, the town started dying. Some of the local shopkeepers had faces as long as Livery Street. I felt sorry for them. They had already had two bad years. The few Brits here were complaining about how prohibitive the extra cost was to come here. One mother with two daughters said that the extra jabs and tests had cost them an extra 500 quid at least. Many places were closed, and those like Sinatra's or The Red Lion were less than a quarter full. It was dire. The week before the town had been full of gipsies, some five or six weddings were being held around the town, and true to form, the gipsies were booking into hotels in small groups of two or four. There were 100s of them scattered around the town trying to keep a low profile. It didn't work. The hoteliers and staff soon caught on. Gipsies are like diarrhoea once they spread out. Whoever gave them protected status made a rod for everyone's back, within a few days. True to form, they were fighting amongst themselves, getting kicked out of hotels and bars. The corner bar had to close due to the fighting and snorting coke in the toilets. The staff at Sinatra's, desperate for a few quid, buttered them up no end to get their tips. They were spending money like it was going out of fashion. Round the hotel pools and bars, they would drink gallons of booze, leaving the tables and floors littered with rubbish. Before just walking away, you just had to wonder at their mindset that made them feel justified in doing that without a care in the world. It just staggered me that they felt they could do that and felt it was acceptable, but then that's what they are like when they set up illegal camps around the country as though they had a given right. After a few days and getting their feet under the table, they started to get worse. I think the whole town breathed a sigh of relief when the last of the weddings took place. They started to leave, then the town really started to die down. Being on my own, it was even worse. I decided to head off, calling into Altea on my way north.

Altea is only a few miles from Benidorm. But a complete contrast, sedate, laid back, more upmarket, the atmosphere more relaxed. Low-level hotels set back from the beautiful sandy beaches and blue sea and a pleasant yet bustling harbour and yacht club. To the far end of the resort is a small car park behind a very nice 4-star hotel, adjoining the beach it is set between shaded trees and is free. Unfortunately, by the time I got there, a Spanish family had nicked the last free spot, so I set off back to the main beach and a campsite marked in the book at 13 euros a night. Maybe because of Covid, but when I asked the price, it was now 25 euros a night. With an ACCI sign on the window, I didn't even bother bringing out my card. We were in troubled times and, on principle, walked away. I headed back down to the harbour, where I pulled in next to the jetty, fishing boats and yachts sitting in the water next to me. I spent an enjoyable couple of nights and days exploring the town. No mobility scooters around here for sure. No, this was a different kind of resort altogether. In El Campello, just a few miles from Alicante, the English tourists and property owners looked down their noses at Torrevieja, oh no, thank you. Here I felt that people in or from Altea would look down their noses at Benidorm.

Just outside of Altea, there is the exclusive development of Altea Heights. So Beverly Hills. According to rumour some very famous singers amongst others wanted a house there. But the man who owned the mountain would only agree on the condition that he built the houses. Apart from the exclusivity, all the houses faced the sun from sunrise to sunset. Amongst some of the famous people who owned a house and lived there was rumoured to be Shirley Bassey and Sticky Vicky. Sticky Vicky? Her fame spread far and wide for appearing at the Benidorm palace pulling all manner of things from her vagina. Very classy, very Benidorm, and she was married to an inspector of police? Hmmm. What did he see in her then? Now both of them lived on the exclusive Altea heights, and

Sticky Vicky's daughter had taken over the mantel of appearing at the Benidorm palace, bringing things down from her vagina. To me, it begs the question who brought up the subject first, "Mommy, could you teach me how to do your job of bringing things down from my vagina?"

"Yes, my dear, but we will have to break you in gently." Yikes, the mind boggles, very classy. Also, outside Altea, and again according to rumour, is the synagogue built by the Russian Oligarch for his mother. Whilst he was enjoying the trappings of his wealth, he wanted his mother to join him and share in his wealth. But she wouldn't leave her beloved church back in Russia, probably praying for forgiveness at how her son obtained his billions. At any rate, a compromise was made, he would build a replica church in Altea, and she would move over to be with her adoring and dutiful son. She now worships in her own church, which is also open for anyone else to worship. After two pleasant and relaxing days in Altea, I set off once again through the mountains to Andorra. The only problem was I put the wrong Andorra into my sat nav.

ANDORRA AND ONWARDS

I don't take notes of what route to take, what towns or cities to avoid, what motorways to take or avoid. I simply put Andorra into my Tom-Tom and sit back and relax, enjoying the journey. What difference does it make whether I take the left-hand fork or the right-hand fork? It's all new to me anyway. It's not like England that I know like the back of my hand. Some travellers can be very precise and diligent when it comes to their touring. It doesn't just apply to how much water they carry or how much they should carry in their fridge. Many weigh everything thinking of the fuel consumption, wear and tear on their tyres, even weighting the motorhome before setting off. I have seen detailed questions on camping forums discussing the merits of weighing the motorhome. Will an extra bag of sugar make a difference, crikey? We are talking about a six-berth motorhome, in most cases with just two people and a Yorkshire terrier. We are light of some 40 stone. No matter how many grandkids or how much I carry, I still never get more than twenty miles to the gallon, uphill or down. I'm quite happy with that. To get me from Altea to Andorra will cost me not much more than a tank full of diesel, some 90 quid. To get from one side of the country to another, I consider that quite good value. Some people insist on keeping an accurate journal of the roads and towns they visit, places of interest and things to do and see, and I think that's great. I sometimes feel I am missing out on a lot more by not being so diligent. I found this even more so in France, where in order to get from A to B, I missed out so much in between.

Andorra was some 360 miles, according to my Tom-Tom. I will do it nice and steady in two days. I don't go into the pedantic or merits of the best route to take. Personally, my feeling is that I've never done that route before, so it's all exciting and new to me anyway. Even if I have done it, and I have a couple of times, it's still fresh enough for me to enjoy the journey, maybe even more so if I recollect some of the places. So no, I just click in Andorra and settle down to enjoy the scenery whilst following my little red car on my Tom-Tom. And what scenery it is, as it varies from one mile to the next. Arid, scorched countryside one minute, rich, arable, country the next. Desert one-minute, dense forests with natural country parks that stretch for miles as far as the eye can see, huge gullies dropping down one minute to sheer mountains rising up the next acres of boulders of all shapes and sizes, thrown up from the bowels of the earth, and dropped back down again, some weighing hundreds of tons covering 1000s of acres. Then there are the towns and place names like Albacete, Acorisa, Huesca Jaca and Arête. The typical Spanish names that you see in those Mexican cowboy films, El Lobo, Rio Grande, evoke such images in mind. I had got some 100 miles to go before Andorra, so I decided to pull into a service station for the night, have a coffee and a meal, and set off fresh the next morning, like France and much of Europe. The Aire in Spain is a welcoming delight. In England, you know you have to get off in two hours or start paying. Get in, eat your overpriced burger or some other poorly cooked food and expensive coffee and get out. Here in Spain, France, there is no such feeling. Here there is plenty of space and plenty of greenery to enjoy and relax. It takes some getting used to. In England, I started to notice many years ago that it's all about money. All these big companies, like the banks, must have little pen pushers getting paid a lot of money just to sit there thinking of ways to make more money. "Ay, why are we letting them park their cars in our car parks for hours on end? It only takes them an hour to walk over, buy a burger, eat it and get back out. I know, let's charge the buggers after two or three hours. That will soon get rid of them." No such attitude here in Europe.

Driving around to get my bearings, I pull in alongside 4 or 5 other motorhomes to the side of the main car park and directly opposite the main restaurant area. The reasoning for this is simple and twofold. I'm amongst others and within walking and shouting distance of the main building with people walking in and out 24 hours a day. It's subconscious. It's automatic. Sometimes I will park amongst the lorries. The problem with that is that they are always starting and running their engines every few hours or moving out with new lorries moving in, which can be noisy. Some of these service stations can spread out over several acres, great if you want peace and tranquillity during the day, not so good to be isolated at night. Walking into the service area and going up to the serving area, I ordered a plate of nice tender ham with frites and a big portion of green beans, very nice too. Heading back to the van, I locked up and put my head down for a pleasant night's sleep. Waking up the next morning, there was no urge to rush, no fear of anyone running over to shoo me off, no. So, there was no rush to get out of bed, another big advantage of Europe. Relaxed, I got up, opened the door, put the kettle on and after my second cup of coffee, was ready to hit the road. Somehow, I had overestimated the final distance to Andorra. It was only 16 miles away. How did I make that silly mistake? But hang about. Something was not quite right. Heading off, I thought something didn't add up. But soon, I saw the sign for Andorra. My mind was playing tricks. Andorra was in the mountains. Maybe I was approaching from a different angle. Soon I was driving into Andorra, but this was not Andorra. In exasperation, I pulled into a layby to try and figure out what I was doing wrong. Then I finally got it, duh, Andorra is a country between France and Spain, this Andorra was a town in Spain. Some distance from Andorra, the country, I had to input Andorra the country itself before it clicked on. I'd never made that mistake before. I had another 100 miles to go. Thankfully, it was en route.

Getting into Andorra, finally, I was surprised to be waved straight through, no customs. Reaching the thoughtfully provided Aire behind the river supermarket, I was impressed to notice it was heaving with motorhomes. The river was not slow. Each motorhome would be buying food and drinks in bulk for their travels. But the river itself was closed. The whole of Andorra was closed for Lords Day. Oh well, I would do my shopping for tomorrow like everyone else, now I know why customs was so quiet. After a good night's sleep, I woke to take myself up into the river supermarket, where I brought my goodies via its thoughtfully provided lifts. It was very easy to spend a couple of days in Andorra just chilling and sightseeing. The parking was plentiful and friendly, the views stunning. But after that, I decided to set off for Martinet some 20 miles away and another beautiful little town with a lovely welcoming Aire. Driving back out the way I came in (the Spanish side), I didn't know what to expect with the Covid. Going through the nothing to declare zone, I was frantically waved down by two customs officers who came rushing over and waving me into one of the bays. Within a few minutes of pulling into the bay, another customs officer came striding across. In anticipation, I had the side door open and the step out. I think that threw him. Looking in, he asked if I had any drinks or tobacco. I do not drink or smoke. That really seemed to piss him off as he grunted and waved me through. Oh well, off I set very shortly reaching Martinet, a friendly and familiar little ski resort. It was packed.

Martinet is beautiful. It's laid back and easy to settle into. The Aires are a delight. A shower room, waste disposal and water, all free, just a small charge for electricity if you needed it. Very few of us needed it. Surrounded by farms and countryside at the rear and side, a lovely river separating us from the town just across the bridge. A pleasant walk around the town, a few euros spent in the shops and café, followed by a reasonable meal in one of the restaurants on the night. I guess it's a win-win situation for both the town and us motor homers. It's a pity a lot of dead resorts in England don't think the same.

MILLAU BRIDGE AND THE GOTHARD PASS

Setting off from Martinet with a full tank of duty-free courtesy of Andorra, I headed off to Switzerland and the Gothard pass via the Millau bridge, the highest bridge in the world. I had travelled over it previously with my wife paying the toll charge for the privilege. Certainly, it's not for the faint-hearted, as for doing it in a force ten gale, well. We had also stood underneath it to get a different perspective. Either way, it is inspiring, awesome. After spending the night in the town, I set off the next day only noticing after I had left Millau way beyond, I was very low on diesel, I was so engrossed in enjoying my journey I hadn't kept my eye on the tank, now I was desperately keeping my eye open for a garage. I could kick myself. Normally I don't let my tank get much below a quarter, then I saw the Carrefour sign. Pulling in, I filled up my tank for 90 euros, a bit of a difference to Andorra at 60 euros. But oh well, pulling out of Carrefour, I was about to set off when I noticed a parking area overlooking the river on the opposite bank. The town was called Langogne, and I decided to spend the night there. I was soon moved along, though, by the truck drivers whose spaces I had nicked. Fair enough. With a pleasant gesture, I got to the end of the lorry park. Setting off the next morning, I saw plenty of Aires all around, including the Carrefour car park. Oh well.

It's typical that after a few hours of driving, I was starting to feel a bit peckish again through the beautiful French countryside, rolling hills and deep valleys with mountains in the distance. Eventually, I pulled up quick sharpish outside a little nondescript patisserie. I grabbed the last and only jambon and cheese baguette and a cake. A few hundred yards further on, I was passing a bigger and better patisserie every few hundred yards, typical. Pulling up in a layby to eat my baguette, I tried to have a nap only to be violently shaken awake every few minutes by the heavy goods lorries passing by. That's it, enough. I set off yet again. Soon I noticed I was surrounded by lakes. I was now in the national park of Villars-Les-Dombes, loads of car parking and motorhome parking surrounding these beautiful lakes. Well, give me a kick, all for the sake of a few extra miles, ahh well.

After another few miles and some 130 miles from Bern in Switzerland, I came into a lovely small village called Joudes with a nice car park next to a pretty church overlooking a nice picnic area, with benches laid out overlooking the green. After a bit of shuffling, I edged into the best position overlooking the green, ready and set to drive off the next morning. Doors open, kettle on, sorted. A couple of hours later, I was joined by a heavy goods lorry that spent the night, no fuss. He just pulled in away from me and also settled down, so typically France. It was now some 130 miles to the Swiss border. The drive, as usual, was delightful, the French roads a pleasure to drive on, wide with tree-lined avenues for mile after mile. Valleys and mountains slip by either side. Surely when those Romans came marching through Europe, they didn't mess about. They marched those soldiers forward in straight lines digging out the roads as they went, south to north, just plough a straight line. If Switzerland had their tunnels, France had their gorges, miles of bridges covering gorges hundreds of feet below, in between quaint little towns and villages that seemed to blend from town to country with hardly a break, even the roads seemed to blend into the footpaths, so laid back is the pace of life. Soon I was entering Switzerland, and the only way I knew was because of the empty border post, empty and almost unnoticeable. I had to drive back out again to double-check I was actually in Switzerland, so I entered the country twice. The change was imperceptible. France has its own distinct character, as does every country. But as you drive out of France, you notice the houses change. From typically French, the houses now morph into each other before turning into the traditional Swiss chalets, the Swiss take on their own particular build. By now, I needed to find somewhere to park for the night, which was easier said than done. The Swiss are sticklers for being correct, and slapstick parking isn't one of them. Pulling into Aldi, I parked up before realising I was only a short distance from the lakes pulling into the side overlooking Lake Lucerne. I put the brakes on and settled down to enjoy the spot. I thought I was sorted until a lady pulled alongside me and told me I was in her spot. Driving on another couple of miles, I pulled into a lovely spot next to a harbour and settled down for the night.

Interestingly there were no signs at all, yet I was the only one parked there. I felt a tad uneasy. I had got the steak under the grill before a friendly couple came over and advised me against stopping there. The police would give me a big fine, big trouble. I knew they were not joking, thanking them. I set off yet again, it was getting late, but within a couple of miles, I came across a garage with a restaurant and parking. I was 100 miles from the Gothard Pass. My next destination.

With the Gothard pass in front of me, I wanted to be fully aware to enjoy the experience of driving over it. The last time I made a mistake somehow of missing it and going through the tunnel, I didn't want that to happen again. Some travellers and camper forums advise against stopping overnight on garage forecourts because of the dangers. OK, maybe I might be proven wrong one day. But with a bit of common sense, I don't think there is much worry or concern. I never park up in some isolated spot, always as close as possible to the main restaurant or garage. After a good night's sleep, a couple of coffees, a wash, I was all good to go. The Gothard Pass is amazing today. It was clear, but it will be impassable in a few short weeks and under deep snow. Winding and snaking across the mountains, the views were awe-inspiring, deep valley's and mountain lakes in brilliant emerald greens and greys, tumbling and bouncing over stones and boulders washed down from the mountains over centuries. I wasn't alone in stopping at many of the viewpoints dotted along the pass. People of all ages, cameras were clicking away, small villages and lakes below us. Of course, my big advantage was the motorhome and the ability to put on the kettle and enjoy a coffee as I soaked up the views.

It wasn't long before I came to the bottom of the pass and set my destination for Poland and Auschwitz. My mistake was using the mapping on my phone, which wasn't very good at all. It took me nigh on 100 miles before I noticed my little car was going in the wrong direction, the kilometres increasing instead of decreasing. Eventually, after lots of trials and mistakes, I made an about-turn and took the motorway back, I think the way I had come. I couldn't bear thinking about it. After another seemingly 100 miles, I pulled into yet another service station and put my feet up, not before I enjoyed a very nice but expensive burger with all the relish. It was now I discovered my sat nav reached as far as Lichtenstein, about another 100 miles east. Perhaps from there, my phone mapping might improve. Either way, I was beginning to panic a bit. After all, I didn't want to turn back. From Lichtenstein, if I couldn't follow my phone map with some 1000 miles to go, I could see Auschwitz receding. Finally, I got to Lichtenstein, an ugly little country I felt, with nothing to praise it for except its castles and low taxes. It seemed to have one road leading in and out and, for some reason, held more millionaires per square mile than anywhere else in the world, apart from Monaco. Strange, all to save a few quid in tax, Lichtenstein is the only country in Europe, a micro country surrounded on all sides by the Alps. I recognised the restaurant that I had called in a few years earlier to enjoy a pleasant stew. On my way out, I recognised the Co-op garage where I had tried to make a little joke a few years earlier. And came right unstuck.

On one of the camping sites, I commented that I couldn't believe how pig-ignorant some of these foreigners are. That I had called into the Co-op, a British business, for the daily Sun newspaper, no one could understand a word I was saying. Well, I thought it was obviously clear it was a joke, so I sat back and waited for the banter to start. Well, it started alright. What a thick ignorant pig I was to expect anyone in a foreign country to speak English. Worse, it was compounded by the fact I was buying the Sun newspaper. The barbs and insults came thick and fast. In the end, I had to ask how stupid they were to fall for something like that. Out of about 40 people, I think one person saw the joke. Needless to say, I was banned from the site.

SEEFELD AND
THE AUSTRIAN TYROL

Setting my route destination on my phone again, I set off through glorious mountain scenery and lush forests, eventually entering Austria with the German border to my left. I soon entered a stunningly beautiful town, so impressed that I knew I had to stop and have a look around. Pulling into a car park, I locked the van up and headed for the shops. It was thriving with a bustling, lively atmosphere. All the restaurants were busy and full. People were sitting outside enjoying a drink or a meal before or after hiking somewhere. It was so typically Swiss/Austrian with those shuttered windows and log framed chalets. I was so enamoured, I found a seat and ordered a coffee. After asking for proof of my jabs, the waiter brought my coffee out. Looking at the menu, I decided to have something to eat. I wasn't starving or even that hungry. I just wanted to soak up the ambience for as long as possible. My choice was either a beef stew with bacon dumplings, interesting, or homemade apple strudel with ice cream. At 4 euros I went for the strudel, it was good value. After enjoying my meal, I asked the waiter where I was, at that point I hadn't a clue. The town was called Seefeld in the Austrian Tirol. Now I had to find somewhere to settle in for the night, it was late and whilst there were plenty of rest areas along the autobahn I had to drive some distance before reaching a service station with adequate parking and restaurant facilities, after a not very nice coffee inside, I settled down for the night with the only bottle of wine I had kept from a few weeks earlier in

Benidorm. Tomorrow I would be on my way to Auschwitz, some 450 miles away. But then I got the knock on the door.

Standing there at the open door were two cops looking suitably serious. I had an immediate joke that they had come to kick me off the service area. No, I had not bought a vignette. A vignette is a pass, a ticket charged by some countries for travelling on the motorways or autobahns. In Switzerland, you will normally be stopped at the border and given the option. If you're using the autobahns, you have to buy a vignette. If you're not, you don't need the vignette. I try to avoid motorways most times. But in this case, I didn't even realise I had crossed over onto the autobahn. These two were not going to give any leeway. I had to pay a fine of 120 euros. 120 euros? Now I wasn't too happy. How was I to know I was on the autobahn and that I had to pay for a vignette? "There are signs," the one cop said.

"Where? I saw no signs, and where do you pay?" A

"At the border or any service station."

"But there was no one at the border."

"Where have you come from?"

"Lichtenstein." That shut him up, he would have known there was no border control, but it did not stop him. "Ok, can I go to a service station or pay for a ten euro vignette here and now?"

"No, you must pay the fine."

Following him round to their van, I could see it was all set up as an office, with a desk and computer. This angered me even more. This was obviously a legal money-making scam, no signs, no notices, no border checks. Just these cops, riding up and down the motorways jumping onto anyone who made the mistake of not paying for a vignette. So much for Austrian hospitality. But when I posted about it on a Facebook camping forum, I got a rollicking for not knowing and not doing my homework. Ignorance is no excuse. Oh well,

After the happy thoughts and memory of Seefeld, I felt it was now spoilt by a couple of greedy cops, obviously backed by a greedy government. Go get 'em, boys. At 120 euros a hit, it's nice money if you can get it. It's like the speed cameras in England. Some are useful. Many are just cash machines. But to listen to the cops, it's all justified. I made it very clear that the last thing I wanted to enter was either Germany or Austria. Apart from Seefeld, I was not really impressed with the Austrian landscape. Setting off the next morning, I had left the mountains way behind and was now eating up the miles of flat or undulating Austrian landscape. Neat and tidy farms and houses passed me in the distance. If I entered any towns or villages, nothing made me want to stop and explore the area. Maybe Seefeld was the only beauty spot, surely not. Maybe this was why Germany and Austria were not on everyone's wish list. Typically, and true to form, I lost myself with my phone sat nav again. It fluctuated between 550 kilometres to 650, then 950 kilometres. Maybe it was sod's law that I seemed destined to be spending forever in Austria or Germany. At least I made sure there were no vignettes for the German roads once I got on them.

POLAND AND AUSCHWITZ

I know what I had done wrong. Somehow, my phone sat nav, being a bit slow on the uptake, didn't really redirect when I did a left turn outside Czechia on the way to Poland. Instead of directing me to keep Czechia to my left, I had turned left, putting Czechia on my right. The route took me north, further into Germany, and the long way round. Obviously, it was my fault as I wasn't reading my sat nav correctly. Oh well, onwards and upwards as they say. As I drove into Poland, the landscape changed from almost flat rolling fields to forests. I had spoken to my friend Ela in Poland, who told me that she, her brother and mother were now on holiday in Macedonia, so it looked like I wouldn't be bumping into them as planned, which was a bit of a disappointment. Only Ela spoke good English, and I was looking forward to treating them to dinner and them treating me to a bit of polish culture from the Polish perspective. Ela and her family lived in Krakow. As they were on holiday themselves, I made directly for Auschwitz and the German concentration camps. Ela had given me the name and directions to a campsite some 7 miles from Auschwitz concentration camp. The campsite was called the Campsite by the Lake, and I found it straight away on my phone.

Calling into the site, I could see it was very quiet and rural but almost empty, not of caravans. There were plenty of them, no, people. The barrier lifted, and I drove through and found a nice spot right by the lake, plugged into the electricity before finding the camp website chat board and sending them a message. Someone would be in the office in ten minutes.

At that stage, I didn't know if I would stop a night or a week. The young, friendly girl told me there was no problem and I could stop as long as I wanted although it was the end of the season. The cost per night, inclusive of Wi-Fi and electricity, was 30 zlotys, which seemed rather a lot until I worked it out. 30 zlotys was about 6 euros a night. Well, with such a beautiful site, I quickly made my mind up that I was going to spend a few nights here. Already, I liked Poland.

I was some 800 miles from Calais, a steady drive spread over maybe four or five days. The next day I had planned to visit Auschwitz, which in actual fact was outside the polish town of Oswiecim. For whatever reason, the Germans had decided to call the camp Auschwitz. My plan was simple, to drive up, get the measure of the camp, my bearings maybe have a look around. The website stated it was free to enter, but a guided tour was advised, and this had to be paid for, the funds helping to cover the cost of refurbishments to the camp. After a look around, I would return the next day for the guided tour. Well, that was my plan. Pulling into the car park, I could see it was rammed, mostly with polish coaches but quite a few from Germany. Just two countries I noticed. By the second day, I was ready to set out for the concentration camp, or really, that should be camps, because there were, in fact, two. Auschwitz itself, that name to me is synonymous with the concentration camp or Birkenau, which is what we are all used to seeing in any German film where the camps are highlighted. Auschwitz itself threw me, approaching it from the outside, and coming from Oswiecim, it just looked like a modern industrial site of two-story buildings surrounded as it was with a ten-foot concrete wall. Approaching it from the car park, it was unrecognisable. Where was the imposing building that I remember seeing in the films, the wide-open tunnel entrance that the trains drove through, packed with poor Jews before disgorging them on the other side of that grim building? Watchtowers every few hundred feet and joined by electrified fencing. It was busy. It was heaving. There were barriers everywhere, with people being shuttled into different lanes and directions. It was not much different to some 80 odd years ago. The dozen or so of two-story buildings had been barracks originally. They looked much like that today, almost a modern army barracks, photos and explanations. Inscriptions were planted everywhere, in and around the entrance and indeed the camp itself of Jewish families who had perished or survived the camp atrocities. The atrocities they had suffered along with the children who had been incarcerated there. It was sobering and very thought-provoking.

Seeing the ticket office, I went over to where a very friendly lady explained the rules to me. First, it was free to enter, for which she gave me a ticket. Then she explained that I could get the free shuttle coach to Birkenau, which was the second part of the visit. This was also free. Having parked my motorhome, I made for the coach, which left every twenty minutes. Birkenau was 3 kilometres away and a ten-minute drive. Pulling up outside Birkenau, I recognised it immediately. The train line leading into the entrance, the watchtowers, the electric fencing was all there as it was in 1944. My first visit was to the bookshop where I purchased the voices of memory, the evacuation, liquidation and liberation of Auschwitz. A concentration camp is not something to rush through or around. Of all the coaches arriving, there is an immediate sense of quietness, anticipation and respect. Most people, even children, know what is expected of them and have some idea of what they are about to witness. As such, I spent some time outside the main entrance of Birkenau, just getting a feel for the place, to try to take in the atmosphere. To try and place myself back in those days of such atrocity. It was impossible.

Both camps covered a total area of some 472 acres. Auschwitz itself has some 49 acres, leaving Birkenau with some 428 acres. In Birkenau, most of the blocks had disappeared or been demolished, leaving just the bases. But at one stage, some 300 blocks had been built over the whole area, all surrounded by electric fencing and watchtowers. Walking in through the main entrance gates, I found it difficult to take in, to comprehend. Various separate groups spread around the land and buildings, many of which remained closed, for whatever reason. I knew and was aware of the tour guides in the main camp of Auschwitz, if it was the main camp, but was completely unaware of how the guide system worked for Birkenau. Seeing the coach tours coming in, in groups, I assumed we in the shuttle buses were left to our own devices. This was until, of course, being close to another group, I heard the guide speaking in English. In English? But the tourists were Polish? Oh well, I decided to latch on to the tour.

Following the train line leading into the camp and behind, the guide first took us to a truck standing near the end of the tracks. A sentry house was built onto the one end for the guard. At this point, the poor Jews were disgorged and sorted. What a horrible term, but they were. Into groups according to their age and physical abilities, the young and fit sent one way, the very young, old and unfit sent another. First, they were herded to the gas chambers and crematoriums very cleverly built and set out at the far end of the camp. The buildings were now destroyed, completely demolished by the Germans when they knew the end was near and the Russians were closing in. But it didn't stop anyone from working out the layout of the buildings, together with eyewitness accounts and drawings by some of the ex-prisoners who had had the misfortune to have spent time in there, and the good fortune? To have survived.

First, they were led into the first section, where false showerheads were fitted. After weeks or maybe months of ill-treatment, the prisoners, mainly Jews, were filthy, many covered in lice or other infestations. The prisoners were relieved at the thought of a shower to wash clean. Too late, they only realised they were being gassed at the last moment.

Conveniently taking all their clothes off and putting them in tidy piles. Once they were dead, the Sonderkommando entered. These were handpicked Jewish prisoners chosen to work on the bodies and cut their hair (used for bedding, etc.). They searched them for any gold or jewellery, even ripping gold teeth out of their mouths. Some of these Sonderkommando even had to guide their own children, relatives or friends, knowingly to their deaths, some trying to placate them, reassure them that everything was fine. Suitcases were sorted along with clothing and put to one side in storage. Then the dead bodies were dragged by the Sonderkommando to the incinerators, where their bodies were burnt. Children were thrown in together to make full use of the incinerators. Once burnt, the ashes were taken outside and placed in a pile at regular intervals. Well, they were burning hundreds of bodies a day. The ashes would be collected up and taken to the local fast-flowing river and tipped, disappearing very quickly.

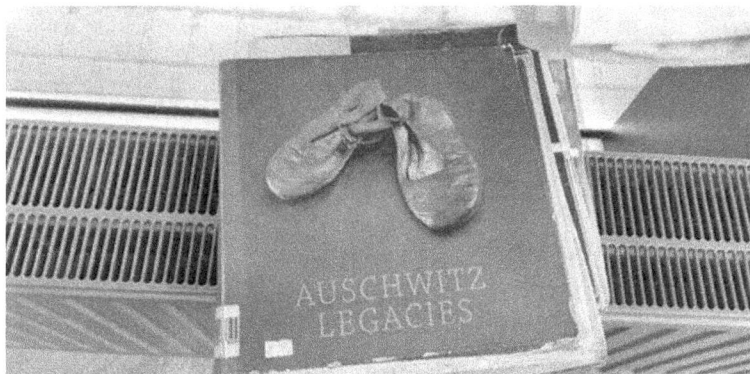

The question that kept throwing up in my mind was? Why didn't anyone know or suspect? At all. I know I am not alone with that thought. Many others ask the same question major factory owners like Volkswagen and Mercedes were offered and used the prisoners as cheap labour. This is a matter of record. Apart from the moral viewpoint, how come not one of these Jewish or other prisoners shout out or whisper, help me? How come no one heard or noticed. I know and understand that the prisoners demolished the houses in the immediate area after the inhabitants were given orders to move out. I can understand the inhabitants having no say in the matter, but the nearest big town of Oswiecim was just a mile and a half away. Now let me tell you, I lived a mile from Aston Cross in Birmingham. Home to HP sauce and Ansell's brewery, you could smell them both on certain days of the week. All over for miles.

London had its bow bells. We in Birmingham had our Ansells brewery and HP sauce. How come no one knew smelt or saw the smoke from the chimneys? Or heard anything? Ok, terrified. But then you watch the films and the documentaries, the Hitler Youth, the Germans who took part in Kristallnacht. We are not talking of a couple of dozen here. We are talking hundreds, whole communities, a whole country working as one. How come there was only one Oscar Schindler? A member of the Nazi party and an industrialist? Were there other Oscar Schindler's? Or was Oscar, being a Nazi, simply covering his own back?

From the gas chambers, the guide took us on to the death houses. These were where the women prisoners were taken to die. They knew it too. It was no secret. Within hours, days or weeks, they were left to starve or taken away to be murdered. Whether through old age, incapacity or simply for being suspected of some crime against the Nazis, some of them scratched or etched their names on the walls in the hope that people would know who they were, be remembered. The wooden bunk beds still there in situ, dozens of them, each being shared by three or more prisoners, crammed in like sardines, all aimed to beat them down and lose their dignity.

By now, I was starting to feel a bit guilty myself for taking advantage of the guide, so I thought it best to introduce myself and offer to pay. I had noticed one or two of the group had clocked me and wouldn't have been surprised if they never said anything. I also noticed they were also wearing a little yellow stick-on badge, which almost amused me, not unlike the badges the prisoners wore all those years ago. The guide was a very nice friendly girl with a shy smile. She lived in Oswiecim, as did her parents and grandfather before her. Her grandfather had been one of the first to enter the camp after the liberation and helped the Jews leave there. The guide still had some of her grandfather's mementoes from that time. She let me know that she had seen me and knew I was not in the group with a smile. How did you know? I wasn't wearing the little yellow badge. We had almost come to the end of the tour now, so she told me I was welcome to continue, and she would not charge me.

Soviet troops had liberated the concentration camp of Majdanek in Lublin in the July of 1944. This set the alarm bells ringing at the Auschwitz garrison. From august of 1944, some 65,000 prisoners were evacuated, among them almost all the poles, Russians and Czechs. Attention was given to destroying all the evidence of prisoner files, registration forms, and lists of Jews deported to Auschwitz for extermination. The SS started killing the Sonderkommando that operated the crematoria and gas chambers since these were direct witnesses to what had happened. A mutiny broke out during which some 450 Sonderkommando died fighting. The rest of the crematoriums were destroyed on the orders of SS Himmler. The rest of the prisoners rounded up and hurriedly shipped out on what became known as the death march. 1,000s of prisoners were forced to march into Germany, many dying or being shot on the way. Most of the prisoners were supposed to be fit and healthy and capable of the hundred-kilometre march. But hundreds more jumped into the queue who were in poor health. Who can blame them? But most of them died or were shot en-route. Some 9000 were left behind, mostly too ill or sick to move. These the Nazis planned to murder, they managed about 700. The prisoners welcomed the Russian soldiers as true saviours, for their part, entered the camp as true liberators and were fully aware of the historical significance of their mission. Personally, I found this quite interesting. The paradox is that the prisoners were being liberated by a totalitarian Stalinist army of and against a Nazi totalitarian army. Soviet soldiers discovered the bodies of at least 600 prisoners in the main camp, many hundreds more in other camps. These were by far not the only traces of crimes committed. Some of the prisoners, in relatively good condition, left as soon as possible and headed to their homes. Many more were left to be treated by the Russians and the Polish red cross. Hundreds more died after liberation. These prisoners were treated in the main camps and had to be given food in small doses like medicine three times a day before eating a full meal. Many prisoners looked like skeletons, had earth or dirt-covered skin and weighed less than half their normal weight.

I visited Birkenau twice in all to let everything, or as much as possible, sink in. In the meantime, my polish friend Ela had been in touch. They were finishing their holiday in Macedonia and planned to come over to the campsite to visit me. Why I don't know, they lived 40 miles further east in Krakow. They had planned for me to visit after and be given a tour of their beautiful city. I was also invited to park up on their mothers land, of which apparently they had plenty. I was looking forward to taking them for a polish meal, seeing some of Poland from the Polish perspective. But I didn't want to impose on them, so I will take it as it comes. I had brought them some gifts, including Danish cookies from Andorra. It was really silly of me when and after I found out how cheap Poland was. Still, the thought counts. They came over to the camp on a weekend, the sun was out, and the camp was busy with visitors, caravan owners who left their caravans full time.

It's cheaper. We had a wonderful day. Ela's mother brought me some lovely polish cake and organic apples from her garden. In return, I gave them some gifts that I had bought in Austria and Andorra. After a nice long day, we visited a restaurant called In the Forest for a nice, typically Polish meal. They drove off, agreeing to meet up again before I left.

Having seen the Birkenau camp, I now wanted to see the Auschwitz camp. But having finally arrived, I stood looking for the famous sign above the camp gates, notorious worldwide. It certainly wasn't what I thought was at the front of the gate, I was soon to find out. Joining the queue, we were herded through the barricades, not a lot of change there then, hmm. The security was as bad as at any airport. First, I had to empty my pockets, put my phone, keys, etc., into a tray that went through a scanner. Whys that? What has been going on here? Weapons? Then another security checkpoint at the far end where my ticket was checked again. Whilst I could understand some of the security, I felt this was a bit over the top. Some years earlier, someone had broken into the camp and stolen the sign.

Soon I was to come to the sign itself, which seemed to be to the side of the camp. The sign itself reads –ALBEIT MECHT FREI— which translates as work sets you free. Yes, those

Germans certainly had a great sense of humour, alright. In this case, in this camp, work killed you. Apparently, the prisoners, being fully aware of what was going on and at great risk, deliberately made the letter B in the sign upside down as some form of protest. I would have thought the last thing on any prisoners' mind entering that camp would be the letter B upside down. Again, the camp was made up of blocks, barracks. It had been a former army barracks with two stories and a cellar. Again, the watchtowers are all surrounded by and connected by electric fencing every few dozen yards. Block eleven was the experimental block where Jews, gipsy twins and Jewish women were experimented on at will by doctors such as Mengele. The only problem I was finding was how to connect the buildings I was looking at to the scenes that took place. I find it difficult to explain it as I write. Maybe I was expecting bloodstains all over the place. Apart from the many pictures and written messages around the camp and barracks, it was difficult to tie the horrors of what had happened with the visual scenes of almost modern plastered walls in modern, well-built buildings. It didn't help that these were two-story buildings with cellars where some of the atrocities had taken place and were yet blocked off from viewings.

In Pompeii and herculean, it was quite easy to imagine and picture the scene of what took place two thousand years before. Both were living history. Even the volcano itself held an aura of fear and malevolence about it, the landscape eerily silent. Oh yes, so was Auschwitz, but differently. Someone once told me that in Auschwitz, the birds never sang. They were right. As in Auschwitz and Birkenau, the birds didn't sing. Is there something more to life and death in the universe that makes it such that the birds don't sing?

Once or twice, I saw young children crying and obviously affected by the scenes they were seeing. I just didn't feel that way. Maybe the government or whoever had thought it better to dilute the horrors, the reality of what we were seeing for fear of being too upsetting. When I mentioned this to Ela, she replied that it was the message that was important and was to be remembered. She was right, of course. In France, we visited a small town called Oradour-Sur-Glane. For some reason, still not explained to this day, a troop of German soldiers made their way to the town, gathered up all the inhabitant's into groups and killed them, then set fire to the town. Fortunately, a couple of witnesses escaped telling the tale. Most of the townspeople were at work in outlying cities like Limoges. Upon visiting the town and seeing the destruction that had taken place, General De Gaul decreed that the town would be left as it was as a living museum and a reminder of the horrors and brutality of the German people, it still serves its purpose walking through the town the brutality and evil were eerily present, oddly enough, here, again, I never heard the birds sing. The only explanation for the brutal murders was that some partisans had attacked and blown up a train days earlier. This was seen as some kind of revenge.

The other thing that struck me, of course, was the modern-day German race of people. One acquaintance I know who is married to a German told me that he just doesn't have a clue as to the truth of what went on. Yet in Oradour-Sur-Glane, I heard German voices, a couple talking? What were they saying? There were coach loads of Germans touring and visiting Auschwitz and Birkenau. What were they saying? What were they discussing? For many, it must have been their fathers who had served in the German army. Maybe some had served in the camps. I just don't think I would like to live with the thought of going to Germany or Poland, and the roles were reversed with my father having committed such acts. You've got to be a certain type of person to be able to carry out acts like that to order. Although I've heard about the black'n'tans in Northern Ireland, some of the British soldiers, and of course, I've seen many a cop who I could imagine could easily carry out such brutality. It's amazing, I suppose, how a uniform can affect so many people. Once, in Morocco, I got talking to a guy who strutted about like he owned the hotel. He told me he was a police officer in Ireland. "Tom, when I first put that uniform on, I felt ten feet tall." Yes, I could imagine.

Back at the campsite, I was settling into a nice comfortable routine, up in the morning, opening the door onto views of the lake right in front of me, kettle on, a cup of coffee to hand before going for a little walk around the campsite or surrounding area, then back to the motorhome and a bit of work on my computer. Maybe it was the time of year, the fact that the site was closed, well, it was supposed to be, but campers were still here, not many, just the odd couple, more would come over at weekends if the sun was shining, the camp had everything. A nice bar, attractive outside eating area and a large function room that appeared to be hired out for the first Saturday night, possibly a birthday party.

A few spoke English, but in the main, they only spoke their native tongue, it didn't matter, I found the polish people very friendly and easy-going. In England and indeed Europe, many campsites turn to full-time campers as they find it more lucrative with a guaranteed income. In England, some £5,000 per year plus. In Spain, £3,000 per year plus. Here, in Poland? I didn't know. At 6 euros a night, i.e., 42 euros a week, I could only take a guess at what the yearly fees would be. But seeing as the camp was full, I could only think that maybe it wouldn't be that expensive. By the first sunny weekend, the site was full of families, the bar busy as people ate food and drank outside. The thought very quickly, and more than once, entered my mind to maybe put a caravan on the site, so cheap was it. The prices in the shops and supermarkets were a revelation. I was buying good quality steaks for what worked out at a few euros. For sure, anyone on a low pension in England could do a lot worse than to consider putting a caravan permanently on-site.

I gave up trying to speak to my neighbours after our first couple of efforts. Friendly as they were, we resorted to good morning, hello. Ela, her brother and her mother came to visit on the Saturday. Maybe it was the language barrier that made things a little bit difficult. Krakow, where they lived, was some 50 miles away. They had initially mentioned my parking on their mothers land and hooking up to their electricity. I was happy and expecting to do that. Still, they wanted to travel over to me for some reason, for how long, I don't know. Still, it ended up they spent all day ending with a nice restaurant meal at the restaurant in the forest, just a mile or so outside the town of Imielin.

Ela, her brother and mother, brought me some gifts of Polish chocolate, fresh organic apples and a homemade polish cake that was very nice indeed, for my part I gave them some biscuits and chocolates that I had brought in Andorra. Too late, I realised Poland wasn't as backward as I thought. Nonetheless, we had a lovely day, the sun was shining, and we sat outside by the lake. Cups of coffee on the go and a couple of oxo drinks that they thoroughly enjoyed. After ten days on the site, I agreed to visit them at their home, hopefully doing a bit of sightseeing around Krakow and having a meal or two out. After ten days and with a little reluctance, I almost had to force myself to pack everything up and make my way to reception and settle my bill. Being the cynic I am, I'm always expecting the little sting in the tail when I go to settle my bill. Surely the electricity can't be included in the six euros a night? After some time, a friendly young polish girl came to the office and worked out my bill. First, she reduced the 10 days to 7 with my discount? Uh, then she gave me the total, 210 zloty, which worked out at some £42. I was almost tempted to say hang on and go back, £42 for ten days, including electric at some five quid a day for food, a pensioner could live here very nicely indeed.

ELA, HER FAMILY
AND KRAKOW

Putting Ela's mom's address into my sat nav, I set off for Krakow. Poland was a constant surprise to me. The small villages I passed through to Krakow were smart, clean and tidy. Nothing like I had expected. As one of the eastern bloc countries, I just lumped it in with Bulgaria, Romania, etc., third world countries living in poverty, right? Wrong. I was totally and utterly wrong. Poland was nothing like that at all. I admitted this to Ela when we met up.

I had met a few polish people in England. All seemed pleasant and friendly. The only contradiction I heard from that was from my friend in Boston, Lincolnshire. Terry ran a flower stall in the Boston market and made a fairly nice living. Initially, and at first, the Poles would come over for seasonal work being put up by farmers who paid them a low wage. The poles would live frugally, sending their wages home to their families. This was fine for a few years until the EU started to widen its net, bringing in and offering membership to Bulgaria, amongst others. The farmers caught onto this bringing Bulgarians in to undercut the Poles. Great for the farmers, stupid and short-sighted as they were. But it started to destroy the town with Poles and Bulgarians vying for work. Those not able to get work hanging around the town drinking vodka by the gallon, fighting and urinating all over the place, and of course, getting full benefits as they were entitled to. Shortly after Terry told me all this, a news documentary covered the town, highlighting the same problem. From a small market town, it had changed and been destroyed out of all proportion. Without a doubt, we have some great sparks running our country. So, in my ignorance, I assumed the Polish people, like the Bulgarians, lived in third world countries, wrong, very wrong. They just had a different monetary adjustment. Drive into Bulgaria. You are entering the third world. Bosnia also, though slightly better, Serbia the same. Yet drive around to Croatia next door, you see happy, contented people growing in prosperity. Yet, all were involved in the Bosnian Muslim conflict just a few short years ago.

Ela's mother did indeed own a very nice house just outside of Krakow. Her husband had died about fifteen years ago. She now lived with her son, Ela lived in Krakow itself. Being made very welcome, I think it was mutually accepted that I was happy to keep to my own camper during my stay. Krakow was an amazing city. I could see why Ela wanted to live in it. Near the Czech Republic, it was surrounded by beautiful medieval walls with a well preserved medieval core centre. A well-established Jewish quarter centred on the expansive stately market square and its site of the clothes hall. The smells and the atmosphere were a heady mix for me. While we spent a good few hours with Ela and her brother showing me around, I made a point of visiting again on my own a few days later. But time flies, and I didn't want to impose on the family's friendship. I had only gotten to know them in Greece a few years before. Whilst it was very nice getting to know them, only Ela could speak English. Her mother and brother none at all, making conversation a bit one-sided. After a few days, we said our goodbyes. Topping my water tank up, I put Calais into my sat nav some 850 miles west. After four months, I was starting to look forward to getting home. Again, I didn't expect or want to rush. I anticipated doing a steady 200 miles a day. So, I stopped at service stations for 4 or 5 days as I went. I had already had the pleasure of filling up with diesel in Poland and enjoying the cheapness of it. I had now got three-quarters of a tank. The Polish border was some 200 miles away. There was plenty enough time for me to refill with a full tank before I got into Germany, where I knew prices would escalate. I just wish I got a couple of ten-gallon tanks, maybe three or four. I'm not greedy.

The drive to the polish border was pleasant, with one overnight stop off at a service station filling up with the last of my cheap fuel. Seeing some large packs of tobacco on the shelf, I asked how much two strong packs would cost? 15 euros. Whilst I didn't smoke, I knew that was cheap, what it would taste like, I don't know, but I guessed my friend's son would appreciate it.

GERMANY AND
THE NETHERLANDS

Initially, going right back to the beginning of the year, my plan had been to visit a few of the concentration camps, the most notorious ones. I researched and checked their positions on the map, Dachau, Buchenwald and Bergen Belsen, before making my way to Poland and the Auschwitz concentration camps. I had cut a couple of them out purely because I knew I couldn't stand the idea of spending too much unnecessary time in Germany. Call me racist. What is racist? What is racist about disliking a group of people because of the country they come from. Why can't I speak my mind in a free democracy? I used to hear all this rubbish with the Welsh, Irish and Scottish. Now the Welsh tend to keep their mouths shut, but years ago, they made their dislike of us English very clear. Now they are more subtle. For instance, for the English, getting a job in Wales is difficult, to say the least. I know. I've spoken to people who have moved and lived in the country. It was one of the main reasons we never bought a smallholding in the country. I suppose, slowly, eventually, throwing everyone into the mix will dilute things a fair bit.

For instance, the Barmouth council is sneeringly looked upon as little Birmingham by the Gwynedd council. So, it might be illegal to express your racism, but it doesn't stop it. The British police have shown their racism against black Caribbean's and Asians for years. It's no secret. It's on record and acknowledged by the government and police themselves.

Don't get me started on Hereford. When we bought a country pub and caravan site in Hereford some years ago, it was made very clear to my daughter Kristy that she could live there for sixty years, and she would never be accepted. That we can dismiss until more than a couple of local outsiders admit the same. We live in a racist world, always have done, and it isn't going to change. But I like the response of an Irish friend of mine many years ago when we were teenagers whose name I have now forgotten. Talking outside my house, he mentioned that he was looking for lodgings. I knew someone was renting rooms nearby and around the corner. "No, Tommy, they have a sign up, no dogs, no Irish." I looked at him and asked if he was offended? "No, Tommy, if they don't want me, then I don't want them. And to be fair, Tommy, you know what we Irish are like, were fighting every Saturday night." My initial reaction was shocked that he could respond like this. But after giving some thought to it, I concluded that it was a reasonable and logical response to take. I had felt and seen the same attitude myself in Wales, some guest houses putting up notices, no English. For the rest of my life, I adopted that very same attitude and response as my Irish friend, if they don't want me, I don't want them. Today it's more subtle. We can't speak our truth or express our feelings, so we express ourselves differently. Maybe that's what makes us more uncertain and more unhappy.

After the war, during the Nuremberg trials when some of those Germans, Nazis, were put on trial, those unfortunate enough to be caught mind, they could only get so many in the dock, some 23 or so, so what the prosecution did was to cherry-pick. They knew that there were 1,000s of Nazis who worked and ran the camps, but because there were only so many seats in the dock, they allowed them to escape, disappear, go off the radar. Those that remained to be tried, some 199, including Martin Borman, Herman Goring, Rudolf Hess and Albert Speer, all pleaded not guilty, all showed no sense of remorse or regret. Out of the 199. 161 were convicted, 37 were sentenced to death. What sticks in my mind is that if those 199 felt no guilt, shame or remorse, what does it say about all the rest who escaped or were never charged? Some to South America, next door to Switzerland. Many even disappeared amongst the population in Germany itself.

But how many knew about these people and never said a word? That, to me, makes them all complicit in their actions. After the concentration camps were opened and discovered after the liberation, the English and American governments were so appalled and shocked they made efforts to video and record it for posterity. Of course, they had heard the rumours, but here was positive proof. Then, quite rightly, they brought in the German population from outside the camps and made them witness the appalling atrocities that had been carried out under their noses. They were also made to carry the dead and bury them. I have been told a few times that the average German, in particular, I suppose, is not aware of what went on in their name. This, to me, is a bit irrelevant. The fact is 1000s did. How many more 1000s spread that sense of defiance and justification out towards the rest of the population? Ok, tell me I'm wrong, tell me I'm paranoid. There are some 84 million people in Germany. I have no doubt that the majority are nice and friendly people. But if I am among them on holiday, I never see them.

We all know they nick the sunbeds around the pool. It's a standing joke. They've even started us off, going to the ridiculous extent of seeing us getting up at five in the morning to throw our towels on the bed. But it's their self-assumed arrogant right to do it that bugs me. Why do people think it's ok to get up, put their towel on the sunbed, then bugger off for half the day. But it spreads further than that. They don't even like each other. This was brought into the open when a photographer took aerial shots around some German beaches for a hotel brochure. Having taken dozens of films, he then got back to developing it. It was at that point he stood back in shock. Among the hundreds of Germans on the packed beach, he noticed that many of them had dug out the sand around them and formed a circular bank. The size is made in accordance with the size of the group, or if single alone. What goes on in the mind to do that? And worse, they have to think to take a shovel to do it in the first place. The photographer was German himself, and he couldn't believe it.

I once had to ask the pool entertainer to help me out in Morocco. The Germans had done the regular thing of getting up in the morning and nicking their little spots. The only problem was they never thought it out. Up at 5 am, they whipped to their little places around the pool, threw the towels on, and then disappeared for the day. The only problem was they didn't realise for a few days that by midday or later when they got back, the sun had disappeared from that side of the pool and moved over to where a small group of us Brits had our sunbeds. That was it. As soon as they clocked on, we lost our small section of sun trap around the pool. They were up at five and nicked all the spaces. Pulling the entertainer over, I bunged him the equivalent of five or six euros in dirhams. "Do not worry, when you go at night, just leave your towel. I will sort it." Our beds were in place when we got there by eleven or twelve.

I don't know whether the entertainer disliked the Germans, but he wanted to organise a ball game in the pool one day. A bunch of English lads were in the hotel for a couple of days, so he set us up against the Germans. A bit of a mistake, really. I quickly realised that none of us knew each other, so I grabbed the English lads telling me to clock my face and look out for me in the pool. I placed myself over in the German half for my part. Every time the English lads got the ball I showed out, they would throw the ball to me, and I threw it right into the net. Boy, were those Germans pissed off. I'd got about five or six balls in the net before the Germans caught on. By then, they all jumped on me and tried to drown me, but too late, we licked them backwards. More than a couple of the English lads shouted, "another loss."

But what I found most interesting was what happened later on in the evening. Most of the Germans in the pool were young guys. Still, the one elder one who approached me came over and congratulated me on our win. He did the strangest thing. He clicked his heels and half did the Nazi salute before lowering his arm. He must have realised. He must have been in the Hitler youth. I was almost tempted to reply with 'Heil Hitler' and raising my arm but thought better of it, but the thought remained. How many of them must there still be in Germany who held onto those same ideals?

Then there's the food they eat. Schnitzel, what kind of food is that? I tried it once in Narbonne, France, for want of something to eat and trying to understand the waiter, I went for the pork schnitzel. The meat is cut thin and cooked in battered breadcrumbs. You can have chicken schnitzel. I guessed this must be a popular spot for Germans by the look of the menu. Maybe I was in a German restaurant. Either way, it tasted disgusting. In India, they have curry. The further south you go, the hotter the curry to disguise the taste, madras, vindaloo, each named after the city where it was created. The Germans had the schnitzel. With the schnitzel, you could be eating anything. Then there is the Schweinshaxe, pork knuckle see, the clue being in the Schwein, as in pig, say no more. Who else would or could eat it? Though I saw it in Poland on the menu at the restaurant, In the Forest, I avoided it and asked Ela about the fish. "Which fish is it?" Ela read out the meal to me. She mentioned cod. Now I love cod. Without thinking I ordered the cod. When it came to my table it was a schnitzel. Unknowingly, I had ordered a fish schnitzel. I didn't say anything as Ela had googled the restaurant and read out the reviews. It looked promising. The fish was cut that thin, it could have been anything. When Ela asked, I just replied, "very nice." They had the same.

Bratwurst, plus all the other disgustingly harsh sausages, I think someone maybe came up with the idea of these foods with some kind of masochistic sense of trying to prove how tough the Germans are. Initially, the difference was subtle but became more and more obvious as I crossed over the border from Poland into Germany. The Polish, I found in general, to be modest and polite. This wasn't just from one perspective. From the many I had observed on the campsite, around the town of Imielin, the shops and restaurants, talking to Ela and her family, I got the impression this personality went across the board. My only minor criticism was the food at the service station where I stopped. I came away with the impression that the Polish were not very adventurous when it came to food, in the main being simple and basic. The restaurant in the park was a bit of a clue. I felt the food was nothing to shout out about, yet Ela and her family were very impressed, and the place was busy. Gordon Ramsay should get over there.

The Polish drivers I found polite and respectful, willing to give way and let you out. This wasn't just because I was an obvious foreigner in a big motorhome. They were the same with their own. With the Germans, it was very different. At first, I never noticed getting onto the motorway. I never even noticed I was in Germany until I realised I had just passed a sign. This was quite regular now in Europe. If you blinked as you passed the sign, you wouldn't know you were in another country. It was a tad disconcerting. I knew firmly I was in Germany when I saw the sign, "ACHTUNG," the only word used in Germany. It was all over Auschwitz. You might think they would drop it from the German language. Nothing shouts Nazi more than the word, ACHTUNG. Because my

Tom-Tom sat nav didn't cover this part of Europe, I had to use my mobile, which was taking some getting used to. Within a few miles of getting driving on the motorway, my navigation system directed me to get off, odd because I could see the sign for Leipzig, which I knew I had to pass by or through.

Ok, so off I go, following my sat nav which was clearly taking me down side roads, and into a village. This was something I did not want. Rightly or wrongly, Germany and its little villages had no appeal to me. Pulling into a car park, I unhooked my mobile and started to try and find out where I was and what was wrong. I soon found the problem, somehow in seeking to avoid toll roads, I also had somehow put in avoid motorways. Why I don't know, but I understood there were no toll roads anyway in Germany. At any rate, I removed the motorway restriction, did an about-turn and got back onto the motorway. It was another few miles before I started to notice the difference. Maybe it was the crossover from Poland to Germany, each getting used to the difference in attitude. I was fully aware of the German autobahns having higher speed limits. I had never given it much thought other than that the German outlook to speeding was more lenient than ours. Maybe the motorways were more superior, maybe the German driver was more efficient. No, sorry, the Germans drive like their personalities, exuding a bombastic and arrogant attitude. They drive like lunatics, 90 miles an hour and up each other's backside, not just one or two. I'm talking about everyone. There seemed to be no accepted gap between them. I had drivers whizzing past me doing 90mph, with some 10 or 15 feet apart. We are talking definite fruitcakes here. Pulling in was easy enough because they were going so fast. Trying to get out was a different matter altogether. No one would let you out. I could see them behind, and in front of me, it was ludicrous. It also made me more determined to get out of the country. My difficulty was trying to figure out how far it was to the Netherlands. I should have done my homework more.

Heading for Poland, I had planned to visit the concentration camp Dachau. Unfortunately, I took the wrong turn in Austria, heading north instead of going straight ahead. Now my plan was to call off my route after Leipzig and visit the Buchenwald concentration camp. I still had my doubts. Seeing the lunatics driving wasn't helping. Ok, I know a million people will argue with me, but I can't help it. At school, we had a teacher named Walker. He worshipped all things German. Why I don't know, they had lost the war. But it was a known fact within the school, stockily and square-built, he even had that Teutonic head. He didn't walk around the school. He marched, upright and rigid, chin stuck out. Many, if not all, had the same view of the German people. Ask anyone to do an impression of a German, and most will put their finger under their nose and march-like Walker. Approaching Leipzig, my doubts were answered for me. I had no fears or worries of parking up and spending the night in the services. The attitude to parking overnight was the same throughout Europe. Plenty of land, plenty of space with no sense of restrictions. I had seen three crashes on the eastbound side of the motorway with queues going back miles. As soon as the services clear the wreckage away, another crash happens a few miles further on. Nutters. Keen as I was to get out of the country, I knew I had to have a break. Finding a spot to settle, I put the kettle on for my first coffee. After an hour or so, I started to question my prejudice, maybe I'm wrong, maybe I'm ignorant and biased? No, that's it, I'm going over to the restaurant for a baguette, maybe a meal.

Straight away, I realised the meal was a no, no. There on the board was schnitzel, schnitzel this and schnitzel that. Then there were the bratwursts. Rows of them, big fat things spread across the hot counter, disgusting, I couldn't understand the rest of the menu, I picked up my baguette, decided to have an ice lolly and enjoy it at one of the many empty tables observing the cliental and proving myself wrong in my attitude. It didn't take long. Sitting down isolated and alone, I took my mask off and started eating my ice lolly. I was halfway down when a member of staff shouted something across to me. I don't know what he was saying, but he didn't look to happy. Pointing to my mask then pointing at the table. Now I didn't have a stamp on my head saying English, so he must have assumed I was German like he was talking to one of his own. I looked around bewildered, trying to figure out what he was yapping and barking on about. I couldn't wear my mask while eating my ice lolly. I could only assume that he was not happy that I was eating an ice lolly in his restaurant. I did consider questioning it but thought better of it. No, I can't be bothered. I finished my ice lolly on the way back to the camper.

The next morning and after a good night's sleep, I set off past Leipzig and, seeing the signs for Dortmund, Essen and Dusseldorf decided to carry on, I gave Buchenwald a miss. There is a big wide world out there, most of which I loved visiting, most of the people I enjoyed saying hello to, even if it was only a smile. Italy, Greece, Spain, France, I still hadn't explored all of it and had more to see. Germany would not be a great loss. The driving hadn't changed. The Germans were still driving like lunatics. They hadn't just been having a bad day. Within hours I witnessed another three crashes. Having to spend another night at the services before entering the Netherlands, I found the two staff at the small restaurant a bit different, not much, the two elderly ladies just ignored me.

I was not sure if, and when I saw a sign, but calling into the next services to fill up with diesel, I was met with a nice friendly smile. In perfect English, "good morning."

It took me a bit before it hit me. I was baffled, "err, excuse me, is this Germany?"

"No-no, you are in the Netherlands now."

"Ahh," I said, "well, how far is the German border?"

Pointing behind me, she said, "about five kilometres." Five kilometres? Yet the difference was amazing, even the food was different. However, it was only basic counter food. I enjoyed a sausage roll and another local hot pie that was equally as nice. Civilisation.

An old school friend, David, had asked if it was possible to call into a cemetery in Arkle in France on my way home and pay my respects to his grandfather on his behalf. Looking at the map, I could see Arkle was a dogleg to the left and about 20 circa miles from Calais, where I was heading. I always felt it was a bit of a duty to visit and pay respects at war graves anyway, so I told him I was happy to do so. The approach to Arkel itself was very pretty. Without a doubt, many French small towns and villages are very pretty and attractive, including and excluding the medieval towns. As I drove into Arkle, I switched from my Tom-Tom, which thankfully had picked up from the Netherlands and Belgium. Once in Arkle, I switched over to my phone, which gave me precise directions to the cemetery just outside the town. Set in the countryside just outside Arkle, I found a small cemetery with some five hundred graves, immaculately looked after behind a low brick wall with two small entrance gates, the peacefulness and serenity were palpable, as I had found with other cemeteries such as Normandy and Germany.

I had pulled into a layby next to the cemetery and, walking in, started at the first row looking for the name Bishop. After finding some indecipherable names after the first two hundred or so, I texted my friend David. In the meantime, I noticed a little cupboard behind a bench backing onto the entrance wall. Inside was a visitor's book and a map of the graves with all the names. But no Bishop. David got back to me, telling me no. His grandfather was named H. Allen and was a bombardier in the artillery field. Second, on the right, two rows in, I found it straight away. David told me his grandfather was killed in 1918 when his mother was just a child of some 8 years of age. Looking down at those graves certainly makes you wonder about the futility of war. It was pleasing to see the graveyard so immaculately maintained and kept my respect for the French again confirmed.

Initially, I considered spending the night in the layby by the graves but felt it might not go down well with the locals. Heading back to Arkle, I found a nice out of the way spot nearby the train station. My plan, after a relaxing and easy night, was to tour the town, maybe have a nice local meal before heading off to Calais and the late-night ferry that I was about to book. The next day I set off for a walk around the town, only to find it closed up, the patisserie, the bar, restaurants, the few places in view, closed. Sometimes the French puzzle me. They seem to close according to their feelings at the time. The Spanish have their siesta. Everyone knows that the French don't have a siesta, but they just close up if it's not busy. They don't even put a sign up saying open at 5pm. No, only the locals know that. Everyone else has to guess. It makes me wonder how the French live. Sometimes they close during the day, at night, after seven pm. Whole swathes of France close down, and everyone disappears, the shutters go up, and the town looks like a ghost town.

By 3pm, I'd had enough. I set off the few miles to Calais, knowing I had a few hours to kill before the midnight ferry. My first checkpoint was the French border security, where I was met by a smiling, pretty French cop. That smile started to disappear after a bit as she examined my passport. Eventually, she looked up whilst pointing to the stamp in my passport. I had been touring Europe for over four months, she pointed out I could only be in Europe for 90 days. Well, I couldn't speak French. She couldn't speak any English, so

I kept looking suitably blank and modest. Well, Europe is a very big place. With the build-up of cars behind me and after speaking to her colleague, she waved me through muttering something about fines. Phew, no one else queried it, and I was put on an earlier ferry to Dover.

From Dover, I had 215 miles to go, which was positively the worst part of touring. I can happily travel thousands of miles all over Europe, but that last 215 miles did me in. Still, I would soon be home, into my nice warm home, which, with some hope, my kids might have kept nice and tidy for me, checking my mail over the time. Some hope. Still, my home is my home, and I was glad to get back to it. Now, where shall I visit next year? A few minor breaks around England, maybe a few days in Wales. The Dales? So many places for short breaks for next year? France again? I love France, but maybe round to Italy? Maybe the ferry over to Greece? The world and Europe are my oysters, without a doubt.

EPILOGUE

Calling into my daughter's house in oxford shortly after we had bought our motorhome, she brought her husband out for a little tour, telling me how much they liked it. This was followed by the next question, can we borrow it, dad? Of course, we will valet it before we hand it back. Now our Autotrail was not cheap, and with all the gadgets, it's not like just hopping into a car. However, I enjoyed the thought of our daughter enjoying trips to some of our favourite places with her siblings.

Without wishing to push the idea, I queried what she had in mind. "Oh, we would invite our friends." Straight away, the alarm bells started ringing. Friends? But where would they sleep?

"Oh, anywhere, Dad. A couple could have your bed. We'd just spread around."

"But, Rach, that is our bed. Me and your mom's personal domain."

"Oh, dad, don't be silly. When you go to a hotel, how many hundreds of people do you think have slept in the bed before you?" She had a point, of course, but that was just one of the main reasons we bought the motorhome.

Oh dear, here comes dad with his conditions again. The word conditional was often thrown at me on occasions.

So I am expected to just hand a very expensive motorhome over without saying a word and just hoping for the best? As usual, I was made to feel guilty about putting conditions down until I started talking to other motorhome owners. One neighbour and owner had a definite rule about anyone using his toilet.

Speaking to many others, I now find I'm not alone in, sadly, having to refuse my daughter the pleasure of sharing and enjoying the use of our motorhome. I've never gone into detail with asking people specifics, but if it's for anything like my reasons, I can only feel saddened. One guy was quite abrupt. "Oh no, no, I tried it once. Never again, I don't think he was too happy."

CAMPING TIPS

1. Always keep your motorhome well stocked with clothes for everyday use. I keep my wardrobe and cupboards stocked with various summer wear, shoes, socks, underpants etc. Jigsaws, games, etc. I have sewing kits, scissors, haircutters, tools, screwdrivers and super glue.
2. Likewise food. I keep all my cupboards full of dried food. Soups, sugar, coffee, tea, powdered milk and Saccharin, even Fray Bentos tinned meals. With a tin of veg, they make a great handy cheap meal. I find powdered milk ideal.
3. My camper is my home. I keep it stocked as I would my house. I keep my 80-litre water tank at least a quarter full, topping up as required. I carry two 13kg gas bottles in my container and another spare, especially for abroad. They will last me at least six months.
4. Whilst my motorhome is my second home, certain rules and common sense must apply. I am quite frugal when it comes to cooking. A Fray Bentos pie will go in the oven and be served in its tin on a plate with a side of vegetables. When finished, the tin goes in the rubbish bag, and the plate is wiped. If I fry an egg with bacon, I simply use a paper towel to wipe the non-stick frying pan. No wasting water. I usually eat out. The idea of cooking a three-course Sunday lunch seems ridiculous in a motorhome.
5. If using water, be even more frugal. For a shower, it's wet hair, turn off, put on shampoo, wash off and turn off. In the sink, I use bottled water to clean my teeth. Wash, brush, rinse. Mostly outside. 80 litres of water might

sound a lot, but it still disappears quickly. I rarely use the shower. Why do you have to clean yourself so often if you are not dirty? If I'm near a stream, I wash in that. A quick dip in the sea, and I'm as right as rain after a swim. Yes, ok, it's your home, but common sense prevails. The way utilities are going up, few of us will be able to afford a bath anyway.

6. If you require water, most garages should be able to help. If not, try the nearest cemetery. In the country, try the local farmer. My go-to place, if nearby, is the marina. All marinas have taps and electric hook-up points.

7. Most of the above applies to me alone, but when my wife was with me, we still more or less kept the same rules. My wife had priority over the toilet and water. And every few days, we would find a cheap site to top up and refresh and empty waste. I never use the toilets to have a pee preferring to use a gallon plastic container, emptying it in some discreet place afterwards.

8. I try not to use sites at all. £30 a night just to park up, empty your waste and use electricity on a patch of grass seems a bit over the top to me. They might as well put up signs saying campers are not welcome in England. Yet I have solar panels, gas, a fridge, a cooker, and a television. I am completely self-contained and sufficient.

9. Finally, treat your outings or expeditions as an adventure. Whether it be a 2 or 3-day break around England or a longer European tour, the attitude to motorhomes is quite different. In France, there are Aires in abundance. I have swum in the sea mere feet from my motorhome. In the Tarn Gorge also, I swam in the river only feet away. On motorways, I always park as close to the restaurants or services as possible overnight. In Italy, parked in a car park by the beach, I was treated to the delightful sight of wild boar coming out of the forest to be fed by the locals. In the mountains of Italy, we saw wild boar and wild bears. You won't get that on a campsite.

www.ingramcontent.com/pod-product-compliance
Lightning Source LLC
LaVergne TN
LVHW091249080426

835510LV00007B/182